WATERING THE VALLEY

DEVELOPMENT OF WESTERN RESOURCES

The Development of Western Resources is an interdisciplinary series focusing on the use and misuse of resources in the American West. Written for a broad readership of humanists, social scientists, and resource specialists, the books in this series emphasize both historical and contemporary perspectives as they explore the interplay between resource exploitation and economic, social, and political experiences.

John G. Clark, University of Kansas, General Editor

WATERING THE VALLEY

Development along the High Plains Arkansas River, 1870–1950

James Earl Sherow

 University Press of Kansas

© 1990 by the University Press of Kansas
All rights reserved

Published by the University Press of Kansas (Lawrence, Kansas
66045), which was organized by the Kansas Board of Regents and is
operated and funded by Emporia State University, Fort Hays State
University, Kansas State University, Pittsburg State University,
the University of Kansas, and Wichita State University

Library of Congress Cataloging-in-Publication Data

Sherow, James Earl.
    Watering the valley : development along the High Plains Arkansas
River, 1870–1950 / James Earl Sherow.
        p.   cm. — (Development of western resources)
    Includes bibliographical references and index.
    ISBN 0-7006-0440-5
    1. Water resources development—Arkansas River Valley—History.
2. Water resources development—High Plains (U.S.)—History.
3. Irrigation—Economic aspects—Arkansas River Valley—History.
4. Irrigation—Economic aspects—High Plains (U.S.)—History.
I. Title. II. Series.
HD1695.A8S54   1990
333.91′009767′309034—dc20   90-12695
                                                                  CIP

British Library Cataloguing in Publication Data is available.

Printed in the United States of America
10 9 8 7 6 5 4 3 2 1

To the memory of my father,
James I. Sherow

CONTENTS

LIST OF ILLUSTRATIONS

PREFACE

Often on hot summer days a Kansas boy would take his father's old patched inner tubes and set off with friends to float miles down the Arkansas River to the northwest of Wichita, Kansas. Once there, the friends would carefully navigate their crafts, trying to remain in the deep channel—the part of the river 6 inches to 2 feet deep. But the sandbars posed a serious challenge to their skills, and seldom did one of these intrepid helmsmen make his journey down the river without grounding to a halt.

The boy could not understand why such a sandy course with water trickling over it was called a river. He had seen pictures of the Nile and the Mississippi. Now those were rivers. But his wiser elders informed him that indeed the Arkansas was also a river and had been mightier in the past. The source of the river lay in the Colorado Rocky Mountains, but irrigators in the same state used so much of the water that little of it made its way into central Kansas. This explanation did not fully make sense to his impressionable mind, but he accepted it anyhow. I had become a true Kansan with all the prejudices against those wasteful water users in Colorado who had deprived me of so many successful floats down the river.

Over twenty years passed before I took up the study of that sandy watercourse as a graduate student at the University of Colorado. My advisor had rekindled a latent interest in the history of the Arkansas River Valley. As I studied the history of the valley, I began to see that the truth of the situation was far more complex than what my elders had offered to me as a youth. These findings ultimately became my dissertation, and that in revised form became this book. I hope that my work will allow people to see some of the valley's past in a different light.

There is one major change in this book from the dissertation. The editors and I decided to drop the tables and charts that undergirded the statistical work. The notes in this volume direct the reader to my dissertation, where he or she can find the appropriate technical material and statistical analysis.

Many people freely gave their time and expertise, which invaluably assisted the research and writing of this study. Archivists, engineers, farmers, lawyers, peers, and family generously gave of themselves so that I might better understand the intricacies of water use on the semi-arid High Plains.

I received fine support from numerous archives and libraries. At the Colorado State Historical Society Jim Lavender-Teliha and Catherine Engel ably assisted me in the exploration of the manuscript collections. Karen Zoltenko and Peggy Turner guided me through the labyrinthine filing system of the Colorado State Archives. Joel Barker of the Federal Record Center in Denver located court and other materials useful to this study. The excellent staff of Western Collections in the Denver Public Library guided me through their holdings. At the Kansas State Archives in Topeka, Terry Harmon lent assistance and always responded quickly to any request. At the La Junta Public Library Dorothy Hewitt made available their collections and indexes of local newspapers, which considerably sped research.

Many people in public offices contributed to my research. Various people in the Colorado Water Conservation Board and State Engineer's Office made accessible many materials relevant to this study. However, because of a renewal of litigation between Kansas and Colorado in the United States Supreme Court, some state documents were withheld from public access. This was not the case in Kansas, where the state's "sunshine law" ensures the availability of public records. Glenn W. Boaz, Jr., of the Division of Water Resources in the Kansas State Board of Agriculture, allowed me freedom to research their holdings and made it financially possible for me to photocopy the material. Mathias A. Scherer, a hydrologist for the Division of Water Resources, also assisted my research. At Garden City, Kansas, Howard Corrigan of the Division of Water Resources explained irrigation in western Kansas, and his assistant, Dale Jacob, gave me an illuminating tour of the ditch systems in the area. Doug Cain and P. O. Abbott, hydrologists for the U.S. Geological Survey in Pueblo, Colorado, gave freely of their time in order to teach me more about linear regression and its application and about the development of water resources in the Arkansas Valley.

I also received considerable aid from the water departments of Colorado Springs and Pueblo, Colorado. Gary Bostrom, an engineer for the Water Division of Colorado Springs, took considerable interest in this project and helped locate many fine sources. Ed Martinez, also in the division, explained how to calculate water consumption in the city. Chet Holbroth took a morning off from work and gave me a tour of, and explained the operations of, the Colorado Springs' reservoir system. Linda Collum in the Department of Utilities made accessible their scrapbook collection of newspaper clippings that related to the Colorado Springs water system and allowed me to freely photocopy from them. Bud

Ohara, the Engineering Division manager for the Board of Water Works of Pueblo, located the nearly forgotten files of the board's former attorney, James Preston. His materials proved very valuable in reconstructing Pueblo's water development. Charles W. Arnot, also of the board, gave me a tour of Pueblo's water system as well as the Bessemer Irrigating Ditch Company's works. Mike Kraska of the CF&I Steel Corporation helped me to locate historical photographs and company reports.

Two irrigating companies opened their records completely for me to research. Bill Mullen, the superintendent of the Bessemer company, explained many of the complexities of the system. Johnnie Weber, the president of the Fort Lyon Canal System in 1985, took an afternoon and showed me the operations of the irrigation system. The company also opened its record vault and allowed me access to any of its materials. Unfortunately, only recently has the Rocky Ford Ditch Company completed a long-drawn-out and tedious court proceeding, which meant that its records were not accessible when I did my research. W. F. Stoeckly, vice-president of the Garden City company, generously provided me with two unpublished papers on the history of his company.

The Hill and Robbins law firm, which is representing the state of Colorado in its newest round of litigation with Kansas over the Arkansas River, made available their complete photocopying of the General Hans Kramer Collection from the National Archives in Washington, D.C., thereby saving me considerable traveling expenses. Mark Wagner, an attorney for the firm, also took time in explaining to me the dogma and ritual of western water law.

Professor H. Lee Scamehorn deserves special recognition for his critical support of and keen insights into this work, along with his continuous support and faith in my ability to bring it to life. Professors John Clark, Patty Limerick, Richard Lowitt, Ralph Mann, Charles Peterson, George Phillips, and Donald Worster also deserve recognition for helping this striving historian with his writing and thinking.

Sections of Chapters 2 and 3 appeared earlier as "Utopia, Irrigation, and Reality: The Plight of the Fort Lyon Canal Company in the Arkansas River Valley," *Western Historical Quarterly* 10 (May 1989). A substantive portion of Chapter 5 was taken from "The Contest for the 'Nile of America': *Kansas v. Colorado (1907)*," *Great Plains Quarterly* 10 (Winter 1990).

Finally, Belinda, my wife, and Brie and Evan, my two daughters, made sacrifices far beyond normal expectations so that I might complete this work. Without their special support and understanding this study would not have been completed.

Even though all of these people have tried to keep me from my seemingly endless and imaginative ways of making mistakes, I alone bear the responsibility for any errors in this work.

CHAPTER ONE

Discord in the Valley of Content

In the late 1890s promoters of irrigation called the Arkansas River Valley, the southeastern quarter of Colorado and the southwest section of Kansas, the "Valley of Content." They saw in the development of water for agriculture, cities, and industry the basis for economic growth that supported learning, religion, and community. They reveled in the way farmers controlled and owned their own irrigation companies. What else could they call such a place, where people in harmonious enterprise undertook the transformation of a "desert" into a garden, but the "valley of content"? There was only one problem with that image—for most people it was also a land of discord. The roots of this content and discord, of conflict and cooperation over water in the Arkansas River Valley on the High Plains, are the subject of this study.

The treatment of water solely as a commodity produced the benefits of water development in the Arkansas River Valley, but it also led to dire consequences seldom considered until recently. Farmers, promoters, and engineers arduously created water systems for farms, industries, and cities. Many of these people had a vision of cooperation and prosperity premised upon the mutual and public ownership of water. Today their operations quench thirsts, water lawns, and cool factories. Farmers irrigate their alfalfa and corn fields, filling the valley's air with humidity during the spring and summer, and their roadside markets offer a variety of fruits and vegetables to passing motorists. But a closer look reveals something far less than a garden paradise. Buildings in the towns look weathered, some farmlands appear pale with alkali and choked with weeds, and irrigators operate canals with worn-out ditch structures. What accounts for this growing wasteland in the midst of a garden?

Unsatisfactorily, the vast majority of scholars have explained the nature of water development in terms of irrigation.[1] One group has built on the thinking of William Smythe, the noted turn-of-the-twentieth-century promoter of the irrigation movement. Smythe saw irrigation resulting in cooperative capitalistic enterprises that, by employing the natural laws of God, would compel the arid lands to bear fruit. He had unbounded faith that material and moral progress would flow from this conquest of nature. More recently, Arthur Maass and Raymond Anderson have fol-

1

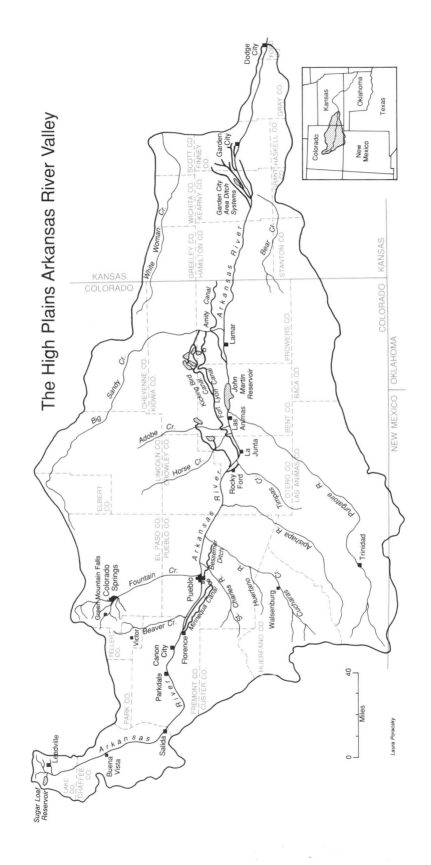

The High Plains Arkansas River Valley

Laura Poracsky

Miles

0   40

lowed Smythe's lead and asserted that a rugged individualism grounded in democratic concepts directed the healthy development of water use in the West. Even if this view is correct, it ignores the harsh environmental ramifications of irrigation.

Karl Wittfogel, associated with the critical theory school of thought, has greatly influenced a second group. Wittfogel argued that irrigation was the root cause of despotism in the ancient Far East. Recently, Donald Worster has built on Wittfogel's ideas and challenged Maass and Anderson's contentions. Worster claimed that after World War II a sinister connection between capitalism and technological manipulation of the western environment produced federally centralized and authoritarian control over water resources that worked in concert with powerful economic elites. He argued that this alliance ultimately degraded people and nature. However, Worster's ideas also do not conform fully with the historical development of irrigation in places such as the Arkansas Valley.[2]

Richard White offers an alternative approach to environmental history. According to White, the goal is to discover the complex and interdependent relationship between economics, society and politics, and nature.[3] In the Arkansas Valley, people have built functioning water systems for their ditch companies and for industries and cities. They have maintained their operations in the midst of countervailing forces marked by conflict and cooperation with nature, aid and control from the federal government, and contention and cooperation among themselves. To those who first settled the Arkansas River Valley, supplying their water needs seemed simple: Construct a small headgate in the riverbank; dig a ditch leading to their farms, cities, or factories; and reap the bounty of nature harnessed. The domination of nature, though, proved considerably more difficult. Each organizational or technological "solution" fashioned through conflict and/or consensus triggered new problems.[4]

Assuredly, the cultural mind-set of the people figured centrally as a molding force. Americans' tenacious beliefs in the goodness of growth, in both social institutions and the economy, were accompanied by opposing tendencies. Smytheian notions resulted in cooperative efforts, including the mutual stockholding company, interstate lobbying for federal water projects, interstate water compacts, and joint efforts among urban planners, industrialists, and irrigators to develop water projects. Simultaneously, adherence to what Donald Worster, in his book *Dust Bowl*, termed "the market culture" promoted destructive aspects of water development. Exploitative attitudes held that nature is capital, that people should use nature to create constant growth in their economy, social institutions, and population.[5] People gave little, if any, thought to the intricate role of water in the ecology of the Arkansas River Valley. Rather, they simply viewed water as something extractable from the valley, a commodity that could be used by them to further their ideas of growth. This pecuniary attitude toward nature premised upon growth encountered difficulties when confronted with the valley's limited water supply. Turning the valley's water into a commodity led to environmental degradation and social conflict and helped give rise to a highly specialized cadre of lawyers who, with one eye on their own interests, devised the legal arrangements to manage disputes over water.

Another aspect of the cultural mind-set—the will to dominate nature guided by engineering expertise—often worked at odds with the environment.[6] The "conquest" of nature always remained incomplete. Indeed, people in the Arkansas River Valley worked in a dialectical relationship with nature. For example, the river reacted in unanticipated ways with each succeeding physical structure or organizational development built to control and to direct its flows. The first headgates were exceedingly simple, inefficient devices. Now huge dams span the river, but still the river does not accept the dominion of people. In short, westerners in the valley have experienced great difficulty in putting together a workable approach that fulfilled their cultural aspirations and corresponded to nature's rhythms.

Residents in the valley attempted to resolve the obstacles to growth by regulating water resource development through their legal system.[7] As the historian J. Willard Hurst first revealed in his path-breaking works, law had an important functional role in the allocation of scarce natural resources. Hurst's approach removed the study of law from the narrow confines of court decisions detached from social reality. Rather, he used legal history, in part, to study the "value judgments about ends and means in men's social relations." Hurst also sought to understand "federal and state legal agencies, legislative, executive, administrative, and judicial," and "those agents in whom the legal system vests particular duties, privileges, or capacities for operating legal processes." Hurst took particular interest in the relationship between the market and law and how one created the other.[8]

As the Hurst approach toward history shows, a complex legal system developed around water as a commodity in the Arkansas River Valley. The legal system fully sympathized with the will to dominate nature and market-culture values. These societal values found expression in prior appropriation and riparian laws, in mutual stockholding companies, in publicly owned city water systems, in state and federal laws and court decisions, and in interstate water compacts. People generally channeled their efforts at cooperation and their conflict over the valley's water through the legal system.

But Hurst's model still falls short of fully describing the water history of this valley. Two additional factors—the niche of a water system and the fluctuation of economic conditions in the river basin—greatly influenced water-using enterprises. To understand the history of water development in the West means assessing not only the mind-set of the valley's water users and their legal system but these two other factors as well, to determine which situations led to cooperation and which to conflict and to understand the consequences for westerners. This study follows the story of water development in the Arkansas River Valley from around 1870 to 1950.

In 1985 over 115 operations supplied water to over 400,000 acres of farmland in Colorado and 50,000 acres in Kansas (about 2.4 percent of the basin's total acreage above Garden City, Kansas), to the cities of Colorado Springs, Pueblo, Trinidad, and Walsenburg, and to the CF&I Steel Corporation. Case studies of several of these areas has revealed the broad sweep of the interrelationship between people and environment.[9] Although the irrigation systems shared many traits that made their operations similar, each was developed under unique circumstances. The histories of three mutual stockholding companies—the Rocky Ford Ditch, the Fort Lyon Canal, and the Bessemer Irrigating Ditch companies—tell of the growth of irrigation and its functioning in the Arkansas River riparian ecosystem in Colorado. The Rocky Ford system irrigated about 8,000 acres of land in the center of the valley, the Bessemer about 20,000 acres toward the upper end, and the Fort Lyon over 90,000 acres below the Rocky Ford's lands. These companies resembled living organisms because each responded to climate and pulsated with water that fed growing crops in soils teeming with organic life. Through these organizations, people invaded an environment and established ecological niches in the valley.

When any invading organism assumes a niche in an environment, it may make alterations to that environment. Quickly or slowly, the changes produced could then destroy the environment and render the organism's occupation difficult or impossible. On the other hand, the organism may successfully adjust to the environment and share a symbiotic relationship with its natural surroundings. What makes a particular organism adaptable or maladaptable depends on its own nature. It is possible to explore how well irrigation companies filled their niches by examining the factors that led to their creation and molded their operations.

The three Colorado companies, all mutual stockholding enterprises, nevertheless differed in experience because they differed in nature. Maass and Anderson's work posits a similarity among mutual stockholding companies that resulted from their governing structure. Yet many factors, such as law, geography, war, regional and national economic change, and social thought and aspirations, created divergence rather than similarities among the companies in the Arkansas River Valley. Only in governing structure did these mutual stockholding companies correspond. In short, how well irrigators filled an ecological niche, and how well their companies adjusted to natural, social, and economic change, determined how well they functioned.

Not all water was consumed by agriculture, and many problems arose supplying the cities of Pueblo and Colorado Springs and the Colorado Fuel and Iron Company, the largest industrial concern in the West, with water.[10] These water users, like irrigation companies, filled and were partly conditioned by their ecological niches in the valley. Their niches, coupled to the goal of growth, kept such water users on a constant prowl for additional water sources.

Clearly, these publicly owned municipal water systems operated to the enhancement of what Samuel Hays refers to as privatism: the making of conditions in a city whereby private gain is promoted. Within the pursuit of privatism engineering plays an instrumental role. Too many scholars have taken the view that somehow engineers have been an objective, neutral force in society. Engineers were anything but that—they were the tools through which the will to dominate nature was expressed in the pursuit of market-culture values.[11]

Irrigation growth and its relationship to the environment in the easternmost part of the valley largely followed the developments around Garden City, Kansas. Five systems irrigated around 55,000 acres, less than the Fort Lyon company's holdings in Colorado. The environmental conditions in western Kansas were strikingly different in many respects from those in Colorado. Consequently, the development of irrigation took a different form from that in Colorado. The differences between the two states gave rise to sixty years of continuous conflict over the division of the Arkansas River flow.

A landmark Supreme Court decision in water law in 1907, *Kansas* v. *Colorado*, was the first interstate suit of *original* jurisdiction to come before the Court.[12] The Court's decision had little to do with justice in an abstract sense; rather, it established the concept of "equity," which has been used in nearly every interstate lawsuit over water since. What is so plain and yet so significant about this case is that it failed to deal with the environmental and social reality of the situation. Instead, it considered only the economic or commodity aspects of the dispute. The decision simply provided a yardstick to measure the division of water between contending states.

The issues raised by *Kansas* v. *Colorado* also included problems in western Kansas. As people around Garden City, Kansas, and those in eastern Colorado pursued their conflicting goals, they engaged in continuing interstate litigation, which proved both expensive and unproductive. Gradually, the participants turned toward cooperation (loosely defined) to achieve a greater domination over nature through technology (the building of John Martin Dam and Reservoir) to support, once again, market-culture values. The path toward this end was complex and often unpredictable.

How could John Martin Dam and Reservoir be regulated for the benefit of all water users in the valley when power was divided among factions of federal and state bureaus, irrigation companies, cities, and industries? By 1950 the development of water had certainly not created a centralization of power in the valley as Worster's theory would predict. What occurred was conflict through *Colorado* v. *Kansas* (1943) and cooperation in negotiating the Arkansas River Compact of 1948, in the overriding interest of preserving market-culture values over the environment. With the signing of the Arkansas River Compact in mid-1949 by Pres. Harry Truman, the valley's residents confidently believed that interstate conflict had found resolution; that further economic growth would follow; and that they had achieved greater control over the river. After 1950 the story changed as the pace of city growth along the Front Range quickened and irrigated agriculture came under more pressing economic and environmental assaults. In 1950 irrigation had reached its pinnacle in the valley. People had failed to consider the ecological niches that each of their enterprises occupied, and how, when an organism weakens the base upon which it feeds, it ultimately weakens itself. In the end, viewing water solely as a commodity held dire consequences for the people and land of the High Plains Arkansas River Valley.

CHAPTER TWO

The Emergence of the Mutual Stockholding Irrigation Company, 1870–1900

The governing structure of mutual stockholding irrigation companies was their only similarity. The owners of a company's water stocks directed its policies. Each stockholder had a voice in company affairs in proportion to his/her ownership of the company's stock issue. The nature of an irrigation project, however, was not the same as its governing structure, and so the nature of all the companies differed.

Three mutual stockholding companies, the Rocky Ford Ditch, the Bessemer Irrigating Ditch, and the Fort Lyon Canal companies, came into existence with diverse character traits. In a sense, each irrigation company had its own personality expressed through the people who owned it. The germ of each system's character was established during its birth. Where a company was built determined its ecological niche and its relationship to other companies in the valley. When a company built fixed the viability of its water rights and how well it survived national and regional economic flux. The social and economic agenda of a company's builders set not only the governing structure but also the ambitions of the system. In sum, the combination of these factors created the temperament of each company.

Colorado irrigators built their ditch systems in a land of climatic extremes, a general condition unevenly affecting the operations of every irrigation system in the valley. On average, depending on locale, between fourteen and twenty inches of precipitation fell annually, but wide variation marked these averages. The rain or snow might come at any time of the year, or not at all. Sometimes searing drought withered flora and parched fauna, and at other times high precipitation nourished a lush growth of short grasses, notably buffalo grass. Sudden torrential thunderstorms might interrupt dry summer days by pounding the land with hail and rain. During extremely hot days, the heat radiating off the land evaporated rain showers before they ever touched earth, and coupled with dry winds, little moisture remained in the soil. Come fall, the morning frost on the summer-withered grass melted away with the rising of the sun to reveal a brownish plains. A balmy autumn day could suddenly turn windy and snowy. In winter, within the span of a few days there could be chilling cold and freezing blizzards, or crystal-clear blue skies and frigid temperatures, or even mild, sunny days. In the spring wet snows and rains, when and if they fell, encouraged the short grasses to cover the plains like a thick velvet green carpet.

More than the region's climate, its river proved unlike anything these builders had ever experienced. Before 1870 people had recorded the peculiar habits of the Arkansas River. Observers most familiar with it noted that it flowed intermittently. The river simply served as a great drainage system for the melting snowpack on the eastern slopes of the Greenhorn, Sangre de Cristo, and Rocky mountains. Generally, from May through June the river brimmed until the sun had finished melting the snows in mountain meadows, forests, and rocky slopes. Winters of unusually deep snowpack fed the Arkansas longer into the summer. Frequent mountain rains and infrequent plains thunderstorms also added their contents to the river and sometimes caused an uninterrupted flow into the subhumid plains.

Often, though, the region's precipitation failed to provide for a surface flow throughout the entire year, mostly because of the nature of the riverbed. It changed from a solid rock base high in the mountains, to boulders in the foothills, to small rocks at the point where it emptied out onto the flats. It became a sandy bottom on the less steeply gradated plains, where the stream slowed and dropped its heavy load of sediment. Usually during the hot summer months, this stretch of the riverbed absorbed the flow in places so that the water seemed to disappear.

During drought, the stream subsided as high up as the river crossing at "old" Rocky Ford, about fifty miles east of the foothills. Before 1860 freighters usually depended on running water there; however, as O. P. Wiggins remembered, in June and July of 1846 and 1854 "the water sunk." Wiggins remembered 1854 as "terribly dry; that is the amount of it. We had to dig for water that year." Freighters knew that they could dig into the sandy riverbed and strike water. In 1846, however, this tactic failed Wiggins, and he traveled north from the Arkansas River to the springs dotting the upper headwaters of the Smoky Hill and Republican rivers before finding adequate supplies. In fact, during dry times, Wiggins and others often observed animals, including wolves, pawing through the sand to find water.[1]

Normally, during the summer the river flowed intermittently below the mouth of the Purgatoire River. In November 1863 the army freighter Edward L. Berthoud noted that the river remained dry from Fort Lyon east to Fort Larned. Great variability, however, existed in the river flow from one year to the next. For example, in July 1853 at Fort Atkinson, Lt. E. G. Beckwith observed the Comanche swimming in the Arkansas, measuring 150 to 200 yards in width, brimming with flow; in contrast, the soldiers informed him that two years earlier they had dug trenches in the riverbed in order to water their stock. The river often disappointed the traveler who expected to find reliable water supplies.[2]

At other times, great floods roared through the river, caused by unusually high runoffs of rainfall in the foothills or on the plains. Possibly the river's greatest flood in the last two centuries occurred in 1844. During the spring, extreme wetness marked the entire region. At the trading post of Pueblo, located at the confluence of Fountain Creek and the Arkansas River, trappers and traders noted flood debris cast high in the cottonwoods and many trees tilted downstream.[3] In 1859 a settler claimed that an Indian had revealed to him deposits of river silt in rock crevices along the mesa bordering the river at Pueblo. The Indian reportedly maintained that the high-water mark of an "old flood"—perhaps the 1844 flood—reached that spot. This level stood twelve feet above the high-water mark of the 1921 flood, which, according to official accounts, killed seventy-eight people and caused millions of dollars in property damage to the city of Pueblo.[4] The point is, the only reliable flow in the Arkansas River occurred during spring runoff; at any other time it flowed erratically depending on the variability of local precipitation.

The river's purity also varied along its length. As a mountain stream it flowed pure and sweet. Even as it entered the plains, despite its turbid appearance, the water retained unspoiled qualities. On 10 September 1868, the *Colorado Chieftain* reported on a series of experiments on river water at Fort Reynolds, located a few miles below Pueblo on the stream, conducted by the post surgeon. The doctor claimed that his results revealed only minute quantities of organic impurities in the water, no alkaline concentrations, a distinct lack of any acidity, and the water's pleasant softness.

Beyond Fort Reynolds, though, the river's quality began to change. The substrata and soils on the plains east of the foothills owed their alkaline nature to the ancient seas that once covered the region. These salt concentrations often found their way to the Arkansas River. For example, the early trappers and army explorers knew Timpas Creek as a bitter water source, barely fit to groom their stock.[5] The river water turned hard with mineral concentrations and somewhat saline as it flowed out onto the plains and its tributaries added their salt loads. Past these brackish inflows, rainfall and sedimentation worked to dilute the briny flavor, and the flow turned sweeter as it surged into present-day Kansas.

This region would prove unsubmissive to those who sought to tame it. Nonetheless, settlers arrived as would-be conquerors, with the belief in the domination of nature guiding their response to the valley. Initially they used words such as arid, harsh, forbidding, the "Great American Desert," sterile, and godforsaken to describe the High Plains. The people knew that less rain fell on these short-grass prairies than on the regions to the east of the 98th meridian. To them, the plains, if left unchanged, was a place of utter desolation, unfit for civilization. The indigenous plants and animals, however, did not know this. To them the land was as it should be, and they had adapted quite well to its moods. But the Americans who came to settle did not want to adapt; they sought to make nature tractable to their will. This objective, so they thought, would not only bring progress to the valley but also improve nature's design by engineering away its shortcomings.

The desire for growth—in population, farms, cities, schools, churches, and private gain—guided the social agenda of this "conquest." The key to American aspirations lay in how market-culture values determined people's view of water. The historian Donald Worster, in his book *Dust Bowl*, provides the best summary. This thinking, he explained, saw nature as capital, gave people the conviction that they had the "right" and "obligation" to use nature for "constant self-advancement," and prodded society to "permit and encourage this continual increase of personal wealth."[6] Nature, especially flowing water, became nothing more than a commodity, something separated from its central role and place in the valley's ecosystems. Water had value to these people only when put to some economic use (in time called "beneficial use"), and the more the region's water was consumed in building American civilization, the better.[7]

Before people had spread a web of irrigation canals throughout the valley, public opinion clearly voiced a market-culture mentality linked to the will to dominate nature. One man expressed these commonly held notions in the *Las Animas Leader* on 20 November 1874. He imagined "the valley on both sides of the river waving with the products of field and garden." However, he thought the valley "*wanting . . .* till the *resources* of the river" were employed in irrigation (emphasis added). On 15 July 1875, the editor of the *Colorado Chieftain* ran an article from *Mines, Metals, and Arts* that compared the Arkansas River to the Nile. The prospects staggered the imagination. "The [valley] may be irrigated by inlet canals that can draw their water from the river level, while the natural declevity [sic] of the river will enable the delivery of the water at any desirable distance back from the river." To such men the transformation of this arid wasteland into a garden meant the possibility of growth.

Obviously, this undertaking was beyond the ability of any one person. For the desert to bloom, the talents and labor of many people would be required. How to harness and guide, or "release," this energy became the question,[8] and the answer was the mutual stockholding company—cooperatively, rather than privately, owned systems. The gospel according to Theodore C. Henry, the great Colorado irrigation promoter of the late nineteenth century, was that the people of a corporation should own and control it. Water, too important to be left in the hands of individuals, should be democratically regulated by granting the shareholders a division of canal flow, assessing them for upkeep, and allowing them a vote in policy formation in proportion to their holdings in the company. For Henry—and later for the noted turn-of-the-century promoter of the irrigation movement, William Smythe—the development of cooperatively owned systems would guide the conquest of the arid West. But the route to cooperation took as many directions as there were companies.

George Swink traveled a relatively simple path in making the Rocky Ford Ditch Company a cooperative enterprise. Thoroughly driven by market-culture values, he left Illinois and in 1871 wandered into the Arkansas River Valley with the intention of ranching. He raised a few cattle but soon entered retailing by joining with Asahel Russel who maintained a mercantile store at a place called Rocky Ford. Some say Kit Carson named this popular ford across the Arkansas River; located about twenty miles above old Bent's Fort, small, rounded rocks covered the river bottom and made an excellent crossing, well known throughout the region. Trading there, as George Swink understood it, meant good business opportunities. In 1876 the Atchison, Topeka and Santa Fe Railway Company laid track near Swink's store but did not connect with it. Consequently, he moved his retail operation three and one-half miles below the old ford to the present site of Rocky Ford, which did have a rail terminal. There he continued both ranching and his mercantile business.[9]

Swink's real contribution to the valley, however, came in his development of irrigation, not ranching and retailing. Among the first to profit from irrigation, he served as an example whom others would attempt to emulate. When he first moved into the valley, there were only two small farming operations near the ford, aside from a few canals in and around Pueblo. A man named Smith tilled unirrigated bottomlands near present-day Manzanola, and a fellow named Snyder worked a spot near present-day Nepesta. Swink bought onions, squashes, and other small vegetables from these men and sold the groceries to local stockmen. Fresh produce, in short supply in the valley, commanded high prices, and Swink wanted to maximize profits by growing his own truck crops. Local ranchers, who feared land competition, tried to convince him of the impossibility of farming. Regardless, Swink cultivated a series of test plots and found that pumpkins, squashes, watermelons, and cantaloupes thrived, whereas corn and wheat fared less well.[10]

Swink's conversion from dry-land farming to irrigation came by chance. He had noticed that plants thrived where he threw waste water from his kitchen window. As a result he concluded that garden crops routinely watered would produce well and yield more profits. He began a test site on the bottomland near his first mercantile store by placing barrels at the head of each of eight or ten garden beds. He filled the containers with water drawn from an alluvial well, let the water stand for a day to warm, then turned it out onto the beds. He had good results with this technique. Although he could not work large acreages with the barrels, he could with an irrigation ditch. On a simple but nonetheless important scale, he sought a greater domination of nature in the pursuit of profits.

As a matter of expediency, not ideological design, Swink promoted cooperation. Lacking capital to underwrite a large privately owned project, he found it easier to organize his neighbors in a collective effort. Consequently, in late 1872 or early 1873, he and others began building the precursor to the Rocky Ford Ditch Company. They located a headgate a couple of miles upstream from the ford. By 1875 they had named the project the "Little Rocky Ford Ditch," and its length stretched just beyond Swink's gardens. By 1877 more farmers had joined Swink and the others, and together they had gradually extended the ditch to an intersection with Timpas Creek. On 28 July 1882, the *Rocky Mountain News* reported that the farmers had legally incorporated their enterprise, naming it "The Rocky Ford Ditch Company." Between 1887 and 1888 the company widened and improved the ditch, giving it a reach of approximately sixteen miles and the capacity to irrigate nearly 10,000 acres.[11]

Nothing became more important to the smooth operation of this company (or for that matter any other company in Colorado) than its proven water rights. In 1890 the stockholders legally fixed the prized nature of their rights. A district court decree gave the company a water right dated May 1874 of 111.76 cubic feet of water per second (cfs), which applied to the original ditch, and another right to 96.54 cfs, dated May 1890, for the farmers' enlargement of the ditch in the late 1880s. Very few water rights in the valley predated 1874, which meant the Rocky Ford shareholders could always divert river flow before nearly anyone else in the basin. The importance of this fact cannot be overstated. Since the farmers could rely on this water right to nurture their crops, they had a degree of economic stability often lacking in other canal systems. Still, the 1890 right, given its junior status, benefited the company only in times of high river flow.[12]

At the same time Swink labored to build the ditch and to secure valuable water rights, he also introduced profitable crops. He excelled as a practitioner of market-culture values. He shoved aside the native Indian turnip and the riparian grasses to make room for the Rocky Ford Netted Gem cantaloupe, alfalfa, and sugar beets. Along with beet farming came sugar refining. He even displaced the native sweat bee with the honey bee. His economic success with these ventures demonstrated to other potential farmers the lucrative nature of irrigation.

Swink's first good fortune came as he pioneered a very marketable cantaloupe, the Netted Gem, that regional farmers grew with great success. He took advantage of the railroad links to other cities and began shipping the fruit. By 1888, as the fame of the melons spread, Swink had helped establish a market well beyond the valley, extending north to Denver and east to Topeka, Kansas City, St. Louis, Chicago, and eventually New York.[13]

Swink used great care in developing his cantaloupe. His first fruit, the "Jenny Lind," shipped poorly because of its shape—flattened and narrowed in front. Looking for an alternative, Swink encountered a man who rented land from him, growing a novelty cantaloupe. Swink remembered it as about the size of a goose egg; however, he also noticed its thick meat, small hollow, and fine color and flavor. He took the seeds from the largest melons, planted them, and continued repeating this process until he had grown one weighing nearly a pound and three quarters. He also culled seeds for proper netting (the fibrous substance grown around the rind that provides protection during shipping). The cantaloupe that Swink developed thrived on irrigation and in the sunny semiarid environment, and in 1904 Swink could recall only four crop failures, all due to overabundant rainfall.

Swink, however, had to overcome an annoying problem in growing cantaloupes. He noticed that the first blossoms never set, whereas the second flowers produced fruit, and that with the second blossoms arrived the sweat bee. Realizing the importance of bees to the pollination process, he convinced a honey bee farmer from Denver to locate in the region. Since honey bees came out earlier in the growing season than did sweat bees, Swink believed the honey bee would pollinate the first blossoms, which would result in more cantaloupes. Afterwards, Swink claimed, he never encountered problems with pollination.[14] Moreover, the bees also thrived upon alfalfa, which Swink took credit for introducing into the valley in 1878. From the flowering plants the bees produced a regionally renowned honey, while farmers produced a fine quality hay for the local ranchers' livestock. Soon thereafter, alfalfa became the valley's predominant crop.

Swink's introduction of sugar beets provided the Rocky Ford farmers with their most viable cash crop.[15] His interest in sugar beets was stimulated when, taking a train to Denver, he read an article in the *Tribune Almanac* on sugar importation into the United States. The article cited Germany as the largest exporter of sugar to the United States, something Swink hardly believed. While in Denver he spoke with an acquaintance who confirmed the report. Always quick to sense an economic opportunity, Swink wrote to some people in the business in Germany inquiring about the nature of beet farming.

Swink subsequently ordered beet seeds from American companies but despaired of the results. The mangel-wurzel, the common blood turnip, and various kinds of reddish beets simply did not produce as Swink thought a sugar beet should. After two seasons of poor results, he purchased sugar-beet seeds from a German source. After two growing seasons, he noted beet size and saccharine content exceeding that reported by German growers for the same plant. Satisfied that he could grow sugar beets successfully, Swink set out to lure capitalists into establishing a sugar refinery in the area.

Encouraged by John E. Frost, a land agent for the Santa Fe railway, Swink met with Prof. T. L. Lyon at the University of Nebraska in Lincoln.[16] Dr. Lyon had gained regional fame as an expert on sugar beets, and Swink knew of his plan to hold a conference of growers and refiners at Grand Island. In 1894, through Frost's arrangements, Swink met with Dr. Lyon and received an invitation to attend the conference. There he paid close attention to the refiners' concerns that building factories in the United States might prove unduly risky. Swink singled out Henry T. Oxnard, a New Yorker who owned an extensive sugar-beet empire in the Midwest. As Dr. Lyon's conference droned on around them, Oxnard informed Swink he knew nearly nothing about the Arkansas Valley, much less Rocky Ford and its ditch. But Swink excited his curiosity when he pulled one of his beets from his pocket. Oxnard fingered the beet carefully and commented that he did not believe Swink had actually grown it. Later, Oxnard decided to take a second look, at which time Dr. Lyon grudgingly turned the floor over to Swink and Oxnard to discuss the beet.

Swink still had to convince Oxnard that his sample represented what could be uniformly grown and that the valley possessed good potential for a sugar factory. Oxnard estimated by examining the root its probable tonnage, purity, and saccharine content and then pronounced to a surrounding group of eastern capitalists: "Gentlemen, I think you had better investigate the valley. If those results can be produced down there it is the best place for a beet sugar plant in the world." With Oxnard's enthusiasm aroused, Swink now had to tell him that no one aside from himself grew beets in the valley. Swink promised to contact Oxnard as soon as he had enough farmers willing to raise the crop. After six years of canvassing the valley Swink had about 1,300 farmers committed to growing beets. He then wrote Oxnard that people were ready for the sugar factory. Oxnard quickly arrived on the scene, and by the fall of 1900, the American Crystal Sugar Company factory was operating.

The Rocky Ford, Fort Lyon, and Amity Systems

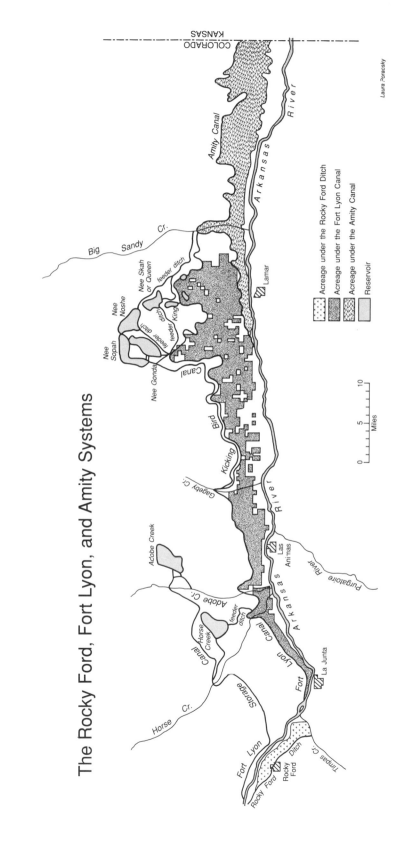

Acreage under the Rocky Ford Ditch

Acreage under the Fort Lyon Canal

Acreage under the Amity Canal

Reservoir

Laura Poracsky

Miles
0   5   10

COLORADO
KANSAS

By 1901 the farmers of the Rocky Ford Ditch Company, under the shrewd boosterism of Swink, found themselves operating the most stable and envied irrigation enterprise in the valley. They never feared a shortage of water, except during extreme drought, and they grew valuable cash crops well suited to irrigation and the environment. The sugar factory, located in Rocky Ford, paid them handsomely to plant beets. Swink and his fellow farmers surely felt like beneficiaries of market-culture values and of the conquest of nature. But not all mutual companies in the valley came into existence under such fortunate conditions, and the purpose underlying Swink's system would work less well for others. A case in point was the establishment of the Fort Lyon Canal Company.

The federal government had established the location for what was to become the Fort Lyon Canal Company with a unique objective in mind. In the spring of 1864, the Bureau of Indian Affairs had Henry Fosdick, an engineer working for the United States Army, construct a small ditch off the Arkansas River located midway between the Front Range and the present-day boundary of Colorado and Kansas. This ditch, built for the use of the Cheyenne and Arapaho, fulfilled one of the terms of the Fort Wise treaty of February 1861. By the end of 1864, however, circumstances had changed: There had been a Cheyenne and Arapaho raid of the system in August, followed in November by the infamous Sand Creek Massacre in which Col. J. M. Chivington's Colorado volunteers slaughtered Black Kettle's encampment. As a result, both bureau and Indians lost all interest in reestablishing the agricultural experiment on the reservation. In 1868 one rancher purchased the canal and its water rights for his stock and the limited irrigation of feed crops, and in 1873 another bought the system for the same purpose. Under their ownership, from 1868 to 1883, the simple ditch structure remained unimproved.[17]

From 1883 to 1887, Otis L. Haskell, a real-estate developer in Denver, organized the Arkansas River Land Town and Canal Company in a bold experiment to enlarge the old ditch in order to rent water to prospective irrigators. An engineer, P. O. Gaynor, designed a massive canal to water over 300,000 acres of "idle" High Plains for agricultural production. In February 1884 forty teams of horses and fifty men began excavation, and over the next few years, the company completed approximately seventeen miles of ditch. The inability to sell water stock to potential investors hindered Haskell's ambitions. In 1886 he reorganized the firm as the Arkansas River Land, Reservoir and Canal Company and purchased several reservoir sites to lend more credence to the project and draw better financial support. He still found it difficult to fund development, and the company lost money from the beginning. Moreover, operating a canal in the semiarid environment of the Arkansas River Valley defied simple arrangements. In 1887 an inexperienced superintendent and ditch runners allowed the headgates to fill with sand. Angry farmers, deprived of water in early summer, physically threatened the superintendent. Unable to cope with the situation, Haskell sold the company in the fall of the same year to investors who renamed the enterprise the La Junta and Lamar Canal Company and who had different notions of irrigation.[18]

Many farmers and political leaders in the state had attacked the corporate approach of renting water to irrigators as too monopolistic. The critics advocated cooperative undertakings similar in scope to those later advocated by William Smythe. Theodore C. Henry, one of the principal investors in the La Junta and Lamar Canal Company, preached cooperative irrigation as the panacea that would transform an arid valley into a garden. A man of unlimited vision and ambition, he had more to do with the development of irrigated agriculture in Colorado before 1900 than nearly anyone else. He pictured independent farmers using the power of human intelligence to transform buffalo-grass plains into a paradise of small-acreage farms. Henry claimed that "on lands . . . under irrigation, in such valleys as the Arkansas or Grand, there are almost infinite possibilities for diversified horticultural and agricultural production." He boasted that a farmer could make a successful living on less than twenty-five irrigated acres (even though the realities of seeking capital later forced him to tie water rights to eighty-acre plots). He envisioned extending the reach of the canal to the Kansas-Colorado state line. Even though his ditch never reached that point, it did measure nearly 110 miles and had the potential of irrigating over 100,000 acres. Henry's figures meant that he hoped to have somewhere between 1,000 to 4,000 farms serviced by his enterprise and to garner substantial profits.[19]

Ditches such as this one were grand construction projects. The contractors erected tent camps, with the cook's and mess tent in the center. M. C. Hinderlider, the state engineer of Colorado from 1923 to 1954, once noted, "A good camp cook was without price." After a hard day of work, ditch diggers expected to eat well. Consequently, cold coffee and bad cooks were more troublesome to contractors than low pay and demanding work. The engineers and foremen usually had private tents; large tents lodged the crews and also served as stables, with corrals nearby, for the teams. As Hinderlider commented, the tents and animals were "never far enough away [from the crews' tents], especially in hot weather." A temporary shed that housed the blacksmith's operations completed this canvas city.[20]

Several hundred teams of horses and sometimes several thousand men might be employed. The workers made the ditch cuts with "wheelers," which they called "horse and man killers." Hinderlider described these machines as "heavy duty plows and scrapers mounted on wheels that could handle much more soil than slips and scrapers." It took at least four horses or mules and one to two men to operate this back-breaking equipment. Scrapers were smaller than wheelers, weighed anywhere from 80 to 135 pounds, and could lift three and a half to seven cubic feet of dirt. When the soil was hard, crews plowed it first, then other crews followed with the scrapers and wheelers.[21]

Henry's ambition to build the biggest ditch in the state, and his faith in hydrologic engineering, produced results by 1890. During the growing season of 1888 the farmers grew a fine yield of alfalfa, and the enterprise seemed on a solid base. During the winter of 1888–89, attracted by the Atchison, Topeka and Santa Fe Railway Company, many new settlers located north of Lamar. These farmers, along with railroad officials, encouraged Henry to resume construction of the canal as far as their holdings. Henry directed over seventy-three miles of extension to a juncture with Sand Creek, where the ditch then reached its present length of 110 miles.[22]

Legal and geographical constraints, however, set a course for a future of conflict. Henry secured two water decrees from the state, but it was not enough to supply sufficient water for such an extensive canal.[23] Furthermore, these water rights were junior to others with earlier dates. Consequently, Henry's weak water rights often proved inadequate for growing cereals and alfalfa on the land served by the long ditch. Moreover, guided by market-culture values, people used prior appropriation to exploit river flow. As historian Donald Pisani has noted, the prior appropriation system fixed a commodity value to river flow.[24] This arrangement separated river flow from its own natural rhythms, and people came to associate a stream with its economic value rather than its part in the natural order. Thinking to dominate nature, irrigators sought to force water to fulfill their economic and social ambitions, rather than to develop a sense of the ecology of the valley and adjust their lives to the seasons of the High Plains. Because of this outlook, irrigators under Henry's project failed to fully comprehend their situation.

Most of the system's farmers simply believed that irrigation problems stemmed from maladministration. Hoping to resolve their difficulties, shareholders united under John Hess, who worked over 600 acres near Lamar, to fight for the cooperative ownership of the La Junta and Lamar Canal Company. Hess and his supporters battled T. C. Henry and the First National Bank of Denver, the most powerful economic institution in the state, which also sought control of the canal through its possession of a defaulted mortgage made with the La Junta and Lamar Canal Company, represented by Henry. At the same time, nature rebuked Henry by filling the headgates and the front portion of the canal with sand, silt, and debris. As a result, the farmers went without water for over thirty days during the 1893 irrigation season. In 1894 the Arkansas River washed out the headgate to the main ditch. No sooner had William C. Burke, the court-appointed receiver of the La Junta and Lamar Canal Company, directed repairs than another flood completely destroyed the headgate. Obviously, Burke's problems sprang from more than the lack of a mutual stockholding company to manage the system.[25]

Burke found a partial solution through a cooperative agreement between two companies when the Fort Lyon Canal Company, a mutual stockholding company formed by the farmers using the La Junta and Lamar canal, assumed ownership of the La Junta company in October 1897. The Great Plains Water Storage Company, incorporated by Denver businessmen Joseph A. Thatcher and James H. Jordan, and Henry C. Vidal, a lawyer who became prominent in the valley, lacked a conveyance ditch for their series of reservoir sites north of the eastern section of the La Junta and Lamar system. Burke agreed to the Great Plains company's plan to enlarge and reconstruct the La Junta company's flood-wrecked canal to just beyond Gageby Arroyo for joint use. There joint use ended, and the Great Plains company continued to deliver its water into the Kicking Bird feeder ditch, which fed the company's reservoirs. In the spirit of cooperation, Burke, with the consent of the stockholders, allowed the Great Plains company two representatives on their five-person board of directors. Burke also sold his mortgage of the La Junta company to the storage company, giving it one additional representative on the board until repayment of the debt. The district court consented to this contract, and in June 1897 the farmers under the La Junta system met in a mass meeting to consider the steps necessary to secure the system. In July they organized a mutual stockholding company, the Fort Lyon Canal Company, which the district court approved in the same month.[26]

From 1898 to 1903 the Fort Lyon farmers fought two Colorado Supreme Court cases before they finally won cooperative control of the canal system and confirmed their contract with the Great Plains Water Storage Company.[27] In effect the court decided that the stockholders serviced by the irrigation system rightfully owned the Fort Lyon Canal Company. Through tortuous litigation they had formed a mutual stockholding company that still functions today. Those farmers believed they had achieved cooperatively controlled irrigation that would lead to material, commercial, and moral progress through the "conquest" of nature. The idyllic conditions of productive farms and orchards supplied by a well-ordered and brimming irrigation ditch, pictured on the company's stock certificates, seemed close at hand.

Dreams of jointly owned ditch systems watering bountiful farmlands also gave rise to the Bessemer Irrigating Ditch Company. William Jackson Palmer, as part of his designs for social reform in the West, envisioned all of his enterprises as cooperative arrangements. Worker ownership of a company, he believed, would make everyone involved "capitalists themselves in a small way."[28] Palmer never abandoned his market-culture values as he pursued what might be called democratic capitalism. He hoped to spread the wealth created through capitalism more broadly by giving workers a direct say in the policy of a company and a proportional share in its profits or losses. Palmer eventually lost control over his enterprises to businessmen more comfortable with standard corporate arrangements, and neither his Denver and Rio Grande Railway Company nor what would become the Colorado Fuel and Iron Company approached a cooperative form of organization. In those companies labor may or may not have earned a decent income, but management certainly excluded it from any voice in policy formation and from the distribution of the company earnings. However, another Palmer venture, the Bessemer Irrigating Ditch Company, was less appealing to corporate buyers. As a result, this left farmers unhindered to develop the canal company as a cooperative enterprise.

Part of Palmer's plans for the Front Range included the building of irrigation ditches. Not only would cooperative institutions proliferate, but so would traffic and freight for his railroad. To achieve this end, he and four others incorporated the Central Colorado Improvement Company in November 1871. The company hoped to develop the Nolan Grant, located south of the Arkansas River near Pueblo, and so it purchased the land in 1872 and platted a new town south of Pueblo, which with great originality it named South Pueblo. Besides the town lots, the Central Colorado Improvement Company gained around 40,000 acres of land through the purchase of the grant. Palmer wanted to colonize this fertile mesa by constructing irrigation ditches to serve as the central inducement for farmers, to make his profits through land speculation, and to leave the operations of the ditch company to the buyers. In fact, the company's reports announced grandiose plans to build a system reaching to the Colorado-Kansas state line, a scheme never realized.[29]

Palmer's cooperative vision fell apart during the sluggish economy of the 1870s. Between 1874 and 1877 the company encountered slow land sales in South Pueblo and on the mesa. The 1873 panic had its impact on Colorado in 1874 and created the region's economic doldrums. Consequently, Palmer "found it necessary to defer . . . the contemplated improvements in the way of additional irrigating canals" to the outlying

William Jackson Palmer (Photographic Collection, Colorado Historical Society)

lands of the Nolan Grant.[30] Moreover, the Central Colorado's ties to the Denver and Rio Grande Railway Company caused problems. The improvement company had issued bonds backed by its holdings of Denver and Rio Grande bonds and lands. Dr. William A. Bell, an officer for both the Denver and Rio Grande and the Central Colorado, sold most of the improvement company's bonds to London businessmen. All went smoothly until the Denver and Rio Grande defaulted on its bond interest payments. The improvement company, which had depended on the interest from the railroad company's bonds for its own operations, defaulted on its financial obligations.[31]

In July 1877 alarmed London investors held a meeting and appointed a committee to investigate the company's affairs and to report their findings. In order to bring greater managerial efficiency and to recover their profits, the financiers recommended the consolidation of several companies. In January 1880 they ordered the improvement company, the Southern Colorado Coal and Town Company, and the Colorado Coal and Steel Works Company (a speculative "paper" company formed by Palmer) to merge into the Colorado Coal and Iron Company.[32]

Even with Palmer no longer in control, the company, under Henry E. Sprague's direction, planned to revive colonization through the construction of large irrigation ditches. Sprague, in keeping with traditional private, rather than cooperative, notions of market-culture values, wanted to continue building an empire that included a steel company and large-scale land speculation. In 1885 the company seemed ready to push ahead with its plans to construct the ditch that was the prerequisite for settlement of the Nolan Grant. The directors ordered the surveying of 9,300 acres east from Florence, most of which were between Florence and the St. Charles River, with 1,800 acres east of the river. The company correctly advertised that the rich sandy loams made possible the farming of all cereals and fruits.[33]

The excitement, however, soon waned as Sprague and company directors found more pressing needs for their limited capital. New coal fields in Garfield and Pitkin counties were requiring large expenditures. Although this delayed the start of work on the ditch, the board felt compelled to resume construction later in 1888. The directors fully realized that the Arkansas River had a limited flow, and since other ditch companies were also building, the number of viable water rights lessened each year. In order to secure reliable water rights for its lands, the board had to act in a hurry, or else forfeit the opportunity to irrigate their holdings.[34]

The directors formed a Committee on Irrigation which filed its report in August 1888. In the 1880s, the report noted, a great irrigation-building boom in valley had created a weak market for irrigated farmland. There was more land on the selling block than farmers willing to buy it, which resulted in falling land values. The report recommended irrigating only a portion of the company's best lands. Apparently by this time the company had already constructed a headgate and called for a ditch terminating somewhere between the St. Charles and the Huerfano rivers. The committee estimated the cost at $92,000 for a ditch capable of irrigating "8,500 acres of [the company's] lands besides irrigating some 30,000 acres belonging to other parties and from which a yearly revenue can be obtained." To the south they also planned to build a series of reservoirs supplied by feeder ditches off of the main canal. The company had an engineer, J. Simons, survey the ditch and oversee its construction.[35]

The board of directors laid the basis for a cooperative irrigation enterprise, the Bessemer Ditch Company. The board reserved to the Colorado Coal and Iron Company the right to build the reservoirs and distribute the water. However, they decided to postpone storage development until they sold the 8,500 acres under the ditch. The directors invested about $100,000 in the irrigation company's stock and hoped to sell steel company lands at $60 an acre (when dry land went for $25, or less, an acre). In this manner they planned to obtain $510,000 on land sales, which would offset the money invested in canal stock. Moreover, the steel company mortgaged its land in such a way that the company's interest in the land ended after purchase and the buyer became a cooperative stockholder in the irrigation company.[36]

More important than establishing the cooperative nature of the system, the board secured good water rights. Over 42 cfs had a priority dated before 1871, and another 34 cfs were dated before 1882. The company acquired the bulk of its water rights (280 cfs) with a decree dated 1887. The limited flow of the river could not adequately fulfill the junior right during dry summer months or in time of drought. Consequently, these rights usually guaranteed that a crop would sprout in the spring, but at times they failed to maintain plants during dry periods.[37]

In three years the Colorado Coal and Iron Company finished the construction of the ditch. Simons had begun excavation in December 1888, and either he or another contractor had completed the canal in 1891. The company underwrote its construction costs in several ways. In April 1890 it mortgaged 500 acres of its land under the ditch to secure the Bessemer's bonds; in September 1891 its vice-president, Henry Grose, transferred the steel company's irrigation stock to whoever purchased its land. The success of Colorado Coal and Iron Company's plans, however, depended upon a healthy real-estate market.[38]

In the early 1890s, a poor regional and national economy wiped out Sprague's irrigation plans. A weak land and steel market created hard times for the Colorado Coal and Iron Company and resulted in reorganization of its real-estate holdings. Sprague set up a collateral firm to handle the steel company's real-estate concerns and thereby unburden the company of losing ventures. This enterprise was named the Colorado Coal and Iron Development Company. Initially the parent company transferred to the development company much of its holdings in South Pueblo; however, Sprague and the board tried to retain possession of the Nolan Grant lands as well as the Bessemer Ditch Company stock and bonds. Sprague was gambling that the grant and ditch properties would eventually pay handsome dividends. The 1893 depression, however, finished any hopes he entertained in making profits from steel, mining, or real estate.[39]

When the Colorado Coal and Iron Company merged with John C. Osgood's Colorado Fuel Company and formed the Colorado Fuel and Iron Company, Osgood, who directed the new firm, decided that a steel company had no business in irrigation or real-estate speculation. The parties worked out an arrangement whereby the Colorado Coal and Iron relinquished all its properties not associated with the production of steel and the mining of coal to the Colorado Coal and Iron Development Company. By 1894 the development company, plagued by poor land sales, failed to pay interest on its irrigation bonds, and the Bessemer Ditch Company folded.[40]

In 1894 both new and original investors formed a new cooperative venture and named it the Bessemer Irrigating Ditch Company. They purchased all the property and water rights of the defunct Bessemer Ditch Company and began operations in July 1894. Gradually, the canal became a mutual stockholding enterprise as the farmers paid off their lands with water rights attached that represented a proportional holding of stock in the company. And even though the steel and irrigation companies remained separate, they would share a symbiotic relationship through the years.[41]

As exemplified by the Rocky Ford, Fort Lyon, and Bessemer companies, the natures and experiences of mutual stockholding companies varied greatly. The Rocky Ford's origins represented a neatly and simply organized system. Largely led by George Swink, the farmers established a solid base upon which they pursued market-culture values through the domination of nature. In contrast, the Fort Lyon's farmers, lured by the cooperative promise of T. C. Henry's promotions, had to struggle to effect a mutual stockholding firm. They also faced inherent weaknesses in their water rights and in the physical complexity of their system. The Bessemer's irrigators inherited William Jackson Palmer's dreams of social progress and John C. Osgood's disinterest in farming. They operated a system neither as strong as the Rocky Ford's nor as weak as the Fort Lyon's.

The Bessemer Irrigating Ditch System

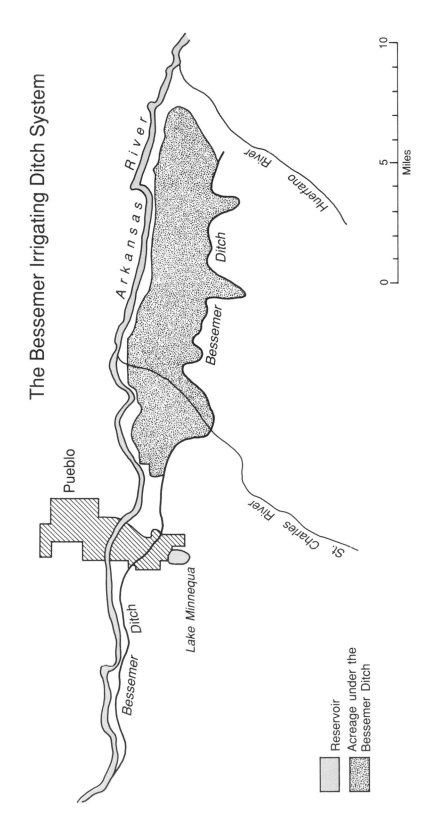

Reservoir

Acreage under the Bessemer Ditch

Arkansas River

Huerfano River

St. Charles River

Bessemer Ditch

Bessemer Ditch

Pueblo

Lake Minnequa

Miles

0   5   10

Laura Poracsky

The differences in each company's personality gave each unique character traits. The Rocky Ford irrigators always had a degree of contentment with their circumstances not shared by the farmers under the other two systems. Circumstances endured by the Fort Lyon shareholders gave them a litigious tendency when confronted by opposition and a willingness to extend their control over nature to improve the weaknesses in their system. Those of the Bessemer company found themselves operating a ditch without the physical weaknesses of the Fort Lyon, but without the simplicity of the Rocky Ford. And the Bessemer irrigators would also discover that their company's historical ties to the steel company would have beneficial results.

Furthermore, *when* these companies built distinguished one from the other, especially in the crucially important matter of their respective water rights. The Rocky Ford ditch operated on a firm base of early-dated water rights. The Bessemer canal relied on some early water rights that guaranteed the emergence of crops, but it also owned later-dated decrees that sometimes failed to meet its farmers' needs. The unwieldy Fort Lyon canal system depended on erratic, junior water rights. The relative strengths and weaknesses of the companies' rights produced legal conflicts over the water supply in the valley. Irrigation promoters, such as T. C. Henry, would not face the fact that it was beyond the capacity of normal river flow to supply all of the decrees obtained for their various enterprises. They had tremendous confidence that their ability to dominate, alter, and improve upon nature would offer the solutions that could maintain and expand what they had built.

Irrigation promoters had wrought remarkable environmental changes in the valley that, in their minds, verified the correctness of their approach toward nature. They firmly believed that their ecological alterations had resulted, and would continue to result, in material and moral progress. George Swink's activities led to alfalfa, sugar beets, and honey bees replacing the riparian grasses, the Indian turnip, and the sweat bee. His work set the standard for the valley. Irrigation also produced unwanted environmental changes as nature resisted people's attempted dominion. Moreover, because too many companies relied upon an overtaxed river flow for their supplies, the policies of mutual stockholding companies often collided with one another and other water users. This set into motion constant conflict and cooperation between companies as each pursued a course forged in its own origins.

CHAPTER THREE

The Incomplete Conquest

Irrigators never fully mastered their own fates in the Arkansas River Valley of Colorado. They intended to create a new environment as they sought to transform the semiarid plains into a profitable, lush green garden. Their work, however, often produced unexpected results. Irrigation reduced the variation in the river flow, narrowed stream banks, raised salinity levels, increased tree growth on the bottomlands, decreased the volume of river flow eastward onto the plains, and increased the rate of sedimentation. In addition, the overextension and proliferation of irrigation companies compounded the effects of environmental change. Finally, the shifting winds of the economy blew both ill and fair for these people. Just as hot southern gusts dried rivers and destroyed fields, a dip in the local, national, or world economy withered pocketbooks—and environmental conditions often worsened along with slumps in the economy. But these factors influenced each irrigation company differently. Although all irrigators might curse drought and low river flows, they did not suffer equally. Likewise, they all despaired of the results of depression, but they encountered unequal losses.

Dictated by its origins, every system occupied a unique niche in the valley. Each operation encompassed a different area of the basin and owned water rights differing in value. These two important factors mitigated the way in which economic and environmental fluctuations affected the operations of the irrigation companies. Early irrigation promoters seldom, if ever, had a good grasp of how their projects would weather changes in the environment and economy. People like T. C. Henry, George Swink, and William Jackson Palmer thought they understood the nature of the river, its erratic flow, and its salinity content. They possessed full confidence that they could conquer the semiarid environment and establish in its place an agricultural paradise—the "valley of content," as promoters dubbed the Arkansas Basin. Believing that irrigation generated economic and social progress, they did not fully foresee the impact of their enterprises on the environment. The reality of their labors stimulated intricate policies of cooperation and conflict as farmers increasingly realized their vulnerability to environmental and economic change.

The main problem for irrigators was that their agenda simply did not coexist well with the valley's environment. If there had been a perfect mesh of social goals and economic systems with the valley's ecology, then little if any conflict between people would have occurred. Obviously, perfect accord is beyond reach, but the extent of conflict or cooperation is one important gauge of how well the conquest of nature and market-culture values worked in the valley.

The domination of nature in the valley did not proceed exactly as planned. Farmers found themselves in increasing conflict with nature each passing year as irrigation tampered with the valley's ecology. For example, by 1900, ditch practices had smoothed the river's erratic flows. Several types of return flow were involved in this development. Groundwater return flow occurred when unconsumed irrigation water permeated the soil until it encountered an underground water table. At this point the flow either contributed to groundwater or seeped to the surface. Tailwater, or surface-water return flow, occurred when irrigation water streamed along the ground, neither absorbed by the soil nor consumed by crops. This water, too, found its way back to the Arkansas River or one of its tributaries.[1]

On the positive side, return flows provided regular supplements to the river and its branches. Once people had established irrigation all along the river, the subsoils and gravels filled with water. These soils gradually released their holds into the nearest streams, and alluviums that had normally held water below the top of the streambed filled and produced surface flows. Because irrigation farmers reused the water repeatedly, the flow of the river changed from intermittent to nearly perennial. By 1905 even tributary streams with highly irregular flows (for example, Big Sandy and Timpas creeks) located near irrigated fields started flowing throughout most of the year.[2]

On the negative side, although irrigation seemed to tame the river, it also sharply reduced the volume of flow on the High Plains. Most horticulturists agreed that crops in the valley, through consumption or transpiration, depleted about 40 percent of the water reaching them. Also, most canal superintendents figured about a one-third loss of water from evaporation and seepage in their ditches. So even if the river flowed throughout the year, its volume decreased as it extended east from the mountains. Consequently, by 1890 the yearly "June rise" for farmers below the Purgatoire River had evolved into something less than a June bump.[3]

More problems arose as irrigation practices altered the nature of the riverbed. Before 1870 the river carried out of the mountains and foothills sand and silt that filled and built up the channel east of Pueblo. The practice of irrigation eroded farmlands, thereby increasing the rate of sedimentation. Riverbanks, once cut sharply, began sloping more gently.[4] All canal superintendents routinely battled sedimentation and, along with it, unwanted foliage. Left unchecked, silt and weeds diminished the carrying capacity of a ditch in a short time. Most superintendents burned weeds during the fall when the plants had withered and dried and fields did not require irrigating. Controlling sedimentation was more difficult. Fine silt build-up along the canal walls and bottom could act as a seal preventing costly ditch leakage, but too much silt and sand reduced the volume of the canal. Before 1900 men drove horse-towed scrapers to clear ditches. After that companies used steam-powered dredges later replaced by tractors equipped with front loaders.[5]

Sedimentation not only clogged ditches but caused serious problems to water diversions. The Rocky Ford company had spent thousands of dollars strengthening riverbanks to prevent floods from shifting the channel. When banks gave way, the debris filled the ditch and sometimes threatened to cut off the diversion works from the main channel. Sedimentation also added to the riverbed, burying diversion works in sand and silt. Engineers designed diversion dams to build up the riverbed so that water would be routed into a headgate rather than impounded. In time, however, a continuously rising bed covered dams and filled headworks. The diversion dam that the Rocky Ford company built in 1923 had stood three feet above the surface of the riverbed. By 1944 no one could locate it in the silt and sand that had completely buried it. At the Fort Lyon headworks, the riverbed measured seven feet higher in 1944 than it had in 1910. Continuously battling siltation drained stockholders' purses and required constant vigilance on the part of the superintendents.[6]

The more people pursued their conquest of the river, the more nature reacted. The very process of irrigation worked to poison farmland as the river's salinity level increased when alkaline salts were leached out of the soils. The more irrigation in the valley, the greater the problem became. Each reuse of the stream through canal diversions brought increased mineral concentrations in the water the farther east the river flowed. Eventually, the salinity level of the river below Timpas Creek achieved the dubious distinction of being one of the nation's highest.[7]

At first, irrigation promoters did not consider salinity a serious problem. George Swink, for example, placed great faith in the practice of leaching—that is, the process of washing the salts through the soil. Soluble salts reduced the amount of clear water that a plant's root system absorbed. As the plant absorbed water, it left greater amounts of soluble salts in the root zone. Unless irrigation water washed the salts down and out of the soil, crop production faltered. Leaching worked particularly well on shallow soils of the Rocky Ford system (or on similar soils in the western portion of the Fort Lyon system) that lay on top of gravel deposits. Once water passed through the root zone, it quickly traveled through the porous substratum toward a surface stream, taking with it dangerous levels of salts. The practice could also increase the fertility of the soil. For example, early irrigation boosters knew that proper leaching turned calcium sulfate and calcium chloride into beneficial fertilizers. Leaching, however, always required a reliable and steady water supply.[8]

When there was insufficient water to dissolve and remove the salt concentrations from the soil, serious crop production problems occurred. The Fort Lyon irrigators in the eastern portion of the system who farmed in deep soils required more water to wash the salts beyond the root zone than did farmers tilling shallow soils. Drainage was also complicated in clays that conducted water slowly. In these soils groundwater levels rose and inundated the root zone with concentrated salt solutions. Moreover, salinity levels in the river flow increased with each reuse of the stream. By 1895 concentrations had reached such a point in the Arkansas River near La Junta that the Atchison, Topeka and Santa Fe Railway quit using river water in its locomotives' boilers, since mineral deposits had resulted in too many costly repairs.[9]

Farmers found their self-made salinity problems difficult enough to handle without an additional assault from nature. Yet rising salinity in the river provided an ideal environment for an insidious phreatophyte. Sometime after 1900 the salt cedar (*tamarix ramosissima*) spread throughout the entire valley, plaguing irrigation farmers. In the early nineteenth century, eastern nurserymen had introduced the tree into the United States as an ornamental. By 1868 the Department of Agriculture grew six species of it in arboretums. In the 1850s the tree was sold in California, in the late 1870s in Galveston, Texas, and in the 1880s in Utah. In 1913 Robert J. Niedrach of the Denver Museum of Natural History recorded the first observation of the tree in the Arkansas River Valley on the High Plains. Whether it was brought by migrating birds or floods, the tree had arrived and was thriving on the saline-rich waters of the basin. When its leaves dropped in the fall, they also contributed salts to the soils. Nearly all of the valley's mammals found salt-cedar groves inhospitable habitats. Moreover, the tree acted as an incessant drain on the valley's irrigation water supply.[10]

Cottonwood growth along the riverbanks caused similar problems for irrigators as did the salt cedar. Before 1870 recurrent prairie fires, freshets, and occasional large floods destroyed most saplings in the riparian ecosystem, except in protected areas. Turning the plains into farms reduced the incidence of prairie fires and smoothed the river flow, which meant that little threatened the survival of cottonwoods along the river and the trees could flourish. Some people, including an engineer who conducted a study for the Fort Lyon Canal Company in 1910, be-

The effects of deforestation in the watershed of the Arkansas River Valley (*Thirteenth Biennial Report of the State Engineer, Colorado, 1905–1906* [Denver: State Printers, 1906], frontispiece).

Protected snowpack in the watershed of the Arkansas River Valley (*Thirteenth Biennial Report of the State Engineer, Colorado, 1905–1906* [Denver: State Printers, 1906], frontispiece).

lieved that cottonwoods prevented costly erosion of ditch banks. They had, however, overlooked the enormous water consumption of these plants. An average cottonwood tree could transpire 1,500 gallons of water a day. In 1905, near Kinsley, Kansas, R. E. Edwards noticed that within twenty years over 200 acres of trees had filled in what had once been grassy river bottoms. By 1923 the Bessemer's board of directors had learned to fully appreciate the dangers cottonwoods posed to their water supply. When the Colorado Fuel and Iron Company proposed to line the Bessemer ditch that passed through its property with trees, the Bessemer board approved, so long as "no cottonwoods or other undesirable trees" were planted. Moreover, through the combination of tree growth and siltation, the riverbanks narrowed considerably in a short expanse of time. For example, from 1880 to 1905 at Syracuse, Kansas, near the Colorado-Kansas state line, the banks constricted from 1,172 feet to 780 feet.[11]

An additional strike at nature through deforestation in the upper regions of the watershed also reduced the river flow. Before large-scale lumbering, the forest acted as a natural reservoir that preserved the snowpack from winter wind and sun. Without the protection of the forest, little of the snowpack remained when the warmer spring weather arrived. Louis G. Carpenter, as Colorado's state engineer, reported in 1905 that less than 20 percent of the original forest remained along the upper reaches of the valley. The cutting of the forest had seriously reduced the river flow to all downstream irrigators, compounding problems with rising salinity levels, siltation, and phreatophytes.[12]

Nature summoned more weapons than these from its arsenal, also impairing the works of irrigators with flood and drought. The 1921 flood wreaked havoc all along the river. An intense downpour in the Upper Arkansas Valley and along the Fountain Creek watershed unleashed a voluminous runoff. A few days afterward, irrigators of the Rocky Ford company, along with all the other farmers in the valley, assessed their losses, which included severe damage to their diversion dam. Within three years the shareholders had put the finishing touches to a new dam and river gates built (to the tune of $50,000) with "a view to withstanding severe flood water." The company's victory was short-lived, as it took the river only twenty years to bury this structure in silt.[13]

The 1921 flood also caused serious damage to the Bessemer system. When the superintendent and the Bessemer's board of directors evaluated the river's destruction, they felt thankful that the headgate and diversion dam had remained intact. The flood, however, had wrecked or swept away four major flumes, caused at least two major breaks in the canal walls, filled sandgates with silt, weakened the spillway at the diversion dam so that it would break within two years during heavy river flow, and flooded the company's office in Pueblo, destroying all but a few of its records.[14] The board had difficulty finding the money needed for repairs, estimated at over $88,000. The federal government, through the Federal Land Bank located at Wichita, Kansas, offered parsimonious aid. The agency made available a mere $250,000 in loans to cover all the flood damage to irrigation systems in the entire valley. With so many concerns clamoring for so little money, the Bessemer's board sought relief elsewhere. It finally arranged a $75,000 loan from the Pueblo Savings and Trust Company and backed the loan by increasing assessments. By the end of summer the company had the ditch in complete repair.[15]

In 1942 another spring flood caused serious damage to the Bessemer canal. A mud and rock slide nearly wrecked the upper end of the ditch. Moreover, the slide almost altered the river's course one and a quarter miles above the company's headgate. Had this occurred, the company's diversion dam would have been left high and dry. Excavation work, however, prevented this, and the river continued to supply the ditch.[16]

A less severe flood than the ones in 1921 or 1942 could still cause a company grave difficulty. In the 1890s freshets provided enough flow to destroy the Fort Lyon headworks. This left the company in such serious trouble that it cooperated in a joint venture with the Great Plains storage company to rebuild the diversion dam and headgates for joint use. Their cooperation to conquer nature, however, soon degenerated into conflict.

During the December 1900 stockholders' meeting of the Fort Lyon company, a majority refused to elect two directors from the storage company, and litigation between the two groups continued for another thirty-nine years. In 1901 the Arkansas Valley Sugar Beet and Irrigated Land Company (part of the sugar-beet empire of the New York Oxnard family) absorbed the Great Plains Water Storage Company and the Amity Land and Irrigation Company; secured the old La Junta company mortgage; and claimed the right to appoint three members to the Fort Lyon board. During the 1902 stockholders' meeting, the Fort Lyon farmers simply refused to seat any of the sugar company's representatives and successfully rebuffed the New York firm in federal circuit and district courts, district state courts, and the Colorado Supreme Court. In 1936 the Colorado Supreme Court converted the New York firm's holdings in the state into a cooperative enterprise called the Amity Mutual Irrigation Company. In 1939 the Amity stockholders relinquished any demands to representation on the Fort Lyon board, resolving one source of conflict. Even so, the Amity company still drew its reservoir water through the headgates of the Fort Lyon, which over the years caused difficulties of its own. The Fort Lyon stockholders, however, rested more easily knowing that their struggle had won for them exclusive control over their system.[17]

Litigation might resolve issues with the Amity company, but Fort Lyon irrigators could not defeat recurring drought—despite their investment of considerable money, time, and effort to combat aridity. Their experiences with dry conditions and with the poor river rights previously secured by T. C. Henry, as well as their tussles with the Amity system, brought the farmers together as they attempted to extend their control over nature. From 1901 until 1927, guided by engineering studies, they constructed a new concrete diversion dam, rebuilt many of the overflows in concrete, bought and enlarged Horse and Adobe Creek reservoirs, and oversaw the construction of a feeder ditch to convey floodwaters from the Arkansas River to the storage sites. In 1915, with the work drawing to an end, longtime president D. S. Nowels claimed in his farewell statement that the technological improvements to the system would finally ensure intensive and diversified farming on holds of eighty acres or less. He insisted that such a system meant "vastly superior social, educational and cooperative advantages for the farmer and his family."[18] In 1916 work was completed on the feeder canal. In commemorating the event the new Fort Lyon president, J. G. Washburn, reflected the common belief that a greater domination of nature led to progress when he stated that as a result of the new canal, the Fort Lyon lands could be "made the garden spot of the Arkansas Valley."[19] The international economic situation also added to Washburn's cheerfulness as World War I created such a demand for food and fiber that prosperity swept the region. As Edward Chew, the state division engineer for the Arkansas Valley, wrote in his 1917 annual report, the farmers felt "the shade of 'easy street.' "[20] International war, combined with the development of flood storage, gave the company its first breath of commercial success.

Nonetheless, the further conquest of nature through the new supplemental systems failed to secure progress and prosperity. By 1930 the Fort Lyon farmers managed a very complex system. The solutions to their problems often lay beyond their capabilities, and consequently they had to rely on hydrologic engineers for answers. But a solution was always elusive. Even though the farmers intended to ensure an adequate supply of water throughout an irrigation season, often the reservoirs remained empty or partially full depending on annual precipitation. Moreover, when full the reservoirs supplied only one complete season's worth of water. Therefore, the storage system, part of the company's effort to harness nature, only augmented the water supply rather than guaranteed it, and the company, as a result, still faced insufficient provisions from the river during extreme drought.[21]

The Fort Lyon farmers, as well as others, faced water shortages because no one had questioned the goodness of growth. Once someone had built a canal, then he or she had a vested property right regardless of

Fort Lyon Headgate System, ca. 1900 (*Thirteenth Biennial Report of the State Engineer, Colorado, 1905–1906* [Denver: State Printers, 1906], facing p. 160).

whether or not the ecology in the valley could support the enterprise. There were simply too many irrigators in the valley, all clamoring for the fulfillment of their water rights. People referred to the Arkansas River in Colorado as "overdecreed," meaning that the total of all water rights in the valley greatly exceeded the normal river flow. River flow could meet all the decreed rights during high flow or floods, but farmers seldom wanted their rights honored during those conditions. Floods caused tremendous damage to irrigation works, and high flows occurred during times of abundant precipitation. The hardship of an overdecreed river came during the growing season. As the river flow lessened, the division engineer began to cut off junior rights. When drought hit, those systems possessing junior rights suffered severe water deficits.[22]

The connection between precipitation and water rights—how this varied between companies and how it promoted either conflict or cooperation—becomes especially clear upon an analysis of how much water each system applied yearly to its lands. Irrigators calculated what they called the gross duty of acre-feet per acre irrigated. This was simply the total annual amount of water that a company applied to its lands divided by the amount of acreage irrigated. The higher the number, the more water the system provided to its land. In the Arkansas River Valley, as a general rule irrigators thought that a gross duty of between 2 to 3 acre-feet a year could adequately supply most crop production needs, so long as the water entered their canals at the right time of the growing season.

Stark differences emerge when contrasting the gross duties of the three case studies. The Rocky Ford Ditch Company, with its early-dated water rights, not surprisingly had the best water supply of the three systems. From 1895 until 1950, it averaged 4.74 acre-feet of water per acre irrigated. During the same period, the Bessemer Irrigating Ditch Company, with some water usually purchased each year from the Colorado Fuel and Iron Company's Sugar Loaf Reservoir located in the mountains along the upper reaches of the Arkansas Valley, provided a mean of 2.84 acre-feet of water per acre irrigated—considerably less than the Rocky Ford. From 1912 through 1950 the Fort Lyon Canal Company, even with its sizable reservoir system, provided only 2.33 acre-feet of water per acre irrigated.[23]

More specifically, drought devastated the companies that possessed weak water rights. During the harsh dry years of 1931–40, the Rocky Ford's farmers may have suffered from low crop prices (aside from sugar beets) but not from a lack of water. Because of their strong water rights, their yearly average gross duty never fell below 3.31 or 4.31 acre-feet of water per acre irrigated (depending on which set of records one chooses to use). The Bessemer, with weaker water rights than the Rocky Ford, never provided less than 2.04 acre-feet of water per acre irrigated, with four years of gross duties above 3 acre-feet. Even in the disastrously dry year of 1934, the company supplied 2.47 acre-feet per acre irrigated. In contrast, the Fort Lyon had only four years with a gross duty *over* 2 acre-feet, and in 1934 the number fell alarmingly to either 1.04 or 1.11 acre-feet of water per acre irrigated—totally inadequate for crop production.[24]

The weakness of the Fort Lyon's water rights placed its operations at the mercy of the river flow. Unlike the other two companies, the Fort Lyon's variation in water diverted onto its lands correlated to the variation in the Arkansas River's flow. If a company owned strong water rights, then normal river flow would always fill them, and variations in stream volume would not be linked to the rise and fall in ditch diversions. Since the opposite case held for the Fort Lyon company, it exhibited a very litigious character, with the board, through its law firm, always responding quickly to any perceived threat to the river flow that could impact the company's operations. Moreover, because both companies were always subject to variable and undependable diversions through the main headgate, the Amity company and the Fort Lyon often disagreed over the accuracy of the flow measurement through the headgate. Miscalculations directly affected the amount of water each received, and neither trusted the other's figures.[25]

During the 1930s the farmers of the Fort Lyon suffered acutely from poor water rights and severe drought complicated by economic depression. Farmers under the system had not experienced such harsh drought conditions since 1901–3, and this dry spell persisted from 1931 through 1939. The Arkansas River flow decreased to nearly one-half that of the previous twenty years. In 1932 H. D. Amsley, the superintendent, tried to manage without any stored water in the reservoirs. He also had to control headgate diversions with river flow fluctuating from 100 to 300 cfs (cubic feet of water per second) during twenty-four-hour periods because of the uneven mountain snowpack melt. Ray McGrath, the company's president, discouraged water-intensive crops, such as corn or beets. Sand built up around the diversion dam, closing off the sand gates and burying a flume. The board raised the dam one foot at the head of the main canal in an effort to keep pace with sedimentation.[26]

If the years 1931 and 1932 seemed like bad ones for the company, then unmitigated disaster was waiting for it in 1934. Amsley attempted to apportion water runs fairly. In spite of his efforts, farmers, desperate from the lack of water, began breaking the locks on their weirs. The ditch runner had the responsibility for locking the weirs after a farmer received his or her share of the run and then for proceeding downstream to unlock the next weir. Lock-breaking presented Amsley with a distinct threat to the equal distribution of scant water supplies. Faced with few alternatives, the board of directors reluctantly initiated lawsuits against many of the lock breakers. Distressed by the ruinous results of drought, Pres. M. M. Simpson commented in the company's 1934 annual report that he "would rather forget than review the past irrigation season."[27]

The financial situation for the canal company appeared as grim as its water supply. In 1932 the board had reduced assessments by ten cents a share to assist farmers. They also investigated the possibility of a $100,000 loan from the Reconstruction Finance Corporation (RFC), but the company failed to qualify. The company's financial condition worsened in 1934. So that the farmers would not have to worry about defaulting on assessments, the board levied very low rates. The company's situation made President Simpson remark: "The old belt is up to the last hole and no corner is in sight; the corners of the mouth will not turn up any more because the teeth are gone. The weather man has taken us off his visiting list. Now, what have you?"[28] During the Great Depression Simpson and his fellow farmers wearily endured a very grim predicament which placed the company on the brink of disaster. The harsh drought and economic conditions of the 1930s revealed to the Fort Lyon farmers how little they controlled their fates.

The Bessemer Irrigating Ditch Company, even though not faced by the same water shortages as the Fort Lyon system, also experienced severe economic strain during the depression. By 1931 the company started cutting the monthly wages of its ditch runners and office staff and the allowances of the directors. Many farmers failed to pay their assessments, prompting the board to toughen the bylaws pertaining to those irrigators who were in arrears. In 1932 out of approximately 250 stockholders, 92 could not pay their assessments. The company threatened to shut off their water, which reduced the number of shareholders in arrears to 51 by 1934. The small stockholders had the most difficulty making payments, and in one instance the board eliminated from the company's rank one small stockholder whom they had found particularly annoying. The board also applied to the RFC for a loan, with the same discouraging result encountered by the Fort Lyon.[29]

The Rocky Ford farmers did not suffer in the depression as did the Bessemer and Fort Lyon farmers. Rocky Ford irrigators usually had ample water because of their early-dated water rights. They also farmed sugar beets, and this crop maintained better prices during the 1930s than crops like alfalfa and cereals.[30] In short, the nature of this system and its niche in the valley sustained flourishing operations even during drought or depression.

The Rocky Ford farmers partook of a cooperative relationship largely influenced by the American Crystal Sugar Company. In 1899 land agents for Henry Oxnard pursued an aggressive campaign to buy land and water rights under the ditch system. Agents worked to provide the sugar company with enough acreage to ensure that it would have a beet crop for its factory regardless of fluctuations in local farmers' beet production. Within a few years it had bought around 4,600 acres. The water rights attached to this land gave the sugar company control over approximately 53 percent of the ditch company's water rights, which meant it also held the same percentage of the ditch company's stock. This gave Oxnard effective control over the policies of the canal system.[31]

The Rocky Ford farmers who elected to retain their lands, however, felt little or no resentment toward the sugar company. Neither Oxnard nor later presidents ever dealt with the farmers in a heavy-handed manner. Attesting to this was the fact that no serious lawsuit ever emerged as a result of disagreements between farmers and the sugar company. The farmers must have never felt seriously cheated or abused by the company's controlling interest in the ditch. When the sugar company had no use for its water, which occurred after it had finished harvesting beets and processing the crop, then the farmers had access to the sugar company's rights for winter watering. Moreover, the proximity of the factory gave the Rocky Ford farmers the opportunity for jobs during the sugar-refining operation in the fall, besides a reliable market for a valuable cash crop. Consequently, a symbiotic relationship between the farmers and sugar company remained healthy through 1950.[32]

Superb fertile soils added to the Rocky Ford Ditch Company's assets. Silty clay loams varying from four to eighteen inches in depth characterized most of the soils under the canal. Their porous nature allowed easy penetration of water and air, as well as plant roots. The majority of these loams lacked any problem with salinity because sandy subsoils, resting on top of limestone or marl, drained the return flows and provided excellent leaching action. The very sandy and saline soils that bordered the creeks and river bottoms yielded the only poor growing conditions under the system. Alkali sacaton, inland slatgrass, and tamarix trees thrived in these areas making them nearly worthless for irrigation practices.[33]

As a result of favorable soil conditions and strong water rights, the Rocky Ford's farmers grew a great diversity of valuable cash crops on 8,000 acres. They could always raise water-intensive plants such as onions, potatoes, beans, peas, sugar beets, and cantaloupes. These plants returned greater profits to the farmer than did the less water-intensive crops of alfalfa and cereals. J. G. Hamilton, secretary of the American Crystal Sugar Company, stated that a farmer cleared more profits from 10 acres of beets than he or she could from 100 acres of corn. Moreover, cantaloupes produced better returns than sugar beets. The farmers faced only one drawback to raising sugar beets and cantaloupes—the manual labor involved in crop production. Without additional hands, one farmer could only work 20 acres in sugar beets. To encourage reluctant farmers to grow beets, the Oxnard sugar company imported Mexican fieldworkers to do the back-breaking thinning of the plants in the spring and the harvesting of the roots in the fall. As a result, of the Rocky Ford company's total acreage under irrigation, beet production ranged from 13 percent (1,190 acres) in 1905 to 38 percent (3,800 acres) in 1907. From 1903 to 1947, the farmers generally kept over 20 percent (around 2,000 acres) of their land in sugar beets. (After World War II the sugar-beet industry suffered severe reversals that caused farmers to reduce their acreages.) Cantaloupes also required extra hands to do the extensive hoeing in the early summer, the precise watering through the summer, and the picking and crating of the fruit beginning in mid August. Thus, even though cantaloupes and melons brought high returns, they accounted for only around 10 percent of irrigated farmlands.[34]

Before the advent of sugar-beet production, the company's farmers had reserved a sizable percentage of the land for orchards. Fruit trees, however, meant long-term investments in money and upkeep before farmers realized profits. With better and faster returns from sugar beets, cantaloupes, and truck crops, farmers began moving away from orchards after 1900. A less water-intensive crop than beets or melons, alfalfa lacked a high cash value and was never allotted the substantial acreage found under other systems—seldom more than 30 percent of their land. Moreover, alfalfa produced less well on the silty loams farmed by the Rocky Ford irrigators than on deep clay loams. Alfalfa, however, had an important place in crop rotation with sugar beets and cantaloupes. From 1906 until 1950 cereals completed the crop production record of the Rocky Ford farmers, who kept about one-quarter of their fields in small grains.[35]

The Bessemer company's nature, and its niche where its 50,000 acres lay, were not as conducive to the superb operations effected by the Rocky Ford. The geographical location of the ditch provided countless difficulties for the Bessemer's superintendent. Before 1950, from its headgate eastward, the ditch traversed ruggedly dissected lands until reaching South Pueblo. The ditch line bisected the city and continued through the Colorado Fuel and Iron Company's property. Beyond the steel plant were located the majority of the Bessemer shareholders' agricultural lands. The direction of the ditch continued eastward to a lengthy redwood siphon built under the St. Charles River. The route of the ditch gave the company persistent problems with its wooden siphons, floods, and its relationship to the city of Pueblo.

The best technology of the 1890s could not fully harness the river. J. S. Greene, the engineer who probably finished the construction of the ditch for the Colorado Coal and Iron Company, designed and directed the building of the redwood siphon under the St. Charles River, a state-of-the-art engineering feat in 1891. The rough terrain that the western portion of the canal passed through required many such structures, and the company had to give constant attention to these important conveyances. By 1920 the redwood staves of the St. Charles siphon had sprung numerous leaks. The board advanced around $3,500 for repair materials, and by the time the crews finished the work the company had spent over $9,000. Even though the redwood staves proved durable over the years, the company still maintained a constant repair program for this essential link in the system.[36]

More troubles arose with the city of Pueblo over how to manage the ditch within the city limits. The increasing use of automobiles and the paving of streets created runoffs into the canal tainted by petroleum products. Whenever it rained, oil, rubber, and anything else on top of the asphalt and concrete streets near the canal polluted the ditch water. In response the company had to design a drainage system that prevented street runoffs from fouling its supply. The more urban growth occurred, which was what irrigation was intended to foster, the more complex the technology became that kept the Bessemer system operational.[37]

While the ditch company worked to protect itself from the city, the

The St. Charles Siphon of the Bessemer Ditch System (Western Research Library, Pueblo Library District, Pueblo, Colorado).

Bridge crossing the Bessemer Ditch (Vallejo Collection, Western Research Library, Pueblo Library District, Pueblo, Colorado).

people of Pueblo likewise regarded the ditch as a serious threat to their safety. In 1926 drownings in the canal led one city newspaper, the *Pueblo Star-Journal*, to label the ditch "a menace to the community." The city and the Bessemer board responded jointly to public complaints. The city's commissioner of public safety hired a special patrolman to keep swimmers out of the canal, and the company erected a high fence enclosing the ditch within the city limits. Moreover, the company also absorbed the cost of maintaining over thirty bridges within the city limits. In 1936 superintendent A. N. Dallimore reported to the board the generally poor condition of the company's bridges, as increased auto traffic was weakening their structural strength. Bridge maintenance presented the company with sizable yearly outlays in capital improvements.[38]

Other people fought the Bessemer company in an attempt to protect their property rights. In 1909 the owners of land located ten miles below the headgate of the ditch threatened to force the company to make costly capital improvements in a series of state supreme court cases. The plaintiffs complained that canal seepage laden with alkali had flooded and ruined their lands. They sought damages from the ditch company and modifications to the canal that would control the problem. Deciding that the plaintiffs had not proven their case, the court ruled in favor of the Bessemer.[39]

Although the Bessemer irrigators stemmed this assault, other battles were more costly. The location of their diversion gates compounded a problem they faced when dealing with transit losses. Simply put, it took water to deliver water. The Bessemer company purchased water on a regular basis from the Colorado Fuel and Iron Company's Sugar Loaf Reservoir in the upper valley. The state engineer calculated how much water would be lost from evaporation and absorption before a given volume reached the Bessemer headgate. This amount was subtracted from the reservoir release, and the Bessemer could divert the remainder as additional river flow at its headgate. If the state engineer estimated too much loss in transit, the Bessemer incurred a loss in water diversions and a correspondingly poor return on their purchases. The Bessemer board seldom agreed with the state engineer's calculation of transit loss. On numerous occasions the board petitioned state authorities and engaged in lawsuits striving to obtain an acceptable standard of measure.[40]

Other facets of the Bessemer farmers' niche were a mixed blessing to their operations. These irrigators worked fertile, sandy clay loams, but the lack of solid water rights focused their attention more on growing alfalfa rather than on raising higher-value and more water-intensive truck crops and melons and the large acreages of sugar beets found under the Rocky Ford. Until the late 1920s, Bessemer farmers put over 40 percent of their lands in alfalfa. From 1935 until after World War II, alfalfa acreage dropped and hovered at around 15 percent of the system's total acreage. The reason for the drop is not entirely clear from the state engineer's records, but it is possible they grew more corn. Regardless, the percentage of alfalfa acreage climbed again after 1947. Bessemer farmers planted significant amounts of sugar beets during World War I and maintained sizable percentages until after the sugar-beet economy had started to fail in the valley in the late 1940s. They planted a smaller proportion of their total land in cereals than did the Rocky Ford farmers. Cereals, however, still formed an important part of the Bessemer's crops and measured somewhere between 15 and 25 percent of irrigated acreage. While farming less profitable crops than in the Rocky Ford system, the Bessemer irrigators still had a fairly stable system, disrupted only by severe drought, depression, and flood.[41]

The niche occupied by the Fort Lyon farmers encouraged as much conflict as cooperation. Differences in geography and water rights on the 90,000 acres within the Fort Lyon system produced opposing attitudes toward capital improvements. From the moment farmers organized the company, two factions of irrigators disagreed over the assessments that generated the funds for canal upkeep and renovations. The nature of the split among the stockholders led to serious disputes.

Before T. C. Henry lengthened the ditch from Gageby Arroyo to Lamar in 1889, the farmers west of the draw possessed adequate water rights for the soils that they worked, so long as the river flowed. The bottoms in this region were characterized by shallow, silty clay loams on top of sand and gravel deposits. Irrigators found this land well suited for growing high-value truck crops and sugar beets. Water also quickly percolated this soil profile to the gravels below which returned the flow to the river. To supply their extensive water needs, the companies, before Henry assumed control of the system, delivered 1 cfs to each 55.55 acres. Irrigators later referred to this amount as "double rights."[42]

Henry created a second group of irrigators when he extended the ditch to the north of Lamar in 1889. He changed the nature of the water rights attached to the land east of Gageby Arroyo because of the pressing need to acquire additional capital and the different geography east of the draw. For this area Henry allowed only 1 cfs per 111.1 acres, a formula irrigators now commonly designate as "single rights." In this manner Henry more than doubled the acreage east of the arroyo using the water decrees that his company had secured from the state. He also generated a great number of individual water rights whose sale he hoped would raise capital. He calculated that this land warranted tying a small volume of water to each acre irrigated. Farmers knew that the deep clay loams of the terraces east of the arroyo held water and produced well when planted in grains and alfalfa—less water-intensive plants than sugar beets or truck crops.[43]

The outcome of the differences in their respective water rights was that the two factions of stockholders often disagreed on the rate of assessments. Assessments, it must be noted, bore no direct relationship to the actual amount of water delivered to each farmer—which varied according to how much river flow the system diverted. The superintendent and ditch runners proportioned the "run" to each farmer based on the percentage of his or her holding of company stock (which was the usual means of water distribution in all mutual companies). Therefore, shareholders east of Gageby Arroyo generally favored higher assessments to achieve ditch efficiencies to their land. Such strategies cost them less per-acre-farmed than the irrigators west of Gageby Arroyo who faced substantially greater costs per-acre-farmed for no material improvements in their water delivery. One eastern farmer summed up this long-standing tension with his western peer: "He wants to wire things up and I want to fix them."[44]

Geography and weak water rights also determined crop production in the Fort Lyon system. As already noted, Fort Lyon farmers tilled quite diverse soils. Farmers west of Gageby Arroyo worked clay loams similar to lands under the Rocky Ford and Bessemer ditches, so they planted crops in percentages similar to those found in the Rocky Ford system. Farmers on lands east of Gageby Arroyo tilled deeper soils on higher terraces farther north of the river bottom than their western counterparts. The majority of the system's acreage lay east of Gageby Arroyo, and these farmers shied away from raising water-intensive crops. Consequently, most of the farmers under the Fort Lyon system relied on sizable plantings of alfalfa and cereals. In the unusual year of 1918 these crops comprised 92 percent of the system's total acreage. Generally, however, farmers devoted around 60 to 70 percent of their lands to the two crops. Lacking suitable soils and water rights they avoided significant acreages of sugar beets. Before the mid-1920s, when the sugar-beet economy still flourished in the valley, these farmers placed as much as 20 percent of their lands in beets. After 1922, however, it never amounted to more than 8 percent, and the sugar-beet acreage continued to fall until it totaled no more than 3 percent of the lands by the late 1940s. Moreover, orchards and melons never figured as more than a minute fraction of the total acreage—seldom exceeding 1 percent.[45]

What seemed to make irrigation profitable, not only for the Fort Lyon farmers but also for most of the irrigators in the valley, were factors lying beyond their control as shareholders in a mutual stockholding company. Just as World War I gave an economic stimulus to the valley's irrigators, the return of war and rain provided renewed relief in the 1940s. World

War II led to an increased demand for food and fiber which helped these companies regain their economic footing, as did the resumption of regular river flow by 1941. As the Arkansas River amply watered crops and filled reservoirs to capacity, Pres. C. N. Troup of the Fort Lyon breathed a sigh of relief and hoped "that we have passed the so-called dustbowl period." By the end of 1944 the board and farmers of the Fort Lyon system approved an assessment sufficient to retire the company's entire bonded indebtedness—the first time the company stood debt-free. Even though many farmers had suffered personal losses from the war, as a whole they welcomed a return of prosperity for their companies. Still, as drought, depression, and war proved, the mutual stockholding form of incorporation did not change the fact that irrigators were often at the mercy of events larger than themselves. No matter how they might regard their "conquest" of nature, they were still some distance from complete victory.[46]

The practice of irrigation had brought environmental change to the Arkansas River Valley of Colorado. Riverbanks narrowed, and cottonwoods and salt cedar proliferated, complicating irrigation practices all along the river. The river's salinity level rose each year, causing companies along its middle and lower reaches problems in crop production. Irrigation companies also lowered and smoothed the Arkansas River flow and produced in places greater regularity in the flow of its tributaries.

Situated in the midst of this ever-changing environment were the irrigation companies. Even though the mutual stockholding form of organization dominated in the valley, the similarity in companies ended there. Of the three case studies, the Rocky Ford Ditch Company, because of its niche and strong water rights, maintained a level of smooth and diversified operations envied throughout the valley. As a farming enterprise it enjoyed a symbiotic relationship with an industrial corporation, the sugar company. The Rocky Ford's precious water rights provided the irrigators with an adequate and reliable supply of water that guaranteed the production of high-value cash crops.

The Bessemer Irrigating Ditch Company, as a result of its niche and its mixture of strong and weak water rights, operated under more trying conditions than did the Rocky Ford. Even though the company enjoyed a mutually beneficial relationship with the region's industrial giant, the Colorado Fuel and Iron Company, and kept up good crop diversity, it could not reliably provide its shareholders the same volume of water per acre as did the Rocky Ford. The Bessemer also experienced trouble in its relationship with Pueblo. The city and ditch company often engaged in acrimonious exchanges over problems that arose from a ditch being located within an urban environment—although they usually reached some compromise. The geographical placement of the company's diversion dam and headgate caused it serious operational problems over the correct measurement of transit loss and costly repairs resulting from floods. Although the stockholders of the Bessemer often celebrated their mutual control of their company and their success at commercial agriculture, they clearly encountered more problems in achieving their prosperity than did the shareholders of the Rocky Ford company.

The operations of the Fort Lyon Canal Company differed considerably from the other two case studies. Weak water rights and tussles with the Amity company compelled Fort Lyon irrigators to build an extensive reservoir system and to improve the delivery capacity and efficiency of the canal. The unique distribution of the company's stock along the ungainly length of the system retarded consensus among the shareholders on capital improvements. Farmers raised more alfalfa and small grains, which were less valuable cash crops than sugar beets or melons. They did this because of the company's weak water rights and because of the clay loams that most of them worked. During any sustained drought junior water rights failed to provide water and damaged the viability of the company. In addition, weak rights contributed to the company's litigious character as the board responded quickly to stop any perceived reduction in the river flow caused by upstream development. The contention between the Amity system and the Fort Lyon alone kept water lawyers well employed. The Fort Lyon board even instructed its attorney to proceed against its own shareholders when their lock-breaking threatened the distribution of water through the ditch during the drought of the 1930s. The history of the Fort Lyon company revealed the difficulties of devising successful commercial irrigation.

In competing for the river flow of the Arkansas River, not only irrigators sought to conquer nature for social and economic growth. Urbanites and industrialists all needed water; as city dwellers multiplied and factory managers increased production, they too demanded more water. By 1900, with far above the normal river flow decreed to agriculture alone, urban and industrial growth meant either clashing with irrigators over the control of river water rights or devising alternatives—such as constructing transmountain projects to pump water west of the continental divide to the thirsty cities, factories, and mills on the eastern slope. Case histories of the water systems of Pueblo, Colorado Springs, and the Colorado Fuel and Iron Company illustrate the character of urban and industrial water development in the Arkansas River Basin.

CHAPTER FOUR

Urban and Industrial Water Uses and Policies, 1870–1950

Urbanites and industrialists, their water plights largely ignored by historians, craved water in the West as much as irrigators. Only Los Angeles has had its water history examined in any detail. In some respects, Los Angeles's development was prototypical of other western cities. The city had few water sources at its disposal. When the population grew beyond the city's ability to supply it, then planners and businesses worked in concert to tap well-water regions with fewer people—for example, the Owens Valley. The economic resources of the city made it possible to raise enormous sums of money to implement water plans and to win costly legal battles with small towns and irrigators, who had difficulty amassing the strength necessary to withstand the onslaught. This scenario of Los Angeles's water history would be played out in other western cities and large industries when they reached the critical mass where local water supplies could no longer sustain their plans for growth.

But just as all mutual stockholding irrigation companies were not alike, the histories of urban and industrial water development in the West differed. The nature of a city or industry—that is, its niche and economics—made for unique experiences in its water development. Pueblo, Colorado Springs, and the Colorado Fuel and Iron Company, though each was smaller and less powerful than Los Angeles, were important urban and industrial centers along the Front Range, second only to Denver. With a history of their water development comes a fuller understanding of water use in the Arkansas Valley.

The pressures of growth often caused conflict when Pueblo, Colorado Springs, and the Colorado Fuel and Iron Company had expanded beyond the capacities of their water systems. By 1900 new viable water rights did not exist in the overdecreed valley, forcing cities and industry to purchase developed agricultural rights, which in turn curtailed farming. Typically, irrigators from an area where rights were to be sold feared the disruption of their water supplies and challenged the buyers' plans in court. To avoid this costly conflict, city planners in particular sought to transport water from the wetter western side of the continental divide to the drier Arkansas River Valley. Sustaining growth turned out to be a complex matter.

The particular niches in the valley occupied by Pueblo, Colorado Springs, and the Colorado Fuel and Iron Company molded their individual approaches to water development. The managers of the three systems faced special water supply problems as they responded to distinct geographic and environmental conditions in the pursuit of common economic ambitions. As seen in each case, planners dreamed of growth through technological water developments secured by strategies of conflict and cooperation.

Initially, the niche of Pueblo afforded its citizens a reliable water supply. Puebloans built where Fountain Creek and the St. Charles River met the Arkansas River as it flowed out of the foothills. This site had served Plains Indians, the Spanish, and fur trappers. In 1859 irrigation farmers, who supplied food to anxious gold miners, settled the area. Soon a few general stores and dwellings were built, and the town was called Pueblo. The residents drew their water from the river, but eventually, as the town expanded, vendors filled barrels with river water and plied it on the dusty streets. This met most Puebloans' early water needs, so long as their buildings did not catch fire.

The business community, faced with poor fire protection, prompted the construction of the city's publicly owned water system. As more buildings sprang up in the city, the potential for conflagration increased. This situation concerned business people more than any others because of the high rates of fire insurance for their buildings. In December 1868 fire swept through the business district of Pueblo and ruined many people. That night, George A. Hinsdale, the editor of the *Colorado Chieftain*, and Mayor James Rice laid their plans for a campaign to acquire a city-owned water system.[1]

A few businesses, however, attempted a privately owned system first. In December 1872 Lewis Conley, the first president of Pueblo's Board of Trustees, joined with Julius Berry, a prominent merchant, and Henry C. Thatcher, a lawyer, to organize the Arkansas Aqueduct Company. Unanticipated costs put the company $40,000 in arrears, and by August 1873 Thatcher began complaining about delinquent stockholders and mounting company debts, which finally bankrupted the company. Worse yet, the open ditch had provided inadequate fire protection. The city, cried the editor, needed a publicly owned water system.[2]

Mayor James Rice had always wanted a public water system, and his work became simpler with the failure of the aqueduct company. Although local capital could not underwrite a private system, brokers could sell municipal bonds to eastern and foreign investors to fund a public project. Besides, as argued in the *Chieftain*, the citizens spent over $5,000 a year purchasing water by the barrel, more than enough to pay the interest rate on a bond issue. Rice's plan was worked out with C. E.

Grey, vice-president of the National Building Company of St. Louis; they would tap the Arkansas River as it flowed through Pueblo with a large steam-generated pumping plant. Grey represented the Holly Manufacturing Company of Lockport, New York, which built massive pumps. Mayor Rice, with the full support of the city's business community, conducted a meeting where the citizens responded by supporting a bond issue to finance the Holly system. When the issue came to a vote in April 1874, it passed with only one dissenting ballot.[3]

The citizens realized the fruits of their cooperative endeavor in 1874. The construction company laid the pumping-house cornerstone at Fourth and High (now called Grand) streets on 24 June, and the city marked the occasion with Masonic ceremonies. On 9 November, to everyone's satisfaction, the final testing of the completed system took place. After a parade led by the newly formed firemen's company, the citizens celebrated amid streams of water thrown hundreds of feet into the air from hoses connected to the fire hydrants. The celebrants retired to the United States Saloon where "speeches were made, toasts drank and everybody had a good time." That evening the Pueblo Fire Department gave a grand ball at Chilcott's Hall where the " 'fire ladies' tripped the light fantastic." The citizens had a right to celebrate; they had acquired a system that protected property and provided for Pueblo's growth.[4]

Even though the public owned the north-side system, the people living south of the Arkansas River remained apart from these waterworks. Until 1886 three contiguous municipalities, Pueblo (north of the river), South Pueblo (south of the river), and Central Pueblo (a tract developed on reclaimed river bottoms), had their own mayors and aldermen, and Pueblo and South Pueblo had their own water systems. In 1886 this inefficient governmental arrangement came to an end when the residents of the three cities voted to form one Pueblo. The citizens north of the river, however, retained exclusive control over their water system as they reorganized it as an independent public agency, the Pueblo Water Works. This left the *privately* owned South Pueblo Water Company to supply the citizens south of the Arkansas River.

The south-side company originated with William Jackson Palmer and his Central Colorado Improvement Company. Palmer, and especially Dr. William A. Bell, solicited capital for the improvement company from far and wide and used the money to enhance the value of their real estate. In 1872 the company located a headgate nine miles up the Arkansas River from its South Pueblo townsite to feed the city's irrigating canal. Palmer's company constructed laterals along every street and watered over 10,000 planted trees in the hope of making the lots attractive to buyers.[5]

South Side Pueblo Water Works (Western Research Library, Pueblo Library District, Pueblo, Colorado).

As a private venture, the south-side company found itself more at the mercy of economic fluctuations than did the publicly owned north-side system. In the mid-1870s a depressed national economy ruined Palmer's plans. No one had money to buy town lots, and real-estate prices took a dizzying plunge. Palmer, nearly oblivious to pending ruin, used the company's remaining capital reserves to complete the St. Charles Canal that supplied Lake Minnequa, a 500-million-gallon reservoir south of the townsite. He had taken steps to slow his capital drain by pressing the town authorities to incorporate a private company called the South Pueblo Water Works to lay iron pipes connecting the business buildings and residences to the reservoir. After 1876 Palmer's plans faltered when depression overtook the region's economy.[6]

When Henry E. Sprague acquired Palmer's holdings, he secured important concessions from the nominally independent South Pueblo Water Company (which had board members representing Sprague's interests) for his Colorado Coal and Iron Company. Just before the iron company took over the properties of the improvement company in 1880, the South Pueblo Water Company had purchased the St. Charles Canal and Lake Minnequa. The improvement company had prudently "reserved in perpetuity" the right to use water from the ditch and reservoir "without cost" for supplying "any manufacturing establishment it may erect." When the Colorado Coal and Iron Company acquired the improvement company, it retained the water provisions made with the

South Pueblo Water Company. In this manner Sprague had unrestricted access to the water stored in Lake Minnequa for iron production and was not burdened by capital improvements for the delivery system.[7]

The south-side company could survive these arrangements as long as the local economy grew. By 1881 a strengthened regional economy brought increasing urban and industrial demands for water, and the South Side Company responded by installing steam pumps and settling reservoirs on the Arkansas River capable of supplying the steel works and filling Lake Minnequa. Its operations proved reliable and profitable. The south side, as a sign of its strength, levied one-dollar-a-month charges for water, whereas the north-side water company asked for two dollars; also, in 1882 and 1883 the Colorado Coal and Iron Company received handsome dividends on its water company stock. In 1887, with population increasing, the South Pueblo Water Company started extensive capital improvements that led to a new pumping station, a diversion dam, and a system of settling reservoirs along the river.[8]

In the economically depressed 1890s, the company found itself hardpressed to pay for its earlier capital improvements. It increased monthly rates to finance its bonds, and by 1901 its rates exceeded those of the north-side water system. The citizens south of the river protested high rates and poor service and organized the South Side Water Consumers' Association in 1903. The interest group demanded public ownership of the system and lobbied the state assembly to achieve their goal. In 1906 the legislature created Public Water Works, District No. 2, and allowed the citizens of Pueblo to buy the system for $1 million, plus the assumption of its bonded indebtedness. North-side taxpayers recoiled from any financial responsibility for the south-side system, leaving those living south of the Arkansas River with no choice but to assume the liability for the works. They elected their own trustees to manage Water District No. 2, then a quasi-public corporation like the north-side company.[9]

From 1914 to 1950, population growth occurred simultaneously with rising water consumption and governed the expansion of both systems. It is useful to note that, during this period, residents used the same amount of water—that is, annual per capita consumption averaged 146,947 gallons. What put pressure on the systems, then, was population growth, not any increases in individual consumption.[10] This simple observation is helpful in explaining the building booms of the two water systems before 1914. From 1880 to 1890, stimulated by increased steel manufacturing, the population of the city rose from over 3,000 to nearly 28,000. From 1900 to 1910 the population jumped from 28,000 to over 41,000. During these growth spurts, the south- and north-side boards enlarged their system to keep pace. By 1900, so boasted the editor of the *Daily Chieftain*, the north-side system could satisfy a city of 200,000 people.[11] These improvements, however, failed to satisfy consumers; consequently, the north-side board made additional improvements to the system, notably a new pumping plant with a total capacity of 40 million gallons per day. Population growth allowed the board to accomplish this construction while at the same time charging lower water rates to its customers than the south side could. This endeared the board to its customers, and virtually without any major modifications, this system supplied the north district into the 1950s.[12]

Even though population trends largely explain the city's water consumption, other factors influenced usage. Normally, annual rainfall did not coincide with how much water people used. Seasonal changes in consumption, however, always occurred, with water usage peaking during the summer months of June, July, and August and bottoming out during November, December, January, and February. Usually, when the river flowed fully, only pumping capacity restricted water consumption. The superintendent ran all the pumps at full steam during the peak demands of the summer months and cut back during winter. Such operations meant higher diversions during dry periods with corresponding reductions in wet times when domestic use lessened. So long as the river flow remained full, nothing prevented the superintendent from satisfying summer demands.[13]

When river flow failed, as it did during the severe drought of the 1930s, operations of both water systems faltered. From 1931 to 1936 annual per capita consumption fell substantially below the average, varying from a high of 139,309 gallons in 1931 to a low of 120,820 gallons in 1935. Moreover, annual water diversions for both companies dropped well below average. Given that maximum water demands always occurred during summer months, the simultaneous failure of river flow multiplied the hardships. For example, in July 1934 the *Pueblo Daily Chieftain* reported a river flow of only 81 cubic feet of water per second (cfs), whereas normally the stream provided 1,687 cfs. In March 1935 the *Chieftain* reported the river dry at Pueblo. The superintendents responded by rationing water, which led to consumer dissatisfaction as lawns browned and trees died.[14]

The severity of the drought caused both boards to secure their water rights. Before the drought, both systems simply pumped from the river whenever they pleased. With scant river flows, however, prior appropriators vigorously asserted their rights, and without legally dated decrees the Pueblo systems could be left dry. In 1932 the attorneys for both boards obtained court decrees to 20 cfs for the north system and 25 cfs for the south side with valuable senior appropriation dates of May 1874. The trustees also took options on agricultural rights offered for sale and acquired an additional 5.52 cfs for District No. 1 and 2.76 cfs for District

No. 2. The north side, though, ran into conflict with irrigators around the Canon City region as it attempted to buy farm rights in the area. The removal of those rights, so the Colorado Supreme Court held, would exact an unwarranted hardship upon local farming practices.[15]

The lack of water rights on the market, and the difficulty in purchasing them, led the north-side board to seek transmountain water. In 1929, on the western slope of the continental divide in Eagle County, Warren E. Wurtz began constructing a small ditch that tapped two tributaries of the Eagle River—Bennett and Mitchell creeks. The ditch would deliver water to a small tributary of the Tennessee Fork of the Arkansas River, thereby diverting western slope water to the eastern slope of the Rocky Mountains. By 1930 he had obtained grants of easement from the United States Forest Service for his ditch in Holy Cross and Cochetopa National Forests. In 1932 a group of investors, who incorporated as the Tennessee Pass Water Association, bought Wurtz's holdings with a view toward enticing the north-side board into a purchase agreement.[16]

The board agreed to buy the ditch, pending an assessment of how much water it could produce. James W. Preston, the board's attorney, and A. Watson "Wat" McHendrie, attorney for the association, worked out an agreement whereby a two-year test study would determine the purchase price. Charles L. Patterson, the region's most acclaimed water engineer and consultant, conducted the experiment. The association hoped to establish water delivery of 6,000 acre-feet per year, thereby justifying an asking price of $100,000.[17] In September 1937 Patterson's report recommended $20 an acre-foot based on an annual delivery rate of 2,500 acre-feet, which amounted to $50,000 for the system. The association bargained for an additional $10,000 but reluctantly agreed to the board's offer of $50,000 in January 1938. North-side voters resoundingly approved the purchase and thus augmented their water supply by around 25 percent. Everyone now hoped to avoid such problems as those associated with the dry decade of the 1930s.[18]

Floods also proved just as difficult to cope with as drought. Nature struck the city hardest in June 1921, when the Arkansas River rampaged for three days. On 5 June, 103,000 cfs poured through the city, over six times the normal flow of the river. The flood carried away 510 dwellings, wrecked 98 buildings, and lifted 61 off their foundations. Rescuers recovered seventy-eight bodies, but no one knew how many people the river had carried downstream and buried in silt.[19]

The south-side water system largely escaped damage, but not so the north. The flood submerged its pumping station to a depth of thirteen feet and filled the intake flume with mud and debris that nearly spilled into the reservoirs. The board spent almost $51,000 in the next year for repairs. It also joined the Pueblo Conservancy District, a state-

Aerial view of the 1921 Pueblo flood (Western Research Library, Pueblo Library District, Pueblo, Colorado).

authorized entity for pooling money and floating bonds, which local businesspeople, bureaucrats, and irrigators organized to construct flood prevention works. For its part, the north-side board contributed $33,000 to the district's construction of a barrier dam along Rock Creek and the channelization of the river through town. On its own the board built levees around the pumping plant. It also lobbied unsuccessfully for federal funding for additional flood control projects.[20]

Besides troubles with river flows stemming from floods and droughts, the niche of the city's two water systems gave rise to three types of river pollution: mine tailings, organic impurities, and hardness. The growth of mining, lumbering, and towns above Pueblo caused all of these problems. In 1929 the local chapter of the Izaak Walton League, a fishermen's interest group, tried to recruit the support of the cities below Leadville to take legal action to stop the Colorado Zinc and Lead Company from dumping in the river. Attorney James W. Preston responded for the north side by stating that even though he shared the league's concern, the board would join the effort only if conclusively shown that the tailings adversely affected their water supplies. Besides, the board generally relied on the threat of lawsuits, rather than actual litigation, to compel industrialists to clean their wastes.[21]

In addition to mine tailings, the untreated sewage from six upstream communities threatened Pueblo's water quality. As late as 1944 both boards attempted to treat their water supplies without expensive filtration systems. Both relied on a series of settling reservoirs to remove suspended matter, using sulphate of alumina for clarification, chlorine gas for sterilization, and chlorine and activated carbon for further sterilization and improvement in taste. The south side added coagulants to its settling reservoirs to remove suspended material. This treatment generally kept water safe for the north-side consumers, but the south side encountered additional problems with old pipe connections to the Colorado Fuel and Iron Company's facilities, which allowed industrial wastes to enter the system.[22]

Also, growing mineral concentrations in the flow caught the attention of Puebloans. As early as 1900 severe erosion of the gypsum beds along the tributaries to the Arkansas River between Canon City and Pueblo—caused partly by heavy runoffs that were prompted in turn by deforestation—contributed large quantities of calcium and magnesium to the water. In 1944 an engineering report calculated that the water at Pueblo averaged a hardness of approximately seventeen grains per gallon, a very high level.[23]

Water hardness had long plagued Pueblo's water supply. In 1903 the board had contemplated installing a filtering and treatment plant but had opted instead for the Pueblo Supply and Water Company's promise of a cheaper remedy through its Fountain Underflow Project. The company planned to tap the alluvium of Fountain Creek with wells, whereupon intake pipes would transport the water into large holding reservoirs. These pipes would connect to the north-side system. E. R. Chew, the engineer of Division No. 2 of the State Engineer's Office, concocted the scheme and persuaded some Chicago businessmen to underwrite the project. Construction crews began work in 1905, but the financiers fell upon hard times and control of Pueblo Supply and Water passed to the Ball Brothers of Muncie, Indiana, who finished the project.[24]

The board had two considerations in mind when they made the contract for water with Ball Brothers. First, they wanted pure and healthful water, and second, they desired a supply abundant enough for future needs, "as every city must make provisions for growth." The contract left the responsibility for collecting and delivering water into the north-side system to the supply company, and in turn the board promised "a certain sum per thousand gallons" delivered. Ball Brothers promised the board 60 million gallons per day, which meant that the north side could leave its Arkansas River plant as a secondary system.[25] Some locals argued that there would be alkali in the company's water, but the company's spokesmen answered with the dubious argument that alkali permeated the soil and not the water.

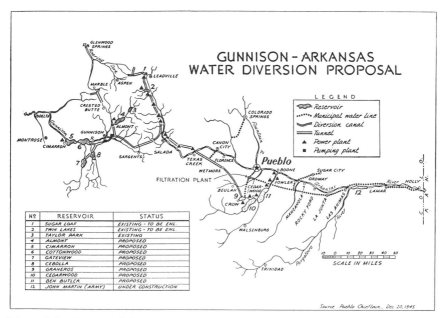

Map of the Proposed Gunnison-Arkansas Water Diversion Project, 1945 (L. A. Henry, "Water: The Second of a Series of Studies Sponsored by the Pueblo, Colorado, Chamber of Commerce," 54, James W. Preston Files, Board of Pueblo Water Works, Pueblo, Colorado).

At the beginning of January 1908 the supply company was ready to test its system. When the first consumers received the water, they found it unpalatable, and for good reason: The water was three to seven times harder than that found in the Arkansas River. Incredibly, the chemists who had conducted the purity tests analyzed only the organic concentrations, not the alkali. The "rumors" of alkaline water in the alluvium of Fountain Creek had proved true. When F. C. Ball, one of the owners of the company, attempted to justify the company's troubles to a mass meeting held at the courthouse, disgruntled citizens drowned him out "in hooting and hisses." The trustees quickly disassociated themselves from Ball Brothers by passing a resolution shutting off the underflow to the north-side system, so ending the board's involvement in the project.[26]

Even though both systems stayed abreast of consumer demands, the people who looked to growth beyond 1950 knew the pressing need for additions to the city's water systems. Some city planners expressed faith in the Gunnison-Arkansas River Diversion Project, a transmountain proposal of the Bureau of Reclamation that if constructed promised to sup-

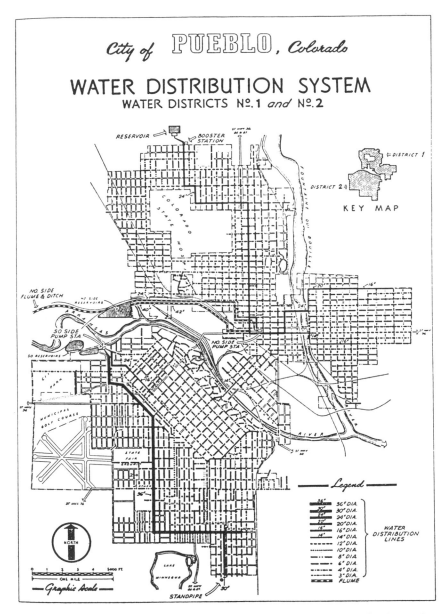

Map of the Pueblo Water System, 1946 (L. A. Henry, "Water: The Second of a Series of Studies Sponsored by the Pueblo, Colorado, Chamber of Commerce," 14, James W. Preston Files, Board of Pueblo Water Works, Pueblo, Colorado).

ply the valley with over 800,000 additional acre-feet a year. In 1949 both boards estimated that the city needed from 15,000 to 20,000 acre-feet to meet projected growth through 1970, a considerable portion of which they hoped to receive from the reclamation plan. In addition, continued public concerns about the quality of water meant that the boards would eventually have to build filtration plants to cleanse and soften the city's supply. Many were beginning to argue that the operation of two separate water systems in the city was an inefficient use of city resources. The city had reached the limits of its local resources, both economic and natural, and now people looked to the federal government to underwrite costly transmountain water projects and sewage systems to support further growth.[27]

As in Pueblo, the water system of Colorado Springs also operated to provide for urban growth. But a difference in niche and economics made this city's drive to develop its water system much more aggressive than Pueblo's. Colorado Springs lacked one important resource possessed by Pueblo: access to a substantial flow of water through the city. The dearth of easily tapped water made people doubt the wisdom of William Jackson Palmer's decision to build a townsite at the eastern base of Pikes Peak. Palmer, taken with the beauty of the place, thought he could overcome any problems of supply through engineering.

In 1871 Palmer initiated the development of the Colorado Springs water system. In the spring he had incorporated a land company, called the Colorado Springs Company, to promote the townsite. He had surveyed 2,000 town lots that he hoped to sell and thereby generate $540,000, $150,000 of which he earmarked for canals, trees, and parks. To design and build a canal system for the townsite, Palmer brought E. S. Nettleton from Greeley, Colorado, since he had devised the irrigation system used at that community. By January 1872 Nettleton had an eleven-mile ditch called the El Paso Canal in full operation. The ditch tapped Fountain Creek west of Colorado Springs, and its path wound through the townsite.[28]

In 1875 city growth required a better supply system than that afforded by the El Paso Canal. The editor of the *Colorado Springs Weekly Gazette* waged a fierce campaign for the building of a public water system that would address the community's twin fears of epidemic and fire. Neither the ditch nor a large public cistern could protect the city from fire, especially during winter months when water froze solid. Moreover, residents drew impure water from their wells. Many in the town found this state of affairs totally unacceptable.[29]

However, conflict with the business community doomed the first attempt at a publicly owned water system. The city had hired George Summers, a local civil engineer, to estimate what amount of water Bear

Creek, located on the south slope of Pikes Peak, could supply to the city. The flow, he concluded, could provide 400,000 gallons per day, enough for a city of 10,000 people. One group of businessmen, however, opposed the system. They had earlier advocated a $250,000 bond issue for the River Bend Railway Company, to subsidize its connection with the Kansas Pacific railroad. Since that bond issue was defeated, they campaigned against the $100,000 bond issue for the public water system wanted by their opponents. Despite the city's concerns over drinking from wells situated among cesspools and over the lack of fire protection, petty revenge helped to defeat the issue in December 1875.[30]

Economic and environmental forces, though, soon shaped a cooperative effort within the business community. In 1876 costly fires in the business district, followed by a drought in 1877, ruined businesses and tarnished the city's image as a health spa. Mayor Matt France, in response, pushed for a publicly owned system, and he based his arguments on the pocketbook-interests of the residents. He and others pointed out that people spent over $6,000 a year for barrel water, more than enough to pay the interest on a bond issue. He also argued that reliance on barrel water gave no fire protection and kept fire insurance rates unnecessarily high for property owners. Moreover, impure drinking water jeopardized the city's tourism—who would come to a health spa where people got sick from drinking the water? The mayor's case met a receptive audience when the propertied voters overwhelmingly approved the bonds in April 1878.[31]

The contracting firm of Russell and Alexander broke ground in Engleman's Canon and laid the foundation in October 1878 for what ultimately became known as the south slope water system. Collection pipes tapped Ruxton Creek just above Manitou and fed a storage reservoir located on the mesa slightly west of Fountain Creek where it entered Colorado Springs. The two newly formed fire companies tested the completed system on 9 December 1878. Residents celebrated under streams of water thrown from hoses attached to fire hydrants, and later that evening the city held a festive ball. Two Sundays before, Reverend Cross of the Congregational Church had given a sermon praising the system for its pure water and arguing that people could no longer claim the need to drink beer and whiskey to avoid tainted supplies.[32]

Between 1880 and 1908, to keep pace with a growing population, the city worked hard to trap the entire supply of water on the south slope of Pikes Peak. The engineering involved showed a sophisticated ability to transport water from one basin to another. Two valuable sources of water, Beaver and Boehmer creeks, lay on the south side of Seven Lakes Divide on the peak, and Ruxton Creek, which supplied the city, flowed to the north. H. I. Reid, the city engineer, designed tunnels—Strickler Tunnel, completed in 1900, and St. Johns Tunnel, finished in 1905—that bored through a hogback rock formation and the divide to carry Beaver and Boehmer creek flows into Ruxton Creek. He also developed Lake Moraine into a high-elevation reservoir to store these transridge waters. Since the lake was within the boundaries of the United States military reservation on Pikes Peak, the city obtained permission from Congress to purchase the site and other large portions of the watershed along the south slope. By 1908 eight high-elevation reservoirs, two major tunnels, miles of flumes and ditches, and two storage reservoirs all collected water to meet the growing demands of Colorado Springs.[33]

However, this elaborate water system raised a thorny legal question concerning rights of water transfer. The city had purchased irrigation rights along Beaver Creek where it emptied into the Arkansas River between Canon City and Pueblo, and it wanted to take the water and reroute it north into Ruxton Creek. Consequently, it had to resolve novel legal questions over the right to transfer into another watershed water that had been formerly diverted downstream in another basin. In a "friendly suit," Mayor John Strickland opened litigation against the city in the Colorado Supreme Court to test the city's plan. The court ruled in favor of the city in 1891. Later, the state legislature enacted laws codifying regulations for such point-of-diversion changes, and the legal basis for transmountain diversions in the state was thus established.[34]

Not all conflict was so easily remedied. The development of Beaver Creek had caused an intercity dispute between the town of Victor and Colorado Springs. Victor drew its water from Beaver Creek, and its residents claimed that the upstream diversions by Colorado Springs depleted their supplies. Colorado Springs hired a caretaker, R. M. Arthur, to operate and guard the high-elevation reservoirs. Allegedly, men from Victor robbed one of the reservoirs in 1902, 1904, and 1909. During the last pilfering raid, Arthur claimed masked men held him at gunpoint and released 25 million gallons down Beaver Creek to Victor's reservoir. Years passed before the two cities resolved their differences.[35]

At about the same time a water "scandal" shook Colorado Springs. The year 1907 had been terribly dry, and so also the summer of 1908. Inexplicably, the water superintendent had failed to restrict water demand. To compound matters, the city had been supplying the Pikes Peak Hydro-Electric Company's generating plant located at Manitou. This privately owned plant used city water and then released it into Fountain Creek without returning any to the city system, thereby depriving the citizens of water for lawns and homes and stimulating a business revolt against the city government.[36]

Members of the Chamber of Commerce, Merchants Association, and the Real Estate Exchange formed a committee to investigate the opera-

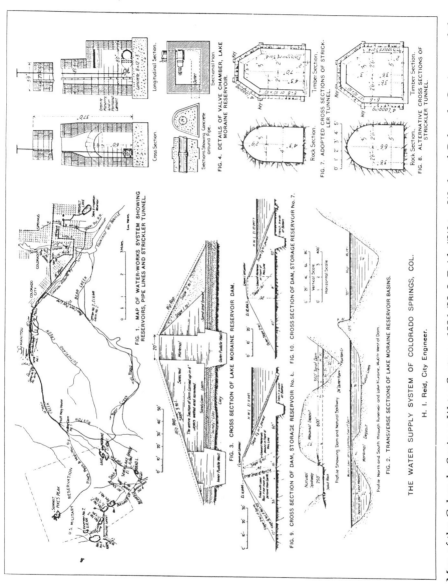

FIG. 1. MAP OF WATER-WORKS SYSTEM SHOWING RESERVOIRS, PIPE LINES AND STRICKLER TUNNEL.

FIG. 3. CROSS SECTION OF LAKE MORAINE RESERVOIR DAM.

FIG. 9. CROSS SECTION OF DAM, STORAGE RESERVOIR No. 6.

FIG. 10. CROSS SECTION OF DAM, STORAGE RESERVOIR No. 7.

FIG. 2. TRANSVERSE SECTIONS OF LAKE MORAINE RESERVOIR BASINS.

FIG. 4. DETAILS OF VALVE CHAMBER, LAKE MORAINE RESERVOIR.

FIG. 7. ADOPTED CROSS SECTIONS OF STRICKLER TUNNEL.

FIG. 8. ALTERNATIVE CROSS SECTIONS OF STRICKLER TUNNEL.

THE WATER SUPPLY SYSTEM OF COLORADO SPRINGS, COL.

H. I. Reid, City Engineer.

Map of the Colorado Springs Water System, 1896 (H. I. Reid, "Water Works of Colorado Springs and the Strickler Tunnel," *Engineering News* 36 [27 August 1896], supplement).

tion of the water system. The propertied interests of Colorado Springs charged the city government with shoddy management of water resources and called for more efficient regulation and use of water. The committee's report concluded that a commission form of government was necessary to prevent a rampant waste of the city's water supply. Indeed, this business uprising employed the rhetoric of democratic reform in a campaign that promoted equally the business interests of all instead of a particular concern, such as the hydroplant. To foster a climate conducive for economic growth required business opportunities for everyone without the waste of water.[37]

For the rest of 1908, the water committee tirelessly criticized the aldermen and mayor with the support of a sympathetic city press. Their efforts bore fruit when a sizable number of citizens petitioned the city's officials to resign their posts. By 1909 the business community of Colorado Springs had spurred the creation of a commission government and was envisioning other vast improvements. In this more "efficient" form of government, each commissioner, who relied on business support to fund his or her election, would administer certain governmental functions. The commissioners hired a city manager, who hired a superintendent for a newly created water department. In typical Progressive terms, the business community saw in these changes the elimination of politics from city government, as neighborhood ward bosses and aldermen lost power. And when the reformers discussed scientific management of the city's water resources in the public interest, they actually promoted their own well-being, since "objective management" meant planning for city growth.[38]

In 1916, for example, influenced by the Chamber of Commerce, the commissioners hired George G. Anderson, a nationally recognized engineering consultant from Los Angeles, to analyze the water system of the city and to make recommendations for its future expansion. His reports would guide Colorado Springs in its development of water resources for the next twenty-five years. Anderson's initial report calculated that the system (basically the south slope) could supply the city's population; however, the business community wanted growth. For this Anderson recommended reducing per capita consumption, which was around 200 gallons per day before 1915, through a greater use of metering and more reliance on the irrigation ditches to relieve pressure on the pipeline system. He also advised the construction of four more storage reservoirs. In a second report issued in 1919, he urged the development of a north slope system and the production of hydroelectric power "as a means to aid the establishment of industrial enterprises."[39]

As the expert engineer, George Anderson provided the means for the city's boosters to pursue a program of growth. In this light, it is important to note that Anderson's work lacked complete objectivity. He took what many historians have called an "instrumental" approach toward controlling nature—"a reasoning about means, not ends." The Chamber of Commerce had set the agenda for Anderson, and he only answered those questions presented to him. Anderson did not weigh all variables equally or objectively as the inquiry principally focused on how to make Colorado Springs grow, not on environmental ramifications, rising conflicts over scant water sources, or the future uses of the water.[40]

The Chamber of Commerce may have had a scientific plan for developing the water system, but Colorado Springs' niche placed limitations on its growth. The system simply drained and stored the watersheds on Pikes Peak, which meant the city drew from a finite water source. From 1917 until World War II, population growth in Colorado Springs was stalled, but water consumption still varied. Unlike in Pueblo, there was little relationship between population and water consumption. Furthermore, as rainfall decreased consumption increased, and vice versa, indicating weak water supplies. The reservoirs were like savings accounts of water: When rainfall increased, the superintendent could keep the accounts filled, and the citizens felt little need to conserve. When rainfall decreased, the residents' demands on the account increased, until demand exceeded supply and the superintendent rationed. Two other factors give a fuller picture of the system. After 1900 the city metered its largest consumers, which encouraged lower use during wet years. In addition, the superintendent permitted those with lawns to receive one free flooding a year from the ditch system, which did not affect the supplies in the reservoirs. Metering and ditch flooding allowed the superintendent to conserve supplies in the mountain reservoirs during wet years in amounts that might be expected to fill higher consumer demands during periods of drought.[41]

The superintendent's careful management of the reservoir accounts, however, could not stem public apprehensions over the city's limited water supply. In the 1930s, browning lawns meant that angry citizens could not transform their little piece of an arid environment into a green garden. During this time E. M. Mosley, the city manager, initiated stiff fines for excessive water consumption along with rationing. Mosley's policies were not well received. Moreover, the Chamber of Commerce knew the lack of reliable water supplies would weaken the city's appeal to new industry. Early in the 1930s the chamber's water committee decided that the city had to develop the north slope resources of Pikes Peak or fail to grow. Working in conjunction with the city commissioners and manager, they pushed ahead with the project.[42]

The North Slope Project had its origin in 1908. An engineer, G. A. Taff, drew up developmental schemes for Catamount, Crystal, and Cascade creeks. He claimed that the watershed produced twenty times what it actually did, thereby luring an eastern concern into buying his reservoir rights. This deal led to the incorporation of the Empire Water and Power Company. The city became alarmed, purchased reservoir sites, and also received from the federal government a grant of around 10,000 acres of the watershed, thereby giving the city near control of the slope. By 1909 the power company had failed, but it would not sell its prime reservoir sites to the city. Colorado Springs controlled the rest of the slope and owned water rights that could fill some of the reservoirs; of course it would not relinquish those holdings to the power company. Not until 1931 did Colorado Springs acquire the reservoir sites by purchasing them for $35,000 from a group of local investors, who had secured the power company's holdings with the covert intention of selling to the city. Now the city could develop the system unimpeded.[43]

Conflict followed as Colorado Springs sought sound water rights by which it could fill its new reservoirs. City manager Mosley intended to buy preexisting rights along the lower reaches of the north slope's creeks and to transfer the diversions from the plains to higher elevations in the foothills and mountains. He accomplished this in spite of the legal obstacles erected by F. F. Schreiber (the attorney for the town of Green Mountain Falls), the El Paso County Taxpayers Association, and the town of Cascade. The city's most formidable opponent was Schreiber, who argued that the upper-elevation diversions planned by the city would ruin the forest by curtailing flows into the creeks of the watershed. Tourists would shun the area, and Green Mountain Falls' main industry would falter. The question, however, was ultimately one of money. Colorado Springs proposed to guarantee Green Mountain's water supply, but Schreiber wanted more money for his client than the city would offer. State courts at every level resolved the issue in favor of Colorado Springs.[44]

To build the north slope system, the city worked cooperatively with the federal government through the Public Works Administration (PWA). In October 1933 the federal government awarded Colorado Springs $285,000 toward an estimated $1.25-million project. The city manager had hoped for more but took what was offered. The PWA ignored protests from Schreiber and his allies and executed the grant in March 1934. The project began delivering water to the drought-parched city that same year. By the time the elaborate system was dedicated in September 1937, the total cost had run to $2 million, to which the federal government had contributed $412,000. Contractors had installed over ten miles of pipeline, two steel-faced reservoir dams, and two major intakes, one on Cascade Creek and the other on French Creek. The editor of the *Gazette* believed that the city was "fixed" for water at least "for several years."[45]

World War II, however, had a striking impact on the economy of Colorado Springs, resulting in the expansion of its water system far earlier than planners had anticipated. The war transformed the city from a tourist attraction to a military center with industrial aspirations. Turning a liability into an asset, Mosley had advertised to the army that the city had 2,500 empty residences waiting to house servicemen and their families. This induced the army to locate Camp Carson and Peterson Field near the city limits. In 1941 Mosley estimated the cost of developing utilities, including water services, for the military at $500,000. The influx of government money into the city, however, more than offset the requirements of capital expansion. A local editor did not know how truly he prophesied when he wrote that the military "will touch everyone in Colorado Springs as it opens up what is destined to be an era in Pikes Peak region history."[46]

World War II had given the city its first real taste of substantial growth, and the citizens liked it. The Chamber of Commerce wanted to avoid a return to the boarded stores and closed movie theaters that had characterized the city in the 1930s. To promote growth the city needed more water. It already owned the majority of the irrigation rights along Pikes Peak and had developed both the north and south slope watersheds. Now the city began a transmountain water search in an effort to overcome the limitations of its niche.

The city commissioners decided to take a gamble on developing the Blue River transmountain system. Mosley was convinced of the need to acquire transmountain water for future industrial growth—and before California, through the Colorado River Compact, laid claim to it. Never before had Colorado Springs considered such an expensive public project. In 1949 city manager C. H. Hoper, Mosley's replacement, predicted the expenditure of $16 million on future water projects in order to promote "new industries, fat payrolls and clogged business establishments." Although this figure included $8 million to build the Blue River project, costs quickly topped $16 million. Planners badly miscalculated how much water development would cost. One consultant, E. B. Debler, formerly with the Bureau of Reclamation in its Denver office, had stated that by the year 2000 Colorado Springs would have to spend nearly $25 million to supply itself with water. Already by 1951, however, the new estimate for the completion of the Blue River project was $18 million, only $7 million short of what Debler thought the city would need for all water development by the end of the century. In three years the estimated cost of the Blue River project had risen by 140 percent! Such rapidly inflating projects tended to make taxpayers nervous.[47]

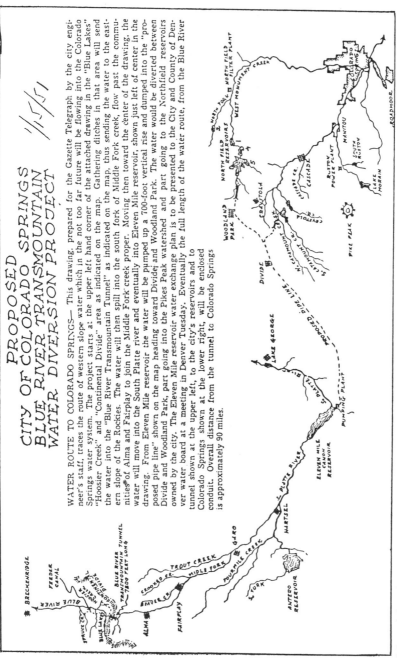

PROPOSED SPRINGS
CITY OF COLORADO SPRINGS
BLUE RIVER TRANSMOUNTAIN
WATER DIVERSION PROJECT

1/5/51

WATER ROUTE TO COLORADO SPRINGS— This drawing, prepared for the Gazette Telegraph by the city engineer's staff, traces the route of western slope water which in the not too far future will be flowing into the Colorado Springs water system. The project starts at the upper left hand corner of the attached drawing in the "Blue Lakes" "Hoosier Creek" and "Continental Divide" area as indicated on the map. Gathering ditches in that area will send the water into the "Blue River Transmountain Tunnel" as indicated on the map, thus sending the water to the eastern slope of the Rockies. The water will then spill into the south fork of Middle Fork creek, flow past the communities of Alma and Fairplay to join the Middle Fork creek proper. Moving then toward the center of the drawing, the water will move into the South Platte river and eventually into Eleven Mile reservoir, shown just left of center in the drawing. From Eleven Mile reservoir the water will be pumped up a 700-foot vertical rise and dumped into the "proposed pipe line" shown on the map heading toward Divide and Woodland Park. The water would be diverted between Divide and Woodland Park, part going into the Pikes Peak watershed and part going to the Northfield reservoirs owned by the city. The Eleven Mile reservoir water exchange plan is to be presented to the City and County of Denver water board at a meeting in Denver Tuesday. Eventually the full length of the water route, from the Blue River tunnel shown at the upper left, to the city's reservoirs and to Colorado Springs shown at the lower right, will be enclosed conduit. Overall distance from the tunnel to Colorado Springs is approximately 90 miles.

Map of the Blue River System for Colorado Springs ("Colorado Springs Proposes Water Exchange with Denver," 15 January 1951, Scrapbook, 1949–51, Public Utilities Office, Colorado Springs, Colorado).

While Hoper pleaded for cooperation from the city taxpayers, he also confronted formidable adversaries—the federal government, Denver, and west slope water users—attempting to block his development of west slope water. In a race with his opponents, he boldly moved to strengthen Colorado Springs' claim to the area's water. First he directed the purchase of water rights in the Blue River region in 1947. Then he approved the construction of Hoosier Tunnel as part of the conveyance system. In 1949 he directed the purchase of the Northfield Company, a private water and power firm, for its reservoirs in order to store transmountain water from Blue River. After these steps he could prove actual intention to put the water to beneficial use in Colorado Springs.[48]

Hoper left the task of legitimating what he did to some of the best water lawyers in state. The proceedings reached Judge William Luby's district court in Breckenridge, Colorado, where Ralph Carr, former governor of the state, well represented the city. Once in addressing the city council, the Chamber of Commerce, and newspaper reporters, he warned: "You've got to fight [for Blue River] or you can give up and stay a nice little residential city which will never grow." A. W. McHendrie, referred to as "the Dean of Colorado water lawyers," was also hired to aid the city's attorney, F. T. Henry. Western slope interests retained Frank Delaney from Glenwood Springs, and Glenn Saunders represented Denver claims to the Blue River. In addition, attorneys for the federal Bureau of Reclamation worked to protect the government's stake in the Colorado–Big Thompson project. The bureau had promised to supply certain irrigators along the Colorado River with water from Green Mountain Reservoir to compensate them for water diverted from the Colorado into the South Platte Valley. The Blue River was to fill Green Mountain Reservoir, but Denver's and Colorado Springs' claims to the same source jeopardized those plans.[49]

McHendrie and Henry pressed the city's cause forcefully, banking on the belief that the judge would not destroy the city's prior claim to beneficial use. Judge Luby listened to their argument that additional water was needed for growth, a recognized good throughout the West. At the time the Nestle Company was planning an eighteen-acre complex, and it seemed certain that the Air Force Academy would locate near the city. But without water, as witnesses pointed out, industries would go elsewhere, as had the Olin Company—soap manufacturers whose plant operations had required more water than the city could deliver. The first indication that McHendrie and Henry had a telling case came when the Bureau of Reclamation, which sensed Judge Luby's lack of sympathy to their cause, moved its plea to the friendlier confines of the federal district bench in Denver.[50]

In November 1951 Colorado Springs won the first legal battle in securing the Blue River project. Swayed by McHendrie and Henry, Judge Luby awarded the city rights that amounted to an estimated 20,000 acre-feet, more than doubling Colorado Springs' resources. He also denied the arguments of the west slope interests, while he satisfied Denver's claims by providing it with most of the water it wanted. Even though McHendrie and Henry still faced the bureau in federal district court, it was clear that they had won big. Hoper would proceed with building the Blue River system, knowing that each foot of ditch dug and tunnel drilled proved a beneficial use that the bureau could not duplicate. Through a bold gamble, Colorado Springs had dramatically increased its water supply and assured future growth.[51]

Ironically, the very growth that Colorado Springs sought and realized necessitated protecting the watersheds on Pikes Peak. Water superintendents sounded as if they were good forest conservationists, and in one sense of the word they were. For example, B. B. McReynolds, the first water superintendent under the commission government, opposed one lumber company's logging on Pikes Peak. In 1918 he wrote, "One green and growing tree is worth more to [the city] than all the money that we can expect to derive from this sale." Trees meant the conservation of water, and when the trees were cut, winds and evaporation carried the snow off the slopes and left little behind for the spring thaw.[52]

The conservation practiced by the city, however, pitted it against outdoor enthusiasts. Some pollution that Colorado Springs experienced came from the tourist industry. Before 1930 the cog railway, which followed Ruxton Creek to the summit of Pikes Peak, provided *open* toilets for its passengers' use, and the excrement made its way into the creek. Guides allowed mules taking throngs of tourists to the halfway house to roam freely in nearby Ruxton Creek. In the 1940s members of the Izaak Walton League asked for greater access to the watershed for fishing, but the commissioners denied their requests. The commissioners primarily feared that one careless match or campfire would destroy the forest. By 1950 the city had nearly finished fencing off the watershed, thereby denying public access to it. In essence, the slopes became one huge tree farm protected from human spoilage. Hence, over time the city felt compelled to restrict public access to the natural beauty that in part fostered Colorado Springs' growth.[53]

Just as cities had struggled to secure and develop their water supplies in the Arkansas River Valley, so did major industry. Most of the industry, which was in Pueblo, relied on the city for water. Two of the four major railroads that were located in Pueblo—the Missouri Pacific and the Denver and Rio Grande Western—supplemented their own water rights with supplies from the South Pueblo Water Company. Some firms, such as the Lincoln Packing Company and the Southern Colorado Power

Company, attempted to control their costs by using only their own water rights. The most notable industrial water system, however, was the Colorado Fuel and Iron Company's.[54]

When William Jackson Palmer organized the Colorado Coal and Iron Company in December 1879, he laid the basis for what would become the largest mining and metallurgical enterprise in the West. He chose South Pueblo as the site for the iron and steel works for two reasons: transportation links and water. The plant was surveyed in 1880; the first blast furnace began operating in September 1881; steel production started up in April 1882.[55]

The company obtained water from three sources. The St. Charles ditch fed Lake Minnequa, the main reservoir, and water pipes linked the steel works with the lake. Second, big river pumps filled settling reservoirs connected to the plant and Lake Minnequa. In 1881 the company added large filtering tanks at the river, since steel production required water without mineral concentrations. Any excess emptied into Lake Minnequa for future use. The third source, two artesian wells, was utilized in conjunction with the ditch and river pumps to cool the company's single blast furnace.[56]

By 1884 Palmer had lost control of the steel company. A weak market in 1883, compounded by erratic plant production, caused major stockholders in the venture to lose faith in Palmer's guidance. Henry E. Sprague, who led the malcontents, won control of the faltering enterprise in April 1884.[57] Sprague encountered many difficulties trying to adjust the production of the Colorado Coal and Iron Company to the capricious economy of the late 1880s. A revived market for steel products gave new life to the company in the summer of 1886. Sprague responded by adding a blast furnace; however, demand sputtered, and steel production was suspended throughout 1889. Moreover, Sprague lacked the water resources necessary for the efficient operation of his second furnace. Under his direction, the company had disposed of its river pumps and was relying on water from Lake Minnequa fed by the St. Charles ditch, which had a capacity of only 10 cfs. Ordinarily, the ditch delivered 2.5 million gallons of water per day, not nearly enough to support the top functioning of two blast furnaces.[58]

Renewed production in 1890 forced the company to augment its water supply. It purchased the Arkansas Valley ditch from an irrigation company by the same name located eighteen miles downriver from the plant, for $7,112.83. This was one of the first successful mutual stockholding companies in the valley, and it had 70 cfs of direct flow rights dated before 1865. These rights promised more than enough water to supply the operational needs of the steel company. Irregular production in a fickle economy, however, returned corporation "earnings . . . not commensurate with the investment." The major stockholders, in response, agreed to a merger with the Colorado Fuel Company, thereby creating the Colorado Fuel and Iron Company.[59]

In 1892 John Cleveland Osgood, the former president of the fuel company, took over the helm of the Colorado Fuel and Iron Company and directed the construction of the only integrated Bessemer-process plant in the West, the Minnequa Steel Plant. Because of depressed economic conditions during the 1890s, he did not initiate his plans for expansion until 1899, at which time he added new blast furnaces along with other enhancements.[60]

The company had to revamp its water system in order to complete these vast capital improvements. By 1905 the partially finished steel plant required between 6 and 9 million gallons of water per day. Upon the completion of all facilities, as reported by a commission appointed to study the company's water-supply problem, full production would require that over 22 million gallons per day be pumped into the plant, in addition to a "liberal re-use" of water within the factory. Including reuse, then, to operate the facilities required a daily supply of at least 48 to 50 million gallons.[61]

Obviously, the St. Charles ditch could not meet the company's water needs. To rectify technological inadequacies, Sprague resorted to further technological improvements. He had two new reservoirs constructed south of Lake Minnequa, to be fed by a new ditch—the St. Charles flood ditch. Plant engineers used one reservoir to settle silt and then released the clear water into another reservoir in an effort to maintain constant water pressure going into the plant; hence it was called an equalizer. Relying solely on the flood ditch, however, was risky, since the St. Charles river flow fluctuated wildly from lows of 2 to 3 cfs to highs of 5,000 to 7,000 cfs. These unpredictable levels could leave reservoirs empty or damaged.[62]

To solve critical water-supply problems, Sprague ventured into complex cooperative arrangements with the Bessemer Irrigating Ditch Company. In 1902 the steel company secured from the federal government the right to construct Sugar Loaf Reservoir, finished in October 1903, in the national forest near Leadville. The company released water from the reservoir into the Arkansas River, then "loaned" it to the Bessemer Irrigating Ditch Company whose ditch ran through the steel plant. Pumping stations drew an equivalent of the reservoir "loan" from the canal for the plant's use, in return for which the ditch company borrowed water from the steel company in times of emergencies and had the right to purchase surplus water from Sugar Loaf. During winter months when Sugar Loaf froze but the irrigation ditch still flowed, the steel company borrowed water from the ditch company, which did not fully use its diversions in winter. The steel company paid the Bessemer farmers back in the summer months with reservoir water when their ditch rights failed. In this case agriculture and industry found it advantageous to cooperate.[63]

Other attempts to remedy water-supply problems resulted in conflict with irrigators, as when the steel company made use of its Arkansas Valley Ditch Company rights. Sprague attempted to "loan" these rights to the Bessemer company and then pumped out the water near the plant for steel production. Irrigators in the area downriver where the Arkansas Valley ditch had been located objected to the steel company's means, believing that their farming enterprises were harmed. Moreover, D. C. Beaman, the steel company's attorney, doubted the legality of "loaning"; another solution had to be found so that the company could use its valuable water rights. The board responded by transferring the diversion point of the Arkansas Valley ditch to a new canal—the Arkansas Valley conduit—above the plant on the Arkansas River.[64]

However, before the Colorado Fuel and Iron Company could relocate the diversion point, the state required tedious and expensive court proceedings. First, in accordance with state law, the company's lawyers sent announcements of the transfer plans to over 2,500 possible objectors. The company also placed notices of their proposal in all the regional newspapers. After the court had considered the company's plans and the objections to it, it ruled that the change in diversion point would not adversely affect any interests in the valley. The judge based his ruling on the astute argument of the company's lawyers that the steel plant returned about 85 percent of the water it used to the stream, whereas agriculture returned only around 33 percent. Therefore, the steel company's use of these rights added more to the supply of the river than did agricultural use. As a result, downstream consumers, by reusing the steel company's water, would have more than they previously had when irrigators had used the water. This was compelling logic. With all legalities decided in favor of the company, it could proceed with the construction of the Arkansas Valley conduit.[65]

The Arkansas Valley conduit, primarily designed by chief engineer R. M. Hosea of the Colorado Fuel and Iron Company, seemed for its time a model of engineering expertise. Construction crews built this $850,000, 37-mile-long conduit through rough terrain above the plant. John Birkinbine, the consulting engineer on the project, helped create a ditch that would carry between 70 and 80 cfs, or over 52 million gallons of water per day. To avoid high filtration expenses, the engineers located the headgate just below Florence where the water quality was purer than near the plant. The water flowed into a series of "skimming basins" designed to remove heavy particles from the water. Since the line of the

The Water System of the
Colorado Fuel and Iron Company

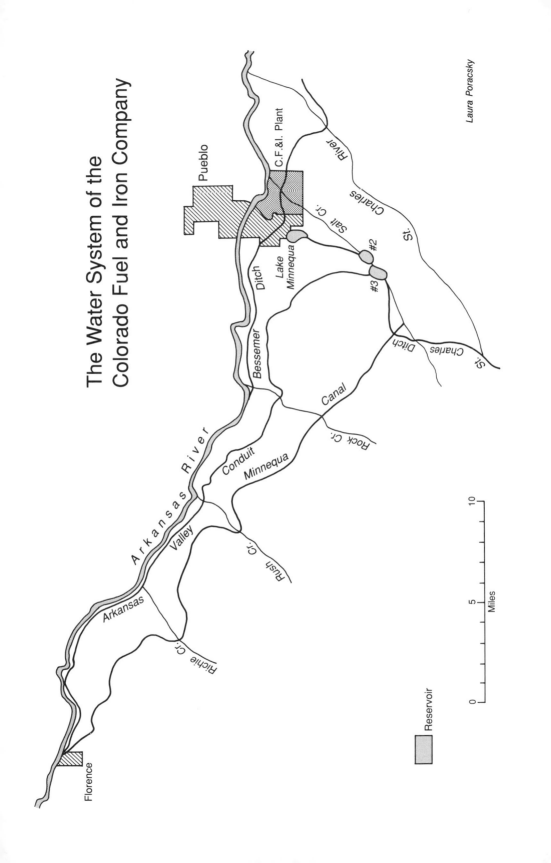

Laura Poracsky

Reservoir

0   5   10
      Miles

ditch stayed close to the southern bank of the Arkansas River, the project required the construction of a 60-inch wooden-stave siphon, 1,000 feet long, under the city of Portland. In traversing difficult arroyo crossings, over 27 siphons were constructed, which amounted to over 43,000 feet of pipe. Five tunnels had to be bored for the ditch to reach its target reservoir. This complex system constituted the vital basis of the Minnequa Steel Plant production.[66]

The water rights of the company proved very reliable, as the conduit delivered a yearly average of 35,253 acre-feet from 1908 through 1942. By 1905 the company, according to Beaman, had acquired rights to nearly 90 cfs, or the capability to produce 58 million gallons per day—more than enough to support full production of the plant.[67] Beaman claimed that the company only purchased water rights dated before 1876. In that year Coloradans had written their constitution, which had established a hierarchy of beneficial water uses. Domestic, or urban, needs were primary, followed by irrigation and then industry. Any rights granted before 1876, though, could be employed in any manner desired by the owner. Therefore, by these early-dated rights the firm protected its steel making from any possible claims from urban or farm interests. Moreover, the company's decrees promised full diversions during regular river flows, which was crucial for steady production. The shrewdness of the purchases made by Beaman and others was borne out as yearly water diversions seldom corresponded to changes in river flow from 1908 through 1942. The company diversions remained constant despite the dips and peaks of river flow near Florence.[68]

The water usage of the plant in one sense was riparian. The riparian doctrine had its origin in English common law and by some accounts was an outgrowth of industrialism. Any person who owned land adjacent to a watercourse had full use of the flow passing that point, so long as that use did not materially affect any property owner downstream. The English may have developed this doctrine to protect water-driven industry. The Colorado Fuel and Iron Company's water use minimally depleted river flow. In 1942 Charles Patterson wrote a report on the plant's water use for the Colorado Water Conservation Board, wherein he figured that the company consumed only 16.9 percent of the water used by the plant between 1927 and 1940. The remainder, 83.1 percent, the company returned into natural watercourses. Even though irrigators did not object to the quantity returned to the river, they feared the water's quality. Until the 1960s, the plant's sewage system dumped untreated water containing tar and oils back into the Arkansas River.[69]

The 1907 Minnequa plant applied the water from the conduit in many different ways to make steel. Company attorney Beaman testified in 1905 that the cooling system for one smelter in the plant required

This rockslide demonstrates one of the difficulties encountered in maintaining the Arkansas Valley conduit. (CF&I Steel Corporation, Pueblo, Colorado)

500,000 gallons of water per day. Water was also condensed from steam for personnel consumption and coal washing. Cooling water also circulated through the numerous open-hearth units, the roll and rod mills, and bolt and spike mills. Yet the Arkansas Valley conduit never dominated nature in the way its planners had intended. First, the plant engineers could never keep the ditch or its reservoir from filling with silt. As a result, the conduit never carried 70 cfs except during floods. Even then, ditch runners had to let this flow out at wastegates before its force and silt load caused damage to the lower reaches of the canal. Ditch personnel faced other problems in keeping the conduit running. For example, hill slides destroyed siphons, and in winter the conduit froze solid in places. From 1931 to 1942 the conduit required more and more maintenance, and it still failed to deliver water on an average of sixty-eight days a year.[70]

In 1931 Harold Christy, superintendent of the company's water division, devised an alternative to the Arkansas Valley conduit. Christy had an extensive background in engineering, including a degree from the Colorado School of Mines at Golden in 1922. Through a personal connection, he came to the Colorado Fuel and Iron Company in 1929 and headed the company's newly established Land, Water, and Power Department. His plan called for a new ditch. He located its headgate at the Union Canal diversion works, an irrigation enterprise near Florence. In this manner the company increased its water supply by buying the Union Canal irrigators' rights and avoided the required court hearings for a point-of-diversion change. He drew the line of the ditch south of the Arkansas River, thereby avoiding many of the engineering troubles associated with the operations of the Arkansas Valley conduit.[71]

In 1933 construction of the new canal began, and it became an exemplar of engineering efficiency, a tribute to Christy's abilities. He placed the headgate at Florence because, as noted, river flows there contained less mineral content than those near the plant; locating a headgate any farther upstream from Florence in an attempt to divert even purer flow would result in unacceptable transit losses. Christy's great skills as an engineer showed in his innovative sandtrap at the headgate that eliminated the siltation problem encountered with the conduit. The dimensions of the ditch—thirty-four feet on top, ten on the bottom, with a depth of eight feet—generated enough pressure to prevent icing problems.[72]

Construction of the Minnequa Canal slackened during the Great Depression, but World War II revived steel markets. The steel plant's wartime production soared, which meant the need for additional water supplies. Christy guided the completion of the Minnequa Canal just in time to avoid really serious troubles with the Arkansas Valley conduit. In 1944, a few days after he first released water into the canal, a major siphon fell out of the conduit. By easing any reliance on the conduit, the canal enabled the steel plant to fulfill its wartime contracts. The Minnequa Canal worked smoothly and enhanced plant production through its 286 cfs carrying capacity. A major capital project that cost $3,154,068 to build, it supplied the Minnequa works with an average of 64,000 acre-feet of water each year from 1944 through 1950. In terms of supplying the corporation's water needs, it stands to this day as an unqualified success.[73]

The case studies of Pueblo, Colorado Springs, and the Colorado Fuel and Iron Company show the high priority each placed on economic growth. Generally, people measured their cities' success by the standards of a growing business community and population, for which the chambers of commerce always fought. Water figured so crucially to growth projections that the Chamber of Commerce in both Pueblo and Colorado Springs had water committees that worked in conjunction with the city governments. The steel company also hoped to sustain growth, thereby commanding ever larger markets. Engineers became the instruments of this expansion, and they provided for the ever-increasing control, development, and use of water.

Given their niches, the Colorado Fuel and Iron Company, Pueblo, and Colorado Springs had to compete for the water rights in the valley or create new ones in other regions. As their economies developed, they bought valuable, early-dated agricultural decrees that placed them in conflict with irrigators. The cities extended their search to the less-developed western slope of the continental divide, often battling irrigators and the federal government. The result? Greater supplies insulated the cities from the effects of drought, satisfying their residents' desires to transform open buffalo-grass plains into urban areas with Kentucky blue grass lawns shaded by maple and elm trees. Businesses multiplied, steel production increased, and the Air Force Academy came to Colorado Springs, along with more and more people.

But population and economic growth in the cities brought problems. By 1950 organic pollution in the river had increased dramatically, as only Pueblo and Colorado Springs treated their sewage. Mining along the upper watershed of the Arkansas River augmented water hardness that plagued both the operations of the Colorado Fuel and Iron Company and Pueblo. Deforestation in conjunction with mining caused heavy runoffs, creating streambed erosion. This led to greater mineral concentrations in the river flow that supplied the cities. Because of increasing numbers of tourists, Colorado Springs restricted access to its watershed along the slopes of Pikes Peak.

However, the Colorado Fuel and Iron Company's growth proved largely unobtrusive to other water-consuming interests in the region, and it even enjoyed symbiotic relationships with some agricultural enterprises. The plant engineers returned heavily filtered river flows used to produce steel to the channel largely undiminished and considerably softer. Factory water, however, contaminated river flows with tars and oils, something the company generally ignored before 1950.

Many pieces composed the full picture of water usage in the valley. Irrigation interests varied considerably depending on geographical location, the organization of their company charters, and the viability of their water rights. Cities and industry in the valley occupied their own niches, shaped by geography, shifting demographics and economics, and cultural values. At times the interests of irrigators, urbanites, and industrialists either collided or coalesced, as each group pursued its own separate way propelled by its unique history.

Irrigators, urbanites, and industrialists always cooperated when mutually threatened by interests outside the state. Thus the activities of the irrigation ditch companies in the Arkansas River Valley of western Kansas had the salutary effect of uniting distinct Colorado interests. Around 1890 irrigators in the Garden City, Kansas, region claimed that water development in Colorado had adversely affected their operations and their state's economy. Coloradans, though, contended that their labor and investments in diverting the Arkansas River onto farms and into cities and industry had established the base of a thriving regional economy. They bound themselves together to resist to the utmost any division of water with Kansas that threatened their plans for growth. But Kansas irrigators believed the conquest of nature should result in growth for them, too; they pressed Coloradans for a more equitable share of the Arkansas River. To understand their actions against Coloradans requires first an examination of irrigation developments in Kansas.

CHAPTER FIVE

Irrigation in Southwestern Kansas, 1870–1950

In the 1890s irrigators in western Kansas began to claim that Coloradans were depriving them of a fair use of the Arkansas River flow. They battled Colorado water users in court cases, negotiated compacts, and lobbied the federal government to solve their predicament. Not all of the problems faced by Kansas irrigators, however, stemmed from developments in Colorado.

Five major ditch companies around Garden City, Kansas, operated within an environmental and economic quandary. Reliable commercial crop production in the semiarid environment of Colorado required the use of irrigation, but the need for irrigation in Kansas was not so clear. At times rainfall did sustain crops, which colored farmers' perceptions about their need for irrigation. They, like their counterparts throughout the nation, managed their lands according to market-culture values: Use nature as fully as possible to maximize production at the lowest cost for enhanced profits. From this perspective irrigation became an expensive liability during wet years. Conversely, during periods of drought farmers viewed it as a necessity and demanded access to it.

Farmers' ambivalence toward irrigation led to corporate control of its initial development. Farmers wanted access to canals but not financial responsibility for them. This left the field open for large-scale enterprises underwritten mostly by out-of-state capitalists unfamiliar with conditions in the Garden City area. Many financiers engaged in mere speculation. Local farmers suffered from such attitudes and yet were unwilling to assume the risk of irrigation development until a more permanent need for it arose.

Local irrigators also suffered from the slow evolution of a legal framework designed to regulate irrigation. Not until 1945 did the Kansas legislature provide a coherent body of water laws to govern ditch and pump irrigation. Before 1945 prior appropriation customs ruled only where they did not interfere with riparian practices. The coexistence of these two doctrines reflected the environmental duality of the state: the semiarid region west of the 98th meridian and the subhumid portion to the east of that line. The lack of unitary legal institutions for the regulation of irrigation practices created considerable conflict between the ditch companies in western Kansas.

Despite severe difficulties, farmers fashioned a workable economic, technological, and legal base for irrigation between 1900 and 1920. The introduction of sugar beets, a reliable cash crop, required the continuous operation of irrigation ditches. Sugar-beet production led farmers to purchase two ditch companies and to reorganize the systems as mutual stockholding companies in an attempt to control their own futures. Irrigators experimented with pumping water from aquifers. By pumping, people had some flexibility in responding to drought or rainfall and some control over their costs. Moreover, federal court decisions gave the various systems enough guidelines for them to coexist. From 1920 through 1950 the companies continued to refine and develop this technological, economic, and legal foundation in the semiarid expanses of western Kansas.

The niches occupied by these five Kansas ditch systems differed from those of their Colorado counterparts, since the Arkansas River Valley was not the same in western Kansas as in eastern Colorado in some important respects. The velocity of the river slowed because of the terrain's reduced gradient, which averaged about seven feet per mile through present-day Hamilton, Kearny, and Finney counties. Over thousands of years the water had dropped heavy loads of sedimentation that built up the area and created what one engineer called an alluvial fan beginning near the former town of Hartland. The river flowed with less volume and reliability than in eastern Colorado. Only floods breached its wide, treeless, and sharply cut banks; once broken, the channel was redirected to nearby depressions, which filled and continued the process of deposition.[1]

The heightened riverbed effectively prevented tributaries from feeding the Arkansas River in western Kansas. To the south the Canadian River flowed at a lower elevation parallel to the Arkansas River and joined it in present-day Oklahoma. The higher elevation of the Arkansas also forced the Smoky Hill and Republican rivers to the north to enter the Kansas River. The two major creeks near Garden City never found their way to the watercourse. Sand hills to the south of the Arkansas prevented Bear Creek from reaching the channel, and Whitewoman Creek flowed beside the river and emptied into a large depression directly north of present-day Garden City. No stream of any significance contributed to the Arkansas River until Pawnee River joined it at present day Larned.

Without tributaries, mountain runoff and local rainfall constituted the Arkansas River flow in western Kansas. The Rocky Mountain efflux reached the region toward mid May and continued flowing through

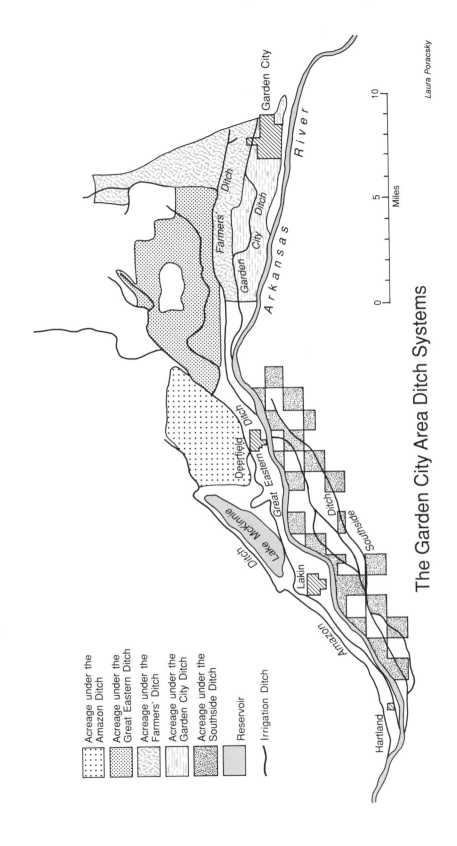

The Garden City Area Ditch Systems

Laura Poracsky

Acreage under the Amazon Ditch

Acreage under the Great Eastern Ditch

Acreage under the Farmers' Ditch

Acreage under the Garden City Ditch

Acreage under the Southside Ditch

Reservoir

Irrigation Ditch

early summer. This "June rise" made fording a hazardous undertaking for freighters and overland travelers but provided an abundance of water for the region's wildlife. Precipitation accounted for the remainder of the flow. In years of above-average rainfall the river brimmed from bank to bank. Frequent, violent thunderstorms released volumes of water that produced sudden freshets or major floods. Otherwise, occasional water holes, or no flow at all, characterized the riverbed until it reached either the mouth of Pawnee River or Walnut Creek.[2]

On an average, more rain fell in the region than in eastern Colorado, but not so much that farmers could rely solely on it for their crops. Severe droughts seared the area in the 1850s, 1870s, 1890s, and 1930s. Higher-than-average precipitation in the 1880s, 1920s, and 1940s caused people to forget that they lived in a semiarid environment. At Syracuse, Kansas, about fifteen miles east of the state line, rainfall averaged just above seventeen inches a year, and farther to the east at Garden City, over eighteen-and-a-half inches from 1894 to 1950. The means incorporated great variations, with a recorded high of 34.81 inches at Garden City in 1923 and a low of 8.87 in 1937.[3]

Sand hills covering large areas south of the river served as a natural reservoir storing rainwater. When rain fell on these porous sandy soils, the water percolated down until reaching an impervious sublayer that channeled the flow underground in an easterly direction toward the river. Sagebrush and prickly pear cactus covered the rolling hills; generally, farmers found the area completely unsuitable for cultivation.[4]

As far as Hartland the topography of the Arkansas River Valley remained much the same as in eastern Colorado. Beyond that to the east the valley opened with contours spreading in a north-south direction. The river had deposited the sediments that formed the soils of this large alluvial fan. Shallow, well-drained, silty clay loams in the flood plain proved very productive under irrigation. Northward were the slope formations that led to the High Plains. The nearly level inclines turned out to be well suited for irrigation practices, as did the silty clay loams on the High Plains.[5]

The permeability of soils contributed to the abundance of alluvium groundwater in the region. The upper layer of groundwater filled the substrata and traveled eastward. When the river flowed fully, it acted like a dam that kept water tables high, sometimes only a few feet below the surface of the bottomlands and slopes. Variations in rainfall also affected the water table, which fell in dry years and rose in wet. The first settlers in the region called this groundwater the "underflow" and erroneously attributed its sole source to the river.[6]

Three major geologic formations held sizable quantities of groundwater. The most important water-bearing layer was the alluvium. The second had its beginnings nearly 100 million years ago when the river deposited thick layers of silt, sand, and gravel that accumulated to a depth of 100 to 300 feet. By the period of recent settlement in the region, these deposits were covered by an additional 50 to 150 feet of loess and silt. This substrata, called today the Ogallala formation, contained an abundant supply of water which was very slowly recharged by percolating surface water. Below this lay the Dakota sandstone formation, which also contained water but with very high mineral content.[7]

From 1880 to 1950 the people who settled and developed the region of western Kansas attempted to transform the area into productive farmland. They diverted the river into irrigation ditches to carry water to their crops. They slowly learned that neither their ditch operations nor rainfall could fully support agricultural enterprises. Because of unsuitable soils, they shunned the construction of storage reservoirs, with one exception. In the search for alternatives they developed a pump technology that exploited the groundwater aquifers. Tapping groundwater augmented ditch flows and rainfall and allowed for more reliable agricultural production. Development of irrigation thus came slowly and painfully.

The humble beginnings of irrigation in southwestern Kansas occurred at Garden City. Richard J. Hinton, a correspondent for *Harper's Weekly*, recalled that Garden City lacked any semblance of a city in 1880. He wrote that "a score of log cabins, or prairie dugouts, with a frame store building, constituted the 'city.'" When he returned in 1888, he noted the community's sizable regional trade and population of 8,000. What helped make this growth possible was the construction of a small irrigation ditch in 1880.[8]

The Garden City ditch had its origins in a fourteen-month drought that struck southwestern Kansas in 1879. The only flow in the river came during a "feeble" June rise. Moreover, not more than 1 percent of the wheat germinated, and the farmers failed to harvest any of it. This frustrated W. H. Armentrout, who had spent a year building a mill race to power a grain mill in anticipation of a large wheat harvest. Seeing no wheat to mill, he allowed Squire Worrell, who had experience with irrigation in California and Colorado, to use the mill race to water a few acres. Worrell's crops survived, and the people who had resolved to stay in Garden City immediately realized the value of irrigation.[9]

Worrell's success with irrigation encouraged others to build ditches. Armentrout persuaded investors to underwrite the conversion of the mill race into an irrigation ditch. He and some local promoters organized the Garden City Irrigation Company in November 1879 and began construction in early winter of 1880. In a drive to lay claim to the river, other speculators filed a total of ten irrigation company charters by the summer of 1881. Many of these enterprises were never more than facades, but some companies actually built.[10]

Charles J. "Buffalo" Jones, a speculator and a half, exerted particular influence on the development of irrigation systems in the area. He took credit for every major advance including the Garden City ditch (which he probably had a hand in digging, but which he certainly did not initiate or fund). Jones had a selective memory that generally recalled events in a manner that enhanced his own reputation. The importance of Jones lay in how his actions mirrored the prevailing market-culture values of his time and the way people applied these values in practice.[11]

A quick summary of one of Jones's projects exemplifies the early development of the ditch companies around Garden City. In October 1880 Jones and four others incorporated the Great Eastern Irrigation, Water Power and Manufacturing Company. Jones attracted outside investment by enticing bankers from Lawrence, Kansas, to join the company. He gave the enterprise respectability when he named Sen. Preston Plumb its president. Frank Marvin, later the dean of the School of Engineering at the University of Kansas, surveyed the ditch. James Craig, a local farmer keenly interested in irrigation, directed the construction. Serving as the first superintendent, Craig let water into the ditch for testing the strength of the banks in 1882.[12]

Ironically regarded by local farmers as the most reliable of the Garden City ditches, mishap after mishap plagued the operations of the Great Eastern. In June 1883 floods destroyed the main headgates, and Craig waited until after the irrigation season before making repairs. During the mid-1880s abundant rainfall lessened the farmers' enthusiasm for contracting for water. In 1886 the company's revenues could not support one-half of its expenses. Nonetheless, the overly optimistic directors kept purchasing acreage from the land company of the Atchison, Topeka and Santa Fe railroad. The investors from Lawrence knew nothing about managing an irrigation system and paid sizable wages to relatives, who were unpopular with the local residents, to manage company affairs. In 1886 drought struck, and farmers flocked to the ditch only to find it in poor shape and dry. They bitterly complained about inadequate water deliveries. In 1887 the company responded by repairing the ditch and extending the length to forty miles, which also pushed the company deeply into debt. In May 1890, unable to satisfy their customers and mortgage holders, investors sold the ditch system to the Southwestern Irrigation Company managed by Frank Denny, a Garden City resident.[13]

Instead of recognizing the limitations inherent in ditch irrigation, Denny attempted a further conquest of the river through technology. He hired B. F. Babcock, a civil engineer associated with the Southwestern company, to devise a means of supplementing irregular river flows. Bab-

Charles J. "Buffalo" Jones (Kansas State Historical Society)

cock concocted the idea of an "underflow" ditch. The principle was simple: Instead of diverting water through a headgate located in the riverbank, dig a trench—at that point and along the same elevation—away from the river headed upstream into the bottomland until striking the alluvium. The level of the underflow intersecting with the groundwater would supply the ditch system at all times. Drought, depression, and bad engineering calculations put an end to the scheme and bankrupted Denny. The local court ordered the ditch system into receivership in 1894.[14]

Thomas E. Dewey was the receiver for the mortgage company, the Security Company of Hartford, Connecticut, and he came to Garden City to undertake repairs on the ditch system. In 1895 plentiful rains hindered Dewey's work, because farmers did not contract for water and in some instances plowed over the company's laterals. Rains failed in 1896, but Dewey did not attempt river diversions into the dilapidated ditch. Subsequently, he leased the system to local farmers in the aspiration of making them responsible for its operation and upkeep. Pinched by years of economic depression, farmers failed to fulfill their agreements, and Dewey lost hope of reviving the system. By 1900 the Great Eastern ditch serviced few farms and badly needed repair.[15]

The farmers' ambivalence toward irrigation explains why only outside corporate ventures undertook the hazardous control of the ditches. Investors wanted only profits from speculation rather than the development of sound operational systems. Farmers compounded their own problems by having no interest in irrigation, unless, of course, drought occurred. The lack of rainfall would raise a chorus of complaints about management, but the poorly maintained systems could not divert the trickles in the river channel. Furthermore, farmers often grew wheat and sorghum without resorting to irrigation. Why, they thought, contract for unneeded ditch water? Until the introduction of sugar beets, a viable cash crop that required constant irrigation, they remained uncommitted to the ditches.

The other systems in southwestern Kansas experienced a similar pattern of nonachievement. James Craig, and others around Garden City, began the construction of the Farmers' ditch (called then the Kansas ditch) in 1880. They sold it to Jones and a group of investors, who incorporated it as the Kansas Irrigating, Water Power and Manufacturing Company. Inadequately designed and managed, the ditch never satisfactorily supplied farmers. In 1890 Denny bought the faltering enterprise along with the Garden City ditch. He combined the Farmers' ditch and the Great Eastern into the Southwestern Company, and he reorganized the Garden City ditch as the Garden City Irrigation Company. In 1894 Dewey, as the receiver of the Great Eastern, also assumed control over the Garden City and Farmers' ditches. These systems, too, fell victim to the same forces that had undermined Dewey's management of the Great Eastern.[16]

The South Side ditch, as local farmers called it, fared little better than the others. In 1880, when Jones began its construction, he named it the Minnehaha ditch. The poorly located headgates, he quickly learned, could not divert water into the ditch. He sold the system to speculators from Topeka, Kansas, who were associated with the Atchison, Topeka and Santa Fe land company. The new investors owned land in the immediate vicinity of the ditch and hoped to boost real-estate values by reorganizing the ditch company. Through the Western Irrigating Company, they relocated the diversion works upriver, which allowed the restoration of the old ditch. C. H. Longstreth, who worked for the railroad's land company, conducted irrigation experiments on his farm and competently managed the system. Farmers, however, refused to contract for water, causing the company serious financial problems. Sensing failure, the investors persuaded imprudent speculators from New Jersey and Ohio to purchase the ditch. The new owners incorporated it as the Western Irrigation and Land Company, which floundered immediately as company-farmer relations worsened over water rental rates. The investors, unable to finance ditch operations, mortgaged their holdings. In 1893 drought and depression ruined the enterprise. In 1894 a loan company took over the South Side ditch and placed it under a receiver.[17]

Jones's last project, the Amazon ditch, also came to nothing. In 1885 he angrily dissociated himself from the Great Eastern and, according to one version of the story, set out to ruin the company. He located the headgate of a new project, the Amazon ditch, so as to deprive the Great Eastern of divertable flows. Edward G. Russell, a prominent banker from Lawrence, Kansas, and his son Percy both managed the Great Eastern. Although they had a few altercations with Jones over his true intentions, these scrapes did not stop him from launching his enterprise. He even filed a suit against the Great Eastern in an attempt to revoke its charter, but the court dismissed his action. His enmity toward the Russells, though, did not produce good results.[18]

Jones directed a poorly constructed and managed ditch. In May 1889 the Amazon ditch walls broke, flooding the railroad tracks and residential sections of Lakin, Kansas. Detecting Jones's lack of interest in providing viable irrigation, the local presses accused him of land speculation and fraud. Before his affairs soured completely—and somewhat confirming his critics' charges—he sold the ditch to a British firm, the Southwest Kansas Land and Irrigation Company of London. The new owners, wholly unfamiliar with conditions in Kansas, made repairs and finished the construction of the ditch by 1891. But drought conditions in 1893 and

1894 hurt their operations, and economically distressed farmers refused to contract for water at the high rates set by the company. The superintendent allowed the system to deteriorate, and the Amazon ditch succumbed to receivership in 1897.[19]

By the late 1890s irrigation was at a low ebb in the Garden City area. Too many farmers refused to use the ditches on a regular basis, which consistently undercut the financial base of the companies. Farmers cried for canal water only during drought, and that was exactly when the companies could not provide it. Moreover, the emphasis of investors on quick returns resulted in poorly managed companies and contributed to farmer discontent. By 1900 farmers only partially used some of the systems, and portions of the Great Eastern ditch stood abandoned. Over the next two decades, however, there would be developments that would rejuvenate interest in irrigation around Garden City. Advances came with pump technology, with sugar beets, with a sugar factory, and with a federal reclamation project.

Although nearly every irrigator complained about the canal superintendents' mismanagement of already-poor river flow into the ditches, a few farmers began experimenting with individually operated pump technologies to supplement chronically weak water supplies. Some tried steam-powered pumps, which proved exorbitantly expensive, but most farmers turned to less costly windmills. E. N. Gause and J. V. Carter experimented with, and helped create an interest in, wind-powered pumps. They marketed their pumps through their local farm-implement firm. But in the hard economic times of the early 1890s, farmers found the initial capitalization prohibitive. Moreover, the early machines could only lift water from the shallow aquifers, which limited their use on the uplands. The drought of 1893 renewed some farmers' interest in windmills, but others searched for more efficient pumping techniques.[20]

A few irrigators had enough money to invest in machines powered by steam, gasoline, and natural gas. Piston pumps could raise deep groundwater, but mineral concentrations in the water fouled the cylinder and piston. Centrifugal pumps handled dirty water well but could not draw from great depths. By 1900 electrical pumps came into vogue, and their greater power produced larger quantities of water. Nonetheless, most farmers continued to rely on gasoline-powered units pumping in the "shallow water district" north of Garden City. Through pumps, many irrigators increased their individual control over crop production while freeing themselves from the erratic operations of the ditch companies.[21]

In addition to water pumps, the introduction of sugar beets encouraged farmers to seize control of their own destinies. In the late 1890s and early 1900s George W. Swink, the indomitable promoter from Rocky

E. J. Pyle's windmill and reservoir system (Kansas State Historical Society)

Ford, Colorado, urged Kansas farmers to grow beets to supply the American Crystal Sugar Company. Impressed with the gains promised from beet production, farmers eagerly planted crops. Beets, however, called for precise watering. Planting occurred at the beginning of April. During germination beets needed moist and warm soil. When the plant had four leaves, it required "a considerable amount of moisture" for the next two months. About one hundred days after planting, the sugar beet needed little, if any, watering. The farmers' past experiences precluded any confidence that the local corporate-controlled ditch companies could provide them with scheduled water essential for beet growing. Before, the farmers had threatened litigation to take over the ditches only to bring better management. This time, however, they meant business.[22]

The first mutual stockholding company came into existence largely through the efforts of James Craig. He knew the local ditch companies well: He had helped build them, he had superintended them, and he owned land as an irrigator under them. Appropriately, he organized those who held lands under the Farmers' ditch (the Kansas ditch at the time) into the Finney County Farmers Irrigation Association. Next, Craig masterminded a plan that led Dewey, the receiver of the Farmers' ditch, to sell it to Craig's new group. Representing the association, Craig threatened to build a new canal with a headgate just above the Farmers' ditch and to dig the ditch on a higher elevation, but parallel, to Dewey's system. Craig's plan would have jeopardized the water supply to the

Farmers' ditch. The lack of enforceable prior appropriation laws with which to defend his water rights left Dewey with few alternatives, so he agreed to Craig's offer for the Farmers' ditch in October 1901. Craig's efforts initiated the longest-running mutual stockholding irrigation company in Kansas.[23]

The Colorado form of mutual stockholding, which guaranteed complete stockholder control over a system, became the model for Kansas irrigators. Craig used it to frame the bylaws of the Finney County Farmers Irrigation Association. In late 1902 local control of the Garden City ditch was achieved when area businessmen and farmers purchased the system. In 1904 the farmers of Kearny County organized the Kearny County Farmers Irrigation Association, bought the Amazon ditch, and set about improving that system. The mutual company was thus an important step in irrigation development in the area.[24]

George Swink's promotions also laid the foundation for a sugar factory at Garden City. Swink knew local bankers wanted a factory but worried about the dependability of the Arkansas River flow for a successful beet crop. These businessmen had taken keen note of the growing numbers of ditch companies and water diversions in Colorado. Swink met with the Garden City investors and convinced them that they could secure a legal right to river flow. The construction of many Kansas ditches pre-dated most in Colorado; hence, he argued, prior appropriation laws should extend beyond state lines. He suggested that the bankers hire lawyers to file a suit seeking recognition of Kansas priorities from Colorado ditch companies. Since the rights of Rocky Ford ditch pre-dated any in Kansas, Swink had little to lose in advancing his argument, and, luckily for him, Colorado irrigators never caught wind of his negotiations in Garden City.[25]

Swink's interest in a sugar factory was purely speculative. In 1905 he and his cohorts incorporated the Arkansas Valley Beet, Land and Irrigation Company through which they purchased and renovated the properties of the Great Eastern and South Side ditches. Swink's group had no intention of keeping the ditches, and they soon sold the properties to Colorado Springs investors, who resold them to R. P. Davie and E. C. Sharer of the same city. Swink achieved his goal—he and his fellow investors profited very nicely on the sale.[26]

Development of the sugar-beet industry came quickly after Davie and Sharer sold their holdings to a syndicate led by the Cripple Creek, Colorado, mining tycoon, Spencer Penrose. One of Penrose's enterprises was the United States Irrigation Company; through it, he bought the South Side and Great Eastern ditches. By September 1906 Penrose had also bought many shares of the Kearny County and Garden City associations. The sugar company directed both associations' policies, which

An aerial view of the Garden City Sugar Factory (Kansas State Historical Society)

took away local farmer control. In addition, Penrose received a $30,000 bonus and 12,000 acres of land from the people of Garden City before beginning the construction of a sugar factory.[27]

By 1920 F. A. Gillespie, the trusted and capable general manager of the company, was directing a sophisticated operation. By 1910 the company had finished building its factory near Garden City, and Gillespie let contracts to farmers, supplied seeds, and brought in migrant workers for beet growing. Gillespie also oversaw a sizable pumping system, powered by a large steam-driven electrical plant, to supplement flows diverted into the ditches. Furthermore, he kept accounts on the surplus electricity the company sold to the local farmers. The success of the company in developing sugar beets in the region boosted the local economy and tied beet farmers to irrigation, either through ditches or pumps.[28]

In addition to the sugar company's influence, the federal government stimulated Garden City farmers' interests in irrigation. In 1889 the United States Senate formed the Committee on the Irrigation and Reclamation of Arid Lands. The committee toured the western states beyond the 98th meridian and took testimony from the residents regarding the development of irrigation. Senator Plumb of Kansas, a member of the committee, owned stock in the Great Eastern, prompting his interest in the committee's findings and recommendations as they applied to southwestern Kansas. In the fall of 1889, as part of their tour, some committee members visited the Garden City region. Several local notables—including "Buffalo" Jones and J. W. Gregory, the influential editor of the Garden City *Sentinel*—gave the committee their views on irrigation in the area.[29]

Gregory presented an elegant case for irrigation in southwestern Kansas and proposed several actions for the government to take. He advocated federally funded studies of groundwater pumping and the construction of government-sponsored demonstration projects. Pumping, he thought, would free irrigators from relying on decreasing river flow. He pinpointed the blame for the diminished flows on the proliferation of Colorado irrigation systems. In its final report the committee took notice of the rising bitterness between Kansas and Colorado interests and recommended surveys of groundwater supplies in the area. But no immediate aid came from the committee's tour and report, and Garden City–area irrigators waited over a decade before receiving any direct assistance from the federal government.[30]

With the creation of the Reclamation Service under the Newlands Act of 1902, Gregory's dream of government-sponsored groundwater pumping found expression. Charles S. Slichter, a consulting engineer for the service, conducted studies of groundwater supplies in the region and concluded that a pumping facility would work. Irrigators of the Finney County Farmers Irrigation Association reorganized themselves as the Finney County Water Users' Association in order to make a contract with the Department of Interior for the water promised through the project. The secretary of interior approved the agreement in October 1905, and the Reclamation Service began construction of the central power station, which eventually supplied twenty-three pumping units, in 1906.[31]

Despite the anticipation of benefits through cooperation, the project worked poorly and created conflict between the local farmers and service officials. The service promised to have the pumps operational for the 1908 growing season; however, when it came time to water germinating crops, the system was not ready. Once the pumps began drawing water from the alluvium, unfiltered sand clogged the machinery. Groundwater, which contained little silt, washed away silt concentrations on the ditch walls, leaving coarser material that leaked water and resulted in large transit losses. Poor river flow in 1908 compounded the problem, but even under such conditions the farmers ended up using more river water than service-pumped water. In 1909 the river flowed so well that farmers refused to contract for government water.[32]

Conflict grew between the farmers and the service and ultimately doomed the project. Unhappy with the farmers' rate of payment, Frederick Newell, the director of the service, ordered the pumps shut down. He also believed that the farmers' irrigation practices were grossly ineffi-

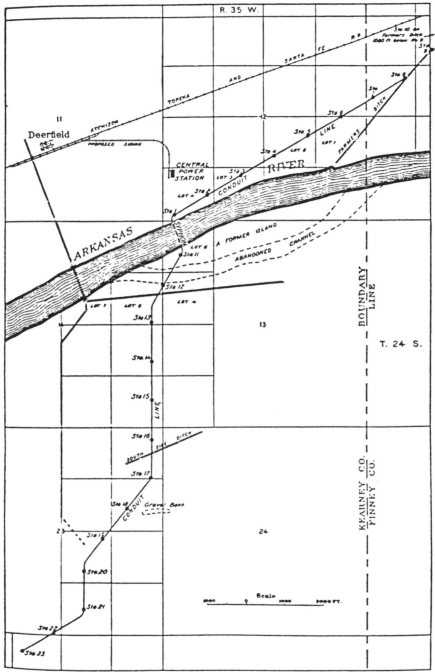

Map of the Garden City Reclamation Project (Charles S. Slichter, "Operations in Kansas," in U.S. Department of Interior, Geological Survey *Fourth Annual Report of the Reclamation Service* (Washington, D.C.: Government Printing Office, 1905), plate 18.

cient and wanted to teach them better techniques. The farmers thought they had little to learn from an operation that had never gotten the pumps to produce as officials had promised. As the farmers saw it, if the service could not deliver water, then they were not responsible for paying. Unable to resolve the differences, the service wrote the project off as a loss and sold its property at public auction. The United States Irrigation Company purchased the most of the land, water rights, and pumps. In 1920 congressional legislation released the company from any further repayment obligations for the project.[33]

Notwithstanding the failure of reclamation, the service, in conjunction with the introduction of sugar beets and the work of the United States Irrigation Company, still whetted an interest in irrigation around Garden City. The potential profits from sugar beets encouraged farmers to purchase local irrigation systems and to manage them through mutual stockholding companies. The sugar factory and the reclamation project created booms, bringing capital and money into the area. Land values rose, and farmers and real-estate speculators prospered. Irrigators, however, still lacked an adequate state institutional system to regulate irrigation practices. This shortcoming guaranteed heated disputes among the companies.[34]

Irrigators in southwestern Kansas wanted some form of prior appropriation doctrine but faced problems trying to achieve this goal. People who lived in central and eastern Kansas had a great deal of difficulty in recognizing or understanding the water problems of western residents. The former inhabited the subhumid and humid regions of the state that seldom experienced rainfall shortages. The prior appropriation doctrine had little appeal to them, and they found more comfort in the notions of common-law riparian practices.[35]

Nonetheless, Garden City–area irrigators did achieve some legislative successes in securing a nascent regulatory structure for irrigation. As early as 1866 and 1876 lawmakers had passed bills that provided for the construction of canals for agriculture and manufacturing. Next, in 1886 the legislature established a weak form of prior appropriation. That act required canal owners to file at a county register of deeds the amount of water claimed and to post the same at the diversion works. Legislators did not create any enforcement agency or adjudication process to test the legitimacy of the water claimed. In 1891 lawmakers established a priority of beneficial use: irrigation followed by industry. However, all of this legislation left intact the riparian doctrine. By and large these acts had little, if any, influence on regulating water use in southwestern Kansas or on stemming conflict among irrigators.[36] Nor did the Kansas Supreme Court add much direction. In the case *Clark et al. v. Allaman et al.* (1905), the court invalidated any customs in conflict with the riparian doctrine. It did allow the statute of 1886 to stand so long as the act did not interfere with previously established riparian rights.

Attempts were also made to create a regulatory agency to administer the hodgepodge of water law. In 1917 lawmakers put together the Kansas Water Commission (to oversee the appropriation of water) and the Division of Irrigation within the State Board of Agriculture (to regulate ditch and pump companies). In 1927 legislation combined the responsibilities of both offices into the Division of Water Resources, which operated under the State Board of Agriculture. Still, the legislature passed all these enabling laws without either changing the 1886 act or dealing with the ambiguities of *Clark v. Allaman*.[37]

Not until the drought of the 1930s did more practical and workable solutions for the regulation of water appear. In 1939 a special commission of the governor called for a statewide plan to regulate the use of both ground- and surface water. In 1941 the legislature responded by repealing the law of 1886 and making the Division of Water Resources responsible for establishing and administering water rights. In 1944, however, the state supreme court ruled that the division was without authority to manage groundwater. In 1945 George Knapp, the chief of the Division of Water Resources and a recognized hydrologist, chaired and heavily influenced another governor's committee which drafted reforms the state legislature enacted that year. Knapp's expertise provided the guidance for new laws that carefully instituted a modified system of prior appropriation procedures. In 1949 the state supreme court upheld Knapp's work, thereby assuring Kansas of a legal structure that could regulate ground- and surface waters.[38]

Before 1945 the absence of effective water regulations had left irrigators in southwestern Kansas to fight among themselves over the division of scarce resources in the region. As discussed earlier, the battle between "Buffalo" Jones (owner of the Amazon ditch) and the Russells (owners of the Great Eastern) serves as a good example. Since no prior appropriation laws such as those in Colorado protected the Great Eastern, the Russells and Jones had many disputes, some violent, over how much water Jones could rightfully divert. By 1891 Denny, the purchaser of the Great Eastern, still had not resolved the issue with the new owners of the Amazon canal and resorted to litigation to protect his interests.[39]

Ultimately, the Great Eastern owners would win their suit; however, the court's decision revealed a distinct lack of judicial sophistication regarding the regulation of surface diversions among contending irrigation companies. Denny filed his suit against the Southwestern Kansas Land and Irrigation Company, the London syndicate that had bought the Amazon ditch. The case began in federal district court in Wichita, Kansas, where some witnesses testified. There the case sat until both systems had passed into receivership. Dewey, the receiver of the Great Eastern, had his lawyer move the suit to the federal court in Topeka. In 1897 the Great Eastern owners won water rights totaling 292,000 inches of water from the Arkansas River for irrigation use. This amounted to between 6,000 and 7,000 cubic feet of water per second (cfs), or nearly *ten times* the maximum diversion capacity of the Great Eastern headworks! Clearly, no other irrigation company could coexist with the Great Eastern, whose right to hog the whole river flow passed to the United States Irrigation Company, which planned to use the water in growing sugar beets.[40]

When the court handed down its decision in 1897, Dewey was managing the Farmers', the Great Eastern, and the Garden City ditches. The court might have intended the decree to apply to all three ditches, not just the Great Eastern. It follows, then, that the three companies should have divided equitably the right to 6,000 to 7,000 cfs. However, by 1909 the United States Irrigation Company, owner of the Great Eastern ditch, was claiming ownership of all the rights attached to the 1897 decree. The Finney County Water Users' Association, the owner of the Farmers' ditch, disputed the absurd water rights claimed by the sugar company. The ruling, the association feared, would strip it of its right to river flow. In 1909 the association filed suit in Kearny County District Court against the sugar company and others, asking for an adjudication of the various water rights to the Arkansas River. The sugar company then had the case removed to the United States Circuit Court at Topeka.[41]

United States Irrigation eventually made a deal with the major ditch companies around Garden City, which temporarily quelled the feuding. The sugar company had persuaded the others that it was working in their behalf, since it was at that moment in federal district court asserting its "prior" right to river flow over several Colorado ditch companies. The sugar company promised to divide whatever water rights it won with the other Kansas companies. In May 1911 the attorneys for the Great Eastern, South Side, Amazon, and Garden City ditches signed a stipulation that divided the water flow of the Arkansas River. The Finney County Water Users' Association signed the agreement two days after the others had and so followed the leadership of the sugar company.[42]

After 1910 the company largely guided the development of irrigation in the region. Not only did it pursue litigation designed to establish all of the local companies' water rights, but it also controlled the local sugar-beet economy. Spencer Penrose, later joined by Charles Tutt, Sr., directed the United States Sugar and Land Company of Colorado Springs, which owned beet farms near Garden City, Larned, and Emporia, Kansas, as well as in New Mexico and around Colorado Springs. Even so, beet production never matched the factory's capacity. To remedy this deficit Penrose and Tutt often required farmers to plant at least *40 percent* of

Sugar beet harvesting near Garden City, Kansas

their lands in beets before the company would supply them with ditch water.[43]

Local farmers under the Great Eastern and South Side ditches, now owned by the sugar company, greatly resented the terms of the beet contracts. They pressed successful suits against the Kansas sugar company, the United States Irrigation Company. Thus in 1910 Penrose and Tutt decided to follow their attorneys' advice and reorganized the company as a Wyoming firm named the United States Irrigating Company (which operated the ditches and factory in Kansas). This maneuver allowed the directors to file interstate suits (a Wyoming plaintiff versus a Kansas defendant) in the less partisan federal courts. By this tactic, the syndicate avoided having suits decided in Kansas district courts, which often leaned in favor of the farmers.[44]

The sugar company also retained the exclusive control of all rights attached to its ditches. Unlike the operation of the mutual companies in Colorado, the United States Irrigating Company rented water to the Colorado Springs sugar and land company, which re-rented it in one-year contracts to farmers who would grow beets. Usually farmers paid $1 to $2 per acre irrigated. By 1913 the company curtailed the amount of land in beets because of chronic water shortages. The directors hoped to increase tonnage on less land with greater amounts of applied water. Farmers found their ties to the sugar gave them little control over ditch water.[45]

After the failure of pump reclamation and the harsh contracts let by the sugar company, James Craig and other leaders of the Finney County Water Users' Association shunned the sugar company. The diversion works of the Great Eastern, South Side, and Amazon ditches were all located above the Farmers' ditch; combined with poor quantities of river flow, the mutual company had difficulty protecting its own interests. People like Craig felt surrounded by hostile interests—the sugar company in Kansas and the ditch and reservoir enterprises in Colorado—which all depleted the river flow. In such a milieu, discord flourished.

The contentious and erratic nature of irrigation enterprises in Kansas sprang from weak irrigation operations. Compared to their counterparts in Colorado, Kansas ditch companies differed markedly. First, Kansas ditch systems maintained far less total acreage than did those in Colorado. Between 1896 and 1949 the largest total of acreage under irrigation in Finney and Kearny counties came in 1944, the height of World War II crop production. In that year the county assessor reported 67,426 acres. This total under five Kansas systems equaled roughly two-thirds of the acreage under just the Fort Lyon Canal Company in Colorado. During the same period, irrigated acreage in Finney and Kearny counties increased by a slight .7 percent compounded annual growth rate; however, this gain came with improved pumping technology and not from increased river diversions.[46]

Poor river flow was the reason why irrigated acreage remained small around Garden City. The gross duty figures for the combined operations of the five ditch system graphically illustrates the point. George Knapp, the chief of the Division of Water Resources, estimated that over 1 million acres in southwestern Kansas, irrigated annually with at least 2 acre-feet of water per acre, could support crop production. In actuality, from 1908 through 1949, ditches supplied an average of around 47,000 acres. In only one year, 1948, did the gross duty top 3 acre-feet; only in four years did it exceed 2 acre-feet. The average for the same time span amounted to 1.47 acre-feet of water per acre of land; in nine of those years it fell *below* 1 acre-foot. When these figures are compared to the Fort Lyon company, the weakest in terms of water resources of the Colorado ditches discussed in this study, the differences are striking. For example, the Fort Lyon company, for roughly the same period, averaged 2.37 acre-feet of water per acre of land. In other words, even if Kansas irrigators had wanted to, they could not solely rely on their canals.[47]

What made it most difficult to get water into the canals was that the river flowed either too much at the wrong time or too little when most needed. That explains why from 1921 to 1949 variations in the river flow at Syracuse, Kansas, correlated weakly to the ditch companies' diversions, even though irrigators claimed the river flow determined their ditch diversions.[48] The companies could divert only so much river flow because of the design of their headgates. From 1921 through 1949 only in a few months did total diversions exceed 30,000 acre-feet of water. Any river flow beyond this amount continued downstream. Often the river carried above 100,000 acre-feet in a month, which meant the occurrence of a freshet or flood. These conditions frequently did more damage than good to the systems. Such a state of affairs meant that the companies were unable to use water when it flowed and needed more when it waned.

Ditch operations in 1921 clearly illustrated the nature of this problem in the extreme. The companies diverted 10,000 acre-feet in October 1920 and decreased the amounts each month through February 1921. This practice constituted in part winter irrigation, applying water to the land in hopes that enough would remain in the ground until spring to germinate the crops regardless of precipitation or river flow conditions. This technique, however, was filled with dangers. Diversions containing slush ice could freeze and wreck headgates and lateral boxes. Even though the river flow at Syracuse supported winter irrigation, it had to be done carefully. When April arrived the river flow fell below 10,000 acre-feet. These were the months that farmers planted sugar beets and had to have water in the soil. They could not rely on the river when they needed it most. Then in June the flood that so damaged Pueblo and the valley below also struck hard in the Garden City area. Unable to handle the over 500,000 acre-feet that passed Syracuse, the farmers attempted to shut out the river from their ditches, yet the flood destroyed headworks and made the canals inoperative. Not until August did they have some of the ditches in order, well after the dry, hot month of July had taken its toll on alfalfa, sugar beets, and milo. By September the operational ditches began the crucial diversions for the newly planted wheat crop. To understate the situation, irrigators had a difficult "go" of it in western Kansas.[49]

Until the opening of John Martin Dam and Reservoir, the companies' individual operations demonstrated an inability to ameliorate their water supply situation. For example, the Farmers' and the Amazon ditches showed a significant rise in rates of diversions between the years of 1916 through 1950. Beginning and ending values of trend lines greatly affect the results; therefore, the operation of John Martin Reservoir (built by the Army Corps of Engineers, in part, to solve the dispute between Coloradans and Kansans over the Arkansas River flow) in the mid-1940s probably contributed to the Farmers' ditch company obtaining more water than it had previously. From 1916 to 1950, however, the Great Eastern, South Side, and Garden City diversions show a fairly flat trend-line. Only in 1942 and 1943 did the diversions of the Great Eastern significantly fall from its average. This came as a result of the April flood in 1942 that completely destroyed its headworks and scoured the upper ditch to "twice its original width and considerably deeper." The river changed course, covering a large portion of former canal and tearing five breaks in the system. Beginning in 1944 the sugar company made agreements with the Kearny County association to use the headworks of the Amazon ditch to channel river flow into the Great Eastern canal. On the whole, between 1916 and 1950, the diversion trends of these companies clearly indicated that they accomplished little on their own to improve their water supplies.[50]

The effects of drought in the 1930s further illustrate the weak nature of the Garden City–area ditches. Although headgate diversions fell somewhat, the operations of the companies remained fairly stable—for three reasons. The ditches already functioned at a low level of efficiency. Only the Garden City ditch sustained below average diversions during most of the decade, and its headgate stood last on the river. The sugar company, now called the Garden City Company, owned the ditch and had a court decree that allowed it to divert some of the ditch rights at the Great Eastern headgate whenever it thought prudent. During drought the sugar company drew from the former to supply the latter, which explains the somewhat steady operation of the Great Eastern and the below-average diversions of the Garden City ditch in dry years. Second, drought disturbed the operations of the companies less than expected because irrigators supplemented ditch diversions with well-developed individual pumping operations. Relatively inexpensive gasoline-powered machines made pump technology possible for large numbers of farmers. Lacking motors, many systems were turned from pulley wheels on tractors. The lift of a single pump was sufficient to irrigate forty or more acres. Third, prices for sugar beets, the area's main cash crop, remained stable during the depression. As dry-land farmers, plagued by dust storms, left the area by the score, irrigators, while by no means making a fortune, remained and prospered in comparison.[51]

World War II added strength to irrigation around Garden City. Prices for commodities rose and did not drop until 1948. Farmers continued investing in pump systems, and as a result, fewer irrigators worked capital-intensive operations on larger acreages. Farmers also started receiving some benefits from the flood and irrigation operations of John Martin Reservoir in Colorado.[52]

By 1949 the attempt by Garden City–area farmers to dominate nature had resulted in an integrated system of ditch and pumping practices. Only a small portion of the farmers relied solely on either ditch or pumping to irrigate their crops. Rather, the vast majority operated systems that practiced sheet irrigation (water let out from an irrigation ditch across a field that lacked furrows to channel the flow) supplemented by pumps that tapped the shallow aquifers. On these lands irrigators raised alfalfa, sugar beets, and cereals, followed by truck crops and fruit.[53]

As in Colorado, however, nature reacted against its "conquest" by western Kansas irrigators. The Arkansas River banks narrowed, spilling water out even during the smallest freshet or flood and damaging fields, canal works, and buildings. For example, by 1930 the riverbanks at Lakin, Kansas, carried only half of what they had in 1890. Salinity levels also rose. Part of the problem stemmed from Colorado operations, since the reuse of water compounded the rate of mineral concentrations in the river flow. What Kansas irrigators received from Colorado was essentially used water. Luckily, little irrigation occurred between the state line and the Amazon diversion works, which allowed some time for the salts to settle on the riverbed before reaching the Amazon headgates. Nonetheless, in the 1930s, as local irrigator T. E. Grable commented, farmers could not convert irrigated fields to dry land because of the build-up of salts in the soil. Moreover, by 1949 untreated river water was unsuitable for drinking, cooking, or washing.[54]

While nature retaliated on some fronts, it fell on others—but in ways that proved troublesome for the victors. Pumping depleted the aquifers. River flow and precipitation recharged the shallow district's groundwater, whereas the Ogallala Aquifer refilled at an extremely slow rate not significantly affected by either streams or rainfall. Most of the wells around Garden City drew from the shallow district. During drought conditions the farmers found that the water table there dropped precariously but rose again after above-average rainfall and river flow. Those who extracted from the more abundant supply of the Ogallala found the water table dropping and not rising. As pump technology improved, more farmers tapped the Ogallala, but they also noticed that table lowered over the years. This translated into higher fixed-capital costs for irrigators investing in pumping. With each passing year, those who pumped found it harder to alter their systems without suffering crippling economic loss.[55]

The salt cedar also caused environmental problems in western Kansas as it had in eastern Colorado. The tree contributed to the saline conditions of the river flow and flourished as the river turned more saline. The plant consumed copious amounts of water and furthered the narrowing of the riverbanks. Farmers found this an insidious problem that defied easy solution. In western Kansas, people began encountering what would became all too commonplace: higher costs of irrigating in an environment less conducive to its practice.[56]

People came to southwestern Kansas determined to remake the area into profitable farmlands, as the name Garden City implies. But crop-destroying droughts in the 1870s and 1880s ruined the dreams of many people and caused them to leave the region in droves. Those who stayed resorted to irrigation in their attempt to subdue nature. Some, like

Charles J. "Buffalo" Jones, hoped to make money from rising land values as irrigation transformed the "desert" into productive farms. Yet plans to build irrigation systems, as Jones's frenzied efforts revealed, showed serious deficiencies before 1910. With Jones, and with other investors in the multitude of irrigation companies that rose and fell around Garden City, speculation ruled and excluded sound management of the ditch systems. Moreover, droughts, depressions, irrigation development in Colorado, and the attitude of local farmers unwilling to rent water from the companies made all the undertakings risky propositions.

After 1900 irrigation around Garden City would probably have died if not for the introduction of sugar beets. Production of this valuable cash crop required precise watering at the proper time, which stimulated a great deal of interest in the dilapidated ditch systems in the area. Irrigators formed cooperatives to own and direct several of the systems, and land speculators thrived again with the arrival of the federal reclamation project and Spencer Penrose's United States Sugar and Land Company. Irrigators also experimented with pumping to supplement chronically weak ditch diversions, and by the 1930s pumping became an integral part of most farms in the area.

Still, irrigation had only a tenuous hold around Garden City. The domination of nature proved incomplete as farmers battled rising salinity, the salt cedar, narrowing riverbanks, and depleted aquifers. Not only did irrigators fight nature, they also fought one another when water became precious for sugar-beet production. Before 1945, haphazard legislation and an unsympathetic state supreme court simply encouraged conflict. A semblance of order—if even that, given the ludicrous decree of 1897—came through the federal courts rather than the state. Not until George Knapp applied his talents to devising a modified prior appropriation system for Kansas did irrigators around Garden City have laws capable of regulating their water use.

Even though irrigation around Garden City was a shaky enterprise at best, the farmers tended to view their problems as coming from elsewhere. They found it easier to blame Coloradans for taking their share of the Arkansas River flow than to fault themselves for the shortsightedness of their own vision. Ever since the droughts in the 1880s and 1890s, Kansans maintained that the development of irrigation in Colorado had robbed them of water and prevented them from operating successful irrigation systems. From 1900 until the signing of the Arkansas River Compact in 1948, Kansans would wage incessant legal war and conduct negotiations, designed to secure what they perceived as their right to the Arkansas River flow.

CHAPTER SIX

The Contest for the "Nile of America": *Kansas v. Colorado*, 1890–1910

The United States Supreme Court took its first notice of interstate squabbling over western watercourses in the suit *Kansas v. Colorado* (1907).[1] The decision failed to stem a steady onslaught of interstate water litigation, but the justices did achieve the means to adjudge water disputes between states. To understand the justices' accomplishment, or lack of it, requires what James Willard Hurst called a "social history of law"—law related to society and to ideas outside the narrow confines of jurisprudence. This approach proves useful for understanding the significance of *Kansas v. Colorado*.[2]

To review, the settlers who came to the Arkansas River Valley of Colorado and Kansas shared cultural beliefs about nature. Kansans and Coloradans held market-culture values and a belief in the domination of nature. Settlers aspired to create a growing capitalistic economy in the valley by conquering nature through hydraulic engineering. Both sides in the case certainly agreed on the values that governed nature and the market.[3] As several historians have noted, Americans ordered their relationship with nature through their legal system. In the marketplace law played an important function in the allocation of scarce natural resources. A complex legal framework, fully sympathetic to the domination of nature and market-culture values, controlled water usage through the general concepts of prior appropriation and riparian rights as defined by state and federal laws and by court decisions. People in the Arkansas River Valley usually developed and protected their interests in the valley's water through the legal system.[4]

By 1900 Coloradans, through the prior appropriation system, had put to use nearly all of the surface water in the Arkansas River Valley. Nearly 100 ditch systems irrigated more than 7,000 farms on more than 300,000 acres. Pueblo and Colorado Springs had built elaborate public waterworks serving approximately 50,000 people. The Colorado Fuel and Iron Company, which employed about 16,000 people and supplied the High Plains region with coal, managed a complex water system for manufacturing steel and mining coal. The company's canal delivered more than 10 million gallons daily to the steel plant. Through prior appropriation, most Coloradans believed they had secured progress with the proliferation of cities, industries, and farms.[5]

The Kansas legal structure, too, had supported the economic development of the Arkansas River. A weak system of prior appropriation laws had permitted irrigation development of more than 30,000 acres in the southwestern portion of the state. In 1905, around the Garden City area, more than $1 million had been invested in irrigation works, with the Reclamation Service committed to spending an additional $250,000 on the development of a pump reclamation project.[6]

Farther down the river at Wichita, Kansas, Marshall Murdock, the powerful editor of the *Wichita Eagle*, and other city leaders sought congressional legislation to deepen the river for the rather boneheaded notion of making Wichita an inland port. From 1879 through 1882, primarily through the active petitioning of Wichitans and residents of Arkansas City (near the Oklahoma-Kansas state line), Congress passed four acts for river improvements along the Arkansas River from Fort Smith, Arkansas, to Wichita, Kansas. In the spring of 1880, when the 500-ton steamboat *Tom Ryan* reached Wichita, the excited townspeople warmly welcomed the captain and crew and rewarded them with all the beer and pretzels that they could consume. An enthusiastic Murdock called the Arkansas "the Nile of America," but the river could never support his expectations. In December 1880 an Army Corps snag boat bottomed on a sandbar within sight of a large crowd of well-wishers. According to Craig Miner, "The passengers leaped out into a raging river 2-1/2 inches deep. Embarrassed, they declared to the crowd that navigation on the Arkansas was closed for the season," and it has remained shut to Wichita ever after. Still, Murdock and others had used law to bring about the economic development of the Arkansas River.[7]

The origins of *Kansas v. Colorado* were the unplanned consequences of instrumental law in the application of market-culture values and the domination of nature. After 1870 people had altered the riparian ecosystem of the Arkansas River Valley on the High Plains. Trouble arose as they erected water-consuming enterprises with no forethought of environmental ramifications beyond the goals of creating a "garden" and achieving commercial prosperity in the arid West through the "conquest" of nature. Consequently, after a period of years water users encountered an environment no longer capable of sustaining the original scope of their operations. Instead of recognizing the inherent flaws in their values, they looked for someone to blame.

The contrived demarcation that separated Kansas and Colorado easily yielded several camps contending for control of the Arkansas River. The boundary plagued both states by neatly but irrationally dividing the

Fully flowing Arkansas River at Garden City, Kansas (Kansas State Historical Society)

Dry Arkansas riverbed at Garden City, Kansas (Kansas State Historical Society)

river basin. All of the upper tributaries remained within the confines of Colorado. Development around Garden City depended in part on the regular flow of the Arkansas River; however, control over the stream sources remained in Colorado. Moreover, the people of central and eastern Kansas had little understanding of, or empathy with, their western counterparts' irrigation practices. People in western Kansas felt isolated between Coloradans, who were "gobbling up" the Arkansas River flow, and residents of central and eastern Kansas, who had a difficult time grasping the irrigation problems around Garden City.[8]

People in southwestern Kansas longed to do something to better their situation. As early as 1890 or 1891, Charles J. "Buffalo" Jones, the most energetic of all irrigation promoters in Kansas, contemplated a suit against Colorado to uphold the prior appropriation status of his enterprises vis-à-vis Colorado ditch companies. However, his attorney, Judge Henry Mason, warned that the case would reach the United States Supreme Court and would cost a bundle to pursue. Jones, who could not even finance his own ditch systems, voiced local sentiment when he stated, "I didn't want such a big job as that on my hands." In the 1890s the feebleness of irrigation in southwestern Kansas precluded people from attempting litigation against the more prosperous systems of Colorado.[9]

Nonetheless, the issue came to national attention. In 1890 irrigators in western Kansas informed the members of the special committee of the United States Senate on the irrigation and reclamation of arid lands about how Coloradans had deprived them of their fair share to the Arkansas River flow. Garden City newspaper editor J. W. Gregory thought the development of groundwater pumping would prevent Colorado from depriving "us of water by continuing in the dog-in-the-man[g]er policy of preventing the water from crossing the State Line." "If our Colorado neighbors would divide with us," opined "Buffalo" Jones, "I think we could have a good deal more [water]." He wanted to establish the prior appropriation rights of Kansas ditches over most canals in Colorado. "If the Colorado ditches had given us a prior right we would have had abundance. The Colorado ditches that have been lately built have been taking the supply of water." Jones, Gregory, and other people around Garden City had found their scapegoat.[10]

Congress considered the simmering resentment around Garden City serious business, and the minority report of the special Senate committee made some recommendations. The states by themselves, the senators believed, could not be trusted to divide interstate river flows equitably. The "National Government," so they wrote, "must, therefore, become the arbitrator between [Kansas and Colorado], and it should immediately intervene to divide the waters in some wise and just manner."

In the minds of these politicians, the allocation of limited water supplies in the arid West logically led to a centralization of power, to be wielded by the federal government over interstate river flows.[11]

Others, however, hoped to avoid the creation of a national regulatory apparatus over western rivers. John Wesley Powell, for one, wanted the major river basins in the West turned into self-governing water districts. The people within each, irrespective and independent of their state governments, would make and administer all laws regarding water usage in the district. In 1895 Orren Donaldson, writing in the *Irrigation Age*, built upon Powell's ideas and suggested, instead of water districts, drawing new states in the West bounded by the contours of river basins. In 1894 Elwood Mead had recommended in the same publication that the states should through "mutual concessions and a disinterested recognition of the rights and possibilities of the respective commonwealths interested" resolve their own differences. But water meant economic growth for whoever owned it, and those who controlled the sources of water were not going to share without a fight.[12]

Irrigators such as "Buffalo" Jones could not afford expensive interstate litigation, but others like Marshall Murdock had the political clout to engage the state of Kansas against Colorado. Murdock was certain he knew the nature of the Arkansas River and who was to blame for the changes in it. As he believed, part of the value of the stream came from its vast "underflow," a subterranean water source that nourished all crops in the valley. In addition, he thought that if the Army Corps of Engineers would properly maintain his "Nile," the flow could support all forms of river traffic. But alterations in the riparian ecosystem around Wichita troubled Murdock. For nearly thirty years he had observed the river flow decreasing, groundwater levels falling, and riverbanks narrowing. In December 1906 S. S. Ashbaugh, an attorney representing Kansas, summarized the disquiet: "Our valley dried out and we no longer have our 'Egypt.' " But what or who had caused this damage?[13]

Initially Murdock held irrigators in western Kansas culpable for changes in the Arkansas River, but later (and more important), he blamed Colorado irrigators. Through the Republican party, he lobbied the Kansas legislature to support a suit of original jurisdiction in the United States Supreme Court to enjoin Colorado interests from any non-riparian diversions. In 1901 Kansas lawmakers heeded Murdock's plea and passed a bill instructing the attorney general to file suit against Colorado. Kansans, by beginning in the Supreme Court, had launched a serious attack against the prior appropriation system governing water usage in Colorado. Interstate suits of original jurisdiction before the United States Supreme Court usually have entailed issues of great importance. In *Kansas v. Colorado*, the justices saw themselves functioning like an international tribunal—an alternative to diplomatic negotiations or armed conflict between sovereign states.[14]

In May 1901 A. A. Godard, the attorney general of Kansas, filed the initial complaint, which made a simple case. Colorado ditch diversions, he argued, had materially depleted the normal Arkansas River flow throughout the entire state to the detriment of the riparian rights of Kansans. The "underflow" of the river, he charged, had sustained major depletion. Reduced surface and groundwater flows, Godard continued, had wrecked the economy all along the river and had ruined navigation below Wichita. He concluded by asking the United States Supreme Court justices to prohibit Colorado from engaging in any form of reservoir and canal building, from issuing any water rights to any interests, from renewing any "expired" rights, or from renewing corporate charters to any company diverting water onto nonriparian land. The only exception Godard allowed was the diversion of water for "domestic" uses onto riparian land.[15]

In June 1903 C. C. Coleman, the next attorney general of Kansas, entered an amended bill of complaint and enlarged the scope of the case beyond simply the state of Colorado. He named seventeen additional defendants including all of the largest water users along the Arkansas River, implicating the Colorado Fuel and Iron Company as well as the irrigation companies. Now the attorney general could press the Kansas suit whether or not the state of Colorado actually built canals and reservoirs or issued water rights.[16]

Colorado lawyers attacked the Kansas position with a strong legal arsenal. When the United States Congress granted Colorado statehood, so Attorney General Charles C. Post argued, it also sanctioned the prior appropriation system of Colorado embedded in the state constitution. Therefore, the riparian doctrine in Kansas had no bearing on water uses in Colorado. Moreover, Post claimed that Colorado possessed complete sovereignty over the unnavigable river with the right to dispose of the flow howsoever it desired. The state of Colorado, as Post also pointed out, did not issue water rights. Rather, the state administered a recognized private and perpetual right to divert water. In large part, Colorado's defense attorneys were elaborating on the "Harmon Doctrine." First articulated by United States Attorney General Judson Harmon in 1895, the doctrine held that a nation possesses sole and absolute jurisdiction within its territory. Building on this line of thought, Colorado lawyers compared their state to a sovereign nation that had the exclusive right to the water within its boundaries.[17]

More telling arguments against Kansas came from the lawyers of the private companies in Colorado. D. C. Beaman, the attorney representing the Colorado Fuel and Iron Company, asked by what right could Kansas

THE EQUITABLE SIDE OF IT.

UNCLE SAM:—It is hardly right to turn fine Kansas farms into arid lands that Colorado may enhance the value of some of her sandhills.

A Kansas view of *Kansas v. Colorado* (*Breeze* [Topeka, Kansas], 15 August 1903).

destroy a multimillion-dollar industry. He believed a decision in favor of
the riparian doctrine would not square with the protection of private
property rights in Colorado. The attorneys for the Arkansas Valley Ditch
Association followed similar reasoning. Fred Sabin and Platt Rogers,
who spoke for this combine of irrigation companies, illustrated how the
economy in the entire Arkansas Valley of Kansas had prospered between
1870 and 1890. Real-estate values had risen, crop production had increased, and so had income and population. Given these facts, how
could Kansans justify tearing apart the economy in the Arkansas Valley
of Colorado?[18]

Francis K. Carey, the president of the National Sugar Manufacturing
Company which operated a large factory in Sugar City, Colorado, gave
one of the clearest expressions of this argument. Carey wrote to N. C.
Miller, the Colorado attorney general who followed Post, that Kansans
had " 'stood by' and allowed enormous sums of money to be invested on
the faith of the [prior appropriation system] adopted by the State of Colorado." Given this, Carey failed to see how the Court would "impair in
any way the vested interests of [Colorado] property holders." Carey's
views here substantiate Hurst's position that the nineteenth-century
concept of protecting vested rights in the United States had "less to do
with protecting holdings that it had to do with protecting ventures." Following Carey's thinking, Kansans' property rights did not deserve the
protection owed to Coloradans' rights, which were superior because
they were obtained through the more energetic exploitation of river
flow.[19]

The case quickly became important to more groups than just Coloradans and Kansans. Frederick Newell, the director of the Reclamation
Service, had taken a keen interest in its development. With the passage
of the Newlands Act in 1902, Newell, along with others in the Department of Interior, worried that either state winning its claim might mean
the destruction of the act's effectiveness. The riparian doctrine would
only allow federal reclamation projects of limited scope. If Colorado's
view of complete sovereignty over the Arkansas River held, then the service would be at the mercy of myriad water laws of arid states, thereby
complicating the management of any interstate project. Newell prevailed
upon the Attorney General's Office to intervene in the case, which the
Supreme Court allowed in March 1904.

The right to intervene in a suit of original jurisdiction comes when a
party, in this case the federal government, has a pecuniary interest in the
outcome of the suit not represented by either of the litigants. When
granted the right to intervene in an ongoing interstate suit, an intervenor
then seeks to act for its own interest independently of the contending
states. P. C. Knox, attorney general of the United States, Frank L. Camp-

bell and A. C. Campbell, assistant attorneys of the United States, and H. M. Hayt, the solicitor general, took the most active roles in representing the federal government's case. Frederick Newell, director of the Reclamation Service, and Morris Bien, supervising engineer in the service, also kept abreast of the developments in the suit and often advised the lawyers in the Attorney General's Office.[20]

All the arguments of federal attorneys alleged the right of the government to regulate interstate streams in the arid states. They denied the navigability of the Arkansas in Kansas and Colorado, the precedence of the riparian doctrine over the prior appropriation doctrine, and the sovereign right of Colorado to control the river flow of any interstate river. Only the federal government, these lawyers claimed, could regulate the flow of interstate streams, regardless of navigability.[21]

To sustain the government's position, A. C. Campbell, an assistant attorney for the federal government, employed the "Wilson Doctrine." During oral arguments, Campbell summarized the doctrine: "The inherent power of the nation exists outside of the enumerated powers in the Constitution in cases where the object is beyond the power of the State, and was a power originally exercised or ordinarily exercised by sovereign nations." Consequently, the fact that the Constitution remained silent about the government's power over interstate streams in the arid West did not exclude the government from exercising regulatory authority over these rivers.[22]

In keeping with the procedures in an interstate suit of original jurisdiction, the justices appointed a commissioner (today called a special master) to take testimony so as to establish the facts of the case. In August 1905 a commission began hearing testimony in Wichita, Kansas. In eighty days in eighteen cities, over 300 witnesses took the stand. The stenographer typed over 8,500 pages of depositions and recorded over 120 exhibits. Seldom in the Court's history had it entertained a case of this magnitude.[23]

Kansas attorneys built their case through the statements of nonexperts. In the closing arguments, C. C. Coleman, the attorney general of Kansas, asserted: "Now, the flow of water is not necessarily a matter of expert testimony." He asked the Court to consider the evidence given by farmers whose experiences in the valley led them all to note the lowering of both the "underflow" and the surface flow of the Arkansas River. Conveniently enough, they all dated this occurrence after the great ditch-building spree in Colorado in the 1880s.[24]

The Kansas attorneys had made a conscious decision to avoid expert authorities, hoping to overwhelm the justices with the testimony of 120 nonexperts who all agreed on essentially the same theory. There were Kansas hydrologists from whom they could have drawn testimony—for

Participants pondering the fruits of their labor (Western History Department, Denver Public Library)

example, Professor Erasmus Hayworth, the state geologist of Kansas; Professor Robert Hay; or Professor Frank Marvin, dean of the School of Engineering at the University of Kansas. However, the studies of these engineers would not have corroborated the attorneys' argument that the groundwater of the valley was the underflow of the river.[25]

Ultimately, the reliance on the farmers' testimony failed. They had trouble remembering in which season they had seen the river full or dry; and in a great many cases, they could not recall the exact year. They failed to explain how surface flow could supply groundwater when much of the underflow lay in elevations above the riverbed. They all noted the narrowing of the Arkansas River banks, the filling of the riverbed with silt, and the lessening of river flows. But had irrigation in Colorado caused these environmental changes, or had the river responded to other variables, such as agricultural development in south-central Kansas? Plowed farmlands absorbed great quantities of rainfall and returned less to the river than native grasslands. Cultivation also diminished prairie fires which gave cottonwoods freedom to grow unimpeded along the riverbanks, thereby helping to shrink the channel. The avoidance of expert testimony cost Kansas dearly in building its arguments.[26]

Colorado attorneys, on the other hand, sought out authorities. Louis G. Carpenter, a professor of irrigation engineering at Colorado Agricultural College in Fort Collins, bore the brunt of presenting the scientific evidence discrediting the Kansans' arguments. Among his important findings was the fact that rainfall contributed more to the underflow than did the Arkansas River flow—an observation that also coincided with the findings of federal witnesses. Carpenter explained how deforestation in the upper reaches of the valley, not irrigation development, had severely reduced spring runoffs. He graphically illustrated the way in which the porous sands of the Arkansas River absorbed surface flows, which meant little, if any, of it originating in Colorado ever reached as far as Wichita. With voluminous historical research, he documented extremely erratic flows in the Arkansas River long before the development of irrigation in the valley. In total, the testimony given by Coloradans painted a picture of minimal harm done to Kansas through irrigation and prior appropriation.[27]

Carpenter, though, could not maintain that irrigation in Colorado had little effect on the Arkansas River flow to the irrigation systems around Garden City, Kansas. Frederick Newell, for one, clearly implicated the growth of Colorado irrigation in the 1880s as a major cause for a falling river flow reaching Kansas ditch companies in the 1890s. The emphasis of Kansas attorneys on the riparian doctrine, however, barely acknowledged the interests of western Kansas irrigators. In December 1904 the editor of one newspaper at Syracuse, Kansas, thought that "this seemed to us to be the object aimed at [by Kansas attorneys]—to knock out all the irrigators—Kansas as well as Colorado." The editor wished that Kansas had taken the position that its western ditches had established prior appropriation rights to the river over most of the ditch companies in Colorado.[28]

Carpenter's research also served to dispute any federal argument that might be made for national control over nonnavigable interstate streams. The notable "Elephant Butte" case, also before the Supreme Court, raised similar questions in a suit concerning interstate and international water development on the Rio Grande. Justice David Brewer, the only Supreme Court justice who had some understanding of western water problems, wrote one opinion during this ongoing litigation that supported federal control over nonnavigable streams under certain conditions. He contended that federal courts could stop the appropriation of water on a river's upper reaches, navigable or not, that depleted the flows to the river in its navigable reaches.[29]

Carpenter countered with a "dual river" theory. His measurements showed that only a minute amount of the water flowing out of Colorado reached the navigable portion of the Arkansas River, which he thought began below Fort Gibson, Oklahoma. Moreover, he continued, on numerous occasions the river failed to flow at all from the western edge of Kansas to the city of Great Bend. Therefore, he claimed that the Arkansas River in reality was two rivers: an upper river fed largely by melted mountain snowpack and occasional runoff from the High Plains, and a lower river, beginning near Great Bend, Kansas, fed by numerous tributaries carrying the runoff from the subhumid prairies. Building on Carpenter's findings, the counsel for Colorado maintained that the federal government could not use Brewer's ruling in the Elephant Butte case to assert any regulation over the upper basin.[30]

Frederick Newell largely agreed with Carpenter's description of the Arkansas River and thus his argument against federal control. Newell had no interest in protecting navigation, a position that benefited the Army Corps of Engineers rather than the Reclamation Service in the Department of Interior. What he wanted was to build dams to store water for the recovery of arid land. Consequently, the testimony given by the federal government's witnesses voiced the need for greater national regulation of rivers in the arid West and the need to protect the newly created Reclamation Service. Frederick Newell and Elwood Mead took the stand to warn against applying the riparian doctrine to arid states, since it would jeopardize the construction of storage reservoirs, a central feature of most reclamation projects. Also, they could not abide Colorado's notion of complete sovereign control over the flow of interstate streams originating within its borders. If the service were to build a reservoir in New Mexico on a stream originating in Colorado, then at some future date Coloradans could decide to use the water formally flowing into the New Mexico reservoir, in effect drying it up. Therefore, to facilitate the operations of the service, Newell wanted the federal government to have the power to regulate all interstate streams in the West.[31]

To illustrate the need for such authority, the federal government questioned witnesses from Wyoming. Along with Coloradans, people in Wyoming had adopted the prior appropriation doctrine. In contrast to Colorado, though, J. A. Van Orsdel, the attorney general of Wyoming, showed how his state recognized adjacent states' priority uses of water. Motivating Van Orsdel's testimony was a situation affecting the Laramie River flow, a stream originating in Colorado and crossing into Wyoming where its water was used in irrigation. He correctly deduced that Colorado's position on sovereignty over all its rivers would seriously threaten developments in Wyoming.[32] The federal attorneys built on this testimony as proof that no state could be left free to use water in impertinent disregard of its neighboring states' economies. The corollary to this view was the argument for complete federal control of interstate streams in the West.

To further bolster their case, the federal attorneys even used Kansans as witnesses. B. F. Stocks, a lawyer representing the Finney County Water Users' Association in western Kansas, believed the enforcement of the Kansas riparian doctrine would make the Garden City area "the desert that it was twenty-five years ago, and the people who have settled here and have expended their money might as well move out." It should be noted that Stocks and his fellow irrigators formed the association to participate in a proposed federal reclamation project to develop pump irrigation that would supplement the available river flow.[33]

Other Kansans besides those around Garden City disagreed with their state's case. In May 1903 J. R. Mulvane, the powerful president of the Bank of Topeka who had helped finance some irrigation projects in the Arkansas Valley of Colorado, wrote to N. C. Miller, the attorney general of Colorado: "Hoping that you may win, as I think the suit never had any merit in it except to put a fee in the hands of some few attorneys." In July 1904 L. A. Young of the Peerless Mining Company in Wichita offered Miller "any assistance," and the following September one farmer from Wichita wrote to Charles Hayt, an attorney for Colorado: "I look upon such a theory [subirrigation from the underflow] as clear humbug." Hayt forwarded this Kansas farmer's letter to Miller, who must have taken a degree of comfort in knowing the dissatisfaction of some Kansans with their state's case. But, as he realized, this discontent did not necessarily spell victory for his cause.[34]

Coloradans also harbored many anxieties about the outcome of the suit. In the late summer of 1903, Colorado Senator Henry H. Teller publicly voiced his concern about the possibility of Colorado losing, since the result would be the destruction of the irrigated economy in the valley. At the same time, Attorney General Miller vigorously opposed any legislative appropriations for a Colorado state canal, which helped remove the state from active canal building. That in turn worked against Kansas' arguments about Colorado construction projects' diminishing the flow of the Arkansas River.[35] In August 1904 D. C. Beaman, the attorney for the Colorado Fuel and Iron Company, even made Miller the extraordinary proposal that he employ the Pinkertons "to hunt up fact." On the other hand, Francis Carey, the sugar manufacturer, could not understand how Miller could "sustain by testimony the broad statement that the method of irrigation adopted in Colorado does not diminish in any material way the flow of the water in the Arkansas River . . . to Kansas." The Denver Post publicly accused Louis Carpenter of graft in serving as an expert witness for the state. In response, many of Carpenter's supporters, fearful of what would happen if his expertise were lost, rallied to retain his valuable contributions to the state's cause.[36]

Together, the Colorado, Kansas, and federal attorneys all had grounds to fear the Supreme Court's reception of their arguments. In 1903, after Beaman first addressed the justices, he perceived their support for the riparian doctrine. During the closing oral arguments in December 1906, Morris Bien, the supervising engineer for the Reclamation Service, detected a divided court. He realized his count might be wrong, but he thought justices Melville Fuller, John Marshall Harlan, and David Brewer all supported the riparian doctrine; justices Rufus Peckham, Joseph McKenna, Oliver Wendell Holmes, William R. Day, and especially Edward D. White seemed to be favoring the prior appropriation doctrine. After the Court's decision, Bien confided in a letter that the justices' shifting views indicated "a very imperfect conception of irrigation and its practical relations to the law." White at times even had difficulty simply remembering how many ditches were involved, inflating the number by 300 during the oral arguments. These justices had only the barest understanding of the nature of rivers, of irrigation, or of the development of the prior appropriation system in the arid West.[37]

On 13 May 1907, the Court delivered a decision amounting to less than what any single party wanted, but clearly Colorado gained the most. Brewer, a Kansan and probably the most learned justice in irrigation law, wrote the opinion for a unanimous Court. Kansas, he stated, was not entitled to a decree restricting the practice of irrigation in Colorado. The reason was that irrigation in Colorado had worked little, if any, economic harm to the majority of the Arkansas Valley in Kansas. The Court agreed with Kansas attorneys that Colorado irrigation had damaged the normal flow of the river into southwestern Kansas; however, the material damages around Garden City did not outweigh the economic gains rendered in Colorado through the use of the stream. In setting out this principle of equity, Brewer became what Justice White called an "amicable compounder"—one called upon "to adjust rights according to [his/her] conception of equity wholly divested of any rule of law." As an "amicable compounder," Brewer had attempted to create interstate common law.[38]

Brewer balanced his award to Colorado by holding that in the event of increasing economic damage, "there will come a time when Kansas may justly say that there is no longer an equitable division of benefits, and may rightfully call for relief against" Colorado water users. Brewer thus denied Colorado's application of the Harmon Doctrine in which it claimed sovereignty over the water originating within its boundaries. Brewer's decision rested on an equitable distribution of the economic benefits derived from the river and sidestepped the issue of which doctrine, prior appropriation or riparian, governed the interstate flow of the river. Each state had the sovereign right to determine for itself the proper institutions for the control of only the water within its respective boundaries. In the event of another suit by Kansas, however, Brewer reserved to the Court the right to apportion the Arkansas River flow between the states in effecting equitable economic benefits.[39]

Brewer's opinion put Colorado on alert. The state could not with impunity develop its river resources to the complete disregard of its neighboring states' economies. By concentrating solely on the economic conditions in the valley, Brewer devised an accounting-procedure solution. He weighed the economic gains registered in both Kansas and Colorado arising from the use of river flow. The economic losses suffered around Garden City had not detracted enough from the total gains accrued throughout the valley in Kansas to warrant a deduction from Colorado. So long as this remained the demonstrable case, Colorado had little to fear from Kansas reprisals. However, if losses persisted in western Kansas while net gains continued in Colorado, then the Court could make adjustments correcting any imbalances.

Only in correcting economic inequity would the Court allow itself a say in the case. This position denied Congress the right to control non-navigable interstate streams in the arid West. Brewer limited the federal government's role to preserving or improving the navigability of the Arkansas River, for which he noted the government had not made a case. Indeed, since the federal attorneys had stipulated the nonnavigability of the river, they could not build an argument on the right of Congress to regulate the Arkansas River to ensure its navigability. Therefore, the federal attorneys had taken Newell's position and had resorted to the Wilson Doctrine to justify federal control over interstate streams west of the 100th meridian, irrespective of navigability. Brewer viewed this approach unsympathetically as he strongly backed a state's sovereign right to devise its own water regulatory institutions.[40]

Predictably, the case greatly disappointed those in the United States Attorney General's Office and in the Reclamation Service. Legal advisors Morris Bien and A. E. Chandler thought the decision would require the service to abide by each arid state's water laws. Moreover, some people at the time erroneously believed the Court had made the Reclamation Service unconstitutional. The enumerated powers of the Constitution, so wrote Justice Brewer in obiter dicta, did not refer to reclamation. From this, A. L. Fellows, the state engineer from North Dakota and a former district engineer for the service in Denver, mistakenly applied the Court's view to the constitutionality of the Reclamation Act. Bien and Chandler knew Brewer's decision did not rule them out of business, but they warned their field agents to gather material in case a suit arose testing the legality of the Reclamation Act of 1902.[41]

Even though the service regretted the decision, most Coloradans hailed it as a vindication of their cause. As Colorado Attorney General

What's The Matter With Colorado? SHE'S ALL RIGHT!

A Colorado view of the decision in *Kansas v. Colorado* (*Times* [Denver], 14 May 1907).

William H. Dickson boasted, "The first man that gets the water keeps it." D. C. Beaman, more reserved in his judgment and with keener insight, thought the Court had divided over deciding which doctrine, prior appropriation or riparian, took precedence over interstate river flows in the arid West. He knew that Brewer's opinion had not exoncrated the Colorado practice of prior appropriation. He believed the justices would wait until "a case arose in which it was clear that irrigation alone was responsible for the lack of water" in a neighboring state. Colorado attorney Charles Hayt correctly observed the key to the decision: "[Kansas] failed to prove damages, and in fact, proved that the lands in Kansas had steadily advanced in value instead of decreased." In addition, Colorado lawyers held the advantage with their expert witness, Louis Carpenter. They regarded his "testimony . . . as one of the most important features" of the case. Moreover, they unanimously, and mistakenly, concluded that Brewer's opinion would "end the controversy."[42]

For some time, the decision severely dampened enthusiasm in south-central and eastern Kansas for ever resuming such a proceeding. However, irrigation interests around Garden City, bitterly unhappy about the manner in which Kansas attorneys had defended them, looked to a new benefactor to press their cause. By and large, they gathered to support the United States Irrigating Company in its suit asking for a federal court decree that would establish the prior appropriation rights of Kansas ditches to Colorado canals. The sugar company, backed by wealthy Colorado businessmen, took on Colorado irrigation enterprises beginning in 1910. Interstate conflict over the Arkansas River flow continued unabated.[43]

Lessons from *Kansas v. Colorado* are many. First, people in the Arkansas River Valley on the High Plains had built beyond the ability of the region's water resources to support their ambitions. Yet the case simply did not address that reality. The justices only considered the economic implications of the suit. Colorado water users possessed certain vested property rights derived from the development of river flow. Kansans owned such rights as well; they just failed to show how the use of river water in Colorado had adversely affected their economy. Nonetheless, as economic development continued—with additional sugar factories, growing cities, more irrigation—the resources to support such expansion thinned even more.

What *Kansas v. Colorado* ignored, and what no one at the time questioned, was whether a capitalistic system premised on growth and the domination of nature could provide for all water users in an area of limited river flow. For Kansans it proved much easier to charge Coloradans with consuming too much river flow than to understand their own impact on the environment. As for Coloradans, they had established the prior appropriation system as a means of economic development, not of environmental adaptation.[44] They reserved the fruits of this growth, and the title to the river flow, solely for themselves. Greedy Kansans, so far as they were concerned, had no right to take from them. But as users claimed more water rights, and as urban, industrial, and agricultural development continued apace, even Coloradans ran out of water for all of their aspirations. Litigation and water lawyers multiplied as Coloradans contended among themselves and with Kansans.

CHAPTER SEVEN

Increasing the Water Supply
for All, 1910–1939

Kansas v. Colorado, the symbol of interstate war waged through litigation, had failed to alleviate the plight of irrigators in western Kansas. Brewer's decision had provided only a means to adjust water between contending states, and moreover, his sense of equity had given no relief to western Kansans. As a result, irrigators in both states faced a messy problem: how to supply their growing economies with a limited water supply. The Court had protected water development in Colorado, but only to a point. Any future water uses could evolve only if they did not injure the economy in western Kansas. Meanwhile, irrigators there still felt cheated by Coloradans.

The people in the valley had three basic choices in resolving their predicament. They could agree to limit their water use to the free-flowing water of the valley and try to adjust their operations to the valley's ecosystems; they could cooperate to apply more elaborate technology to trap more water to supply rising demand (a greater domination of nature); or they could fight one another for every drop of water through expensive litigation. People never really considered the first option because it would have entailed a fundamental reevaluation of the market culture and the domination of nature. The second option proved more promising for water users since their capital would be protected and growth could continue until the additional water resources had been claimed and consumed. The second option also steered clear of costly and often unproductive lawsuits.

The third option appealed to western Kansas irrigators as they sought to protect their rights. The unpredictable decisions of judges and the complex nature of water problems made litigation risky business. But this gamble affected Kansas irrigators less than Coloradans, who had more to lose. Kansans' willingness to use the courts, then, made Coloradans more amenable to cooperation. Consequently, both sides would join together to wring more water out of the valley and to negotiate agreements among themselves for the division of new supplies, in order to avoid having their disputes settled in court. Water users in both states would find the route toward protecting market-culture values through the domination of nature difficult and often uncertain, but it led to the building of John Martin Dam and Reservoir and the written agreements designed to divide the project's water between the two states.

There is no reason to believe that "objective" science guided the construction of the dam merely because engineers built it. Rather, well-entrenched interests in the valley demanded more water to protect their investments and to support future growth. Scientifically trained hydrologists, who fully acquiesced in market-culture values and the domination of nature, simply provided the techniques. Engineers had been doing this for some time. By 1890 the normal flow of the river could not supply all of the water rights in the valley; however, no one wanted to lose his or her investments in those water rights. As the shareholders in the Fort Lyon Canal Company had done, people hired consulting engineers who dammed greater supplies of water through the construction of flood storage reservoirs on the minor tributaries to the Arkansas River. Beginning in the 1920s transmountain diversions played a bigger role in supplementing the river flow. By the mid-1920s the state engineer had improved regulation of river flow by obtaining better measurements of canal diversions. These developments helped Colorado irrigators to improve their productivity—but what of western Kansans' vested property rights in irrigation? They too wanted to enhance their capital investments. Could they expect Coloradans to share an already overextended resource? Gradually people in both states decided not to share at all but to get more water for everyone. Engineers certainly had no qualms about these ambitions and lent their considerable talents to the building of John Martin Dam and Reservoir, funded by the federal government.

John Wesley Powell originated the ideas that would lead to the construction of John Martin Dam and Reservoir. Powell, as historians such as Donald Worster have observed, took basically an instrumental approach toward engineering. Powell believed applied technology could solve the water dispute between Colorado and Kansas, and in 1889 he proposed constructing dams and reservoirs in the foothills of the valley to douse the smoldering controversy. Water was nothing more than a commodity to Powell. The irrigation season, he assumed, lasted about three months, and the stream went to "waste" during the other nine. Store this water in mountain reservoirs, and both Kansans' and Coloradans' needs for growth could be met. He warned against locating any reservoirs on the High Plains since he calculated that the evaporation rate on the flats was three times that in the mountains. Furthermore, he thought that silt would rapidly fill any plains reservoir.[1] Powell's plan, though, went largely unnoticed as the Reclamation Service tried pump technology, rather than reservoir construction in Colorado, to solve irrigation problems in western Kansas. Besides, western Kansans had come to believe they had prior appropriation rights to the river flow to most of the adjudicated rights in Colorado. This conviction arrived along with the sugar factory near Garden City.

Before investors around Garden City would consider a sugar factory in the area, they wanted a reliable water supply. In 1903 George Swink discussed his plan with several influential businessmen in the city. Once they finished revamping the Great Eastern, the investors should, according to Swink, ask Coloradans to recognize the Great Eastern's prior right to river flow over any ditch constructed in Colorado at a later date. If Coloradans declined to share, then the Kansas firm should inaugurate a lawsuit in federal court to fix a priority for the Great Eastern. Swink's approach completely disregarded state boundaries in the establishment of appropriations—the same position the United States took in *Kansas v. Colorado*. He and his fellow investors, however, never launched their plans for litigation. They had barely begun cleaning and reconstructing the headworks of the Great Eastern before they sold it.[2]

When the United States Sugar and Land Company (USS&LC), under the direction of Spencer Penrose of Colorado Springs, acquired the Arkansas Valley Beet, Land and Irrigation Company, the directors resolved to follow Swink's scheme.[3] They wanted an appropriation for the Great Eastern dated 1881, which would antedate the majority of water rights in Colorado. Penrose had the United States Irrigating Company (the Wyoming branch) hire Walter F. and Karl C. Schuyler to handle the case. The USS&LC also hired the knowledgeable engineer Louis G. Carpenter to research the hydrologic aspects of the case. In 1910 Schuyler and Schuyler initiated the suit *United States Irrigating Company v. Graham Ditch Company, et al.*, against the Colorado ditches.[4]

Through this interstate suit, the United States Sugar and Land Company saw a way to also ease its problems with the Amazon and Farmers' ditch companies. The sugar and land firm had incorporated the United States Irrigation Company in Kansas to run the Great Eastern and South Side ditches for the benefit of their sugar-refining plant at Garden City. The subsidiary encountered numerous suits in Kansas district courts with other local ditch companies and irrigators. Penrose had the parent firm form the United States *Irrigating* Company in Wyoming. His move made future suits interstate disputes under the jurisdiction of federal courts—a tactic that removed the suits from the more partisan Kansas district courts where his interests seldom found a sympathetic hearing. But the sugar company also held out an olive branch to its rival ditch companies around Garden City. In its suit against the Colorado ditch companies, the USS&LC promised to secure the water rights of its Kansas rivals.[5]

In August 1910 the United States Sugar and Land Company had all the pieces in place for its legal assault in federal court against Colorado ditches. Through Spencer Penrose and Charles Tutt, Sr., it had the financial strength needed to engage a formidably organized opponent. The sugar company had the backing of the other ditch companies around Garden City, so long as it won. Moreover, through this suit the company might actually obtain an adjudicated right to reliable surface flow in the Arkansas river.

In federal court the Schuylers made a direct and compelling argument for a water right predating those of twenty ditch and reservoir companies in Colorado. All the defendants were members of the Arkansas Valley Ditch Association (AVDA), formed in 1901 during the litigation of *Kansas v. Colorado*. Through the association the ditch companies along the main stem of the Arkansas River had hired Fred Sabin, a capable La Junta attorney, to protect their interests. The Schuylers maintained in their complaint and briefs that the Kansas sugar company had "the prior and paramount right and title" to divert 250 cubic feet of water per second (cfs) into the Great Eastern and a similar right to 100 cfs for the South Side ditch. The court, they argued, should award both Kansas systems appropriation dates of 1881. In practice, this would have required any Colorado water user who owned rights dated after 1881 to forego diverting stream flow until the river had filled the Kansas ditch rights. Furthermore, the Schuylers alleged that by 1907 the Colorado ditches' "junior" rights had reduced the river flow to 25 percent of its 1895 flow. If this depletion was verified, the Schuylers could show that Coloradans' growing use of the river flow had proven injurious to the sugar company's prior development of river flow as well as that of other Garden City ditch companies.[6]

The defendants, represented by attorneys Fred Sabin, Henry A. Dubbs, and Platt Rogers, charged that the sugar company had no grounds for their case. Penrose had formed the Wyoming company, so the trio contended, simply to bring the suit against Coloradans. In reality, the suit was a conflict between Colorado companies—an intrastate affair, not an interstate suit. The Great Eastern, they further maintained, had fallen into a condition of near, if not actual, abandonment from the late 1890s to 1905, when Swink and others had rebuilt the system. Consequently, water flow had not been in a constant state of beneficial use, which meant the sugar company did not have an 1881 right to the river flow.[7]

On 19 March 1912 Judge John River decided the jurisdictional question. The Wyoming firm, he ruled, was an enterprise independent of the United States Sugar and Land Company of Colorado. As such, the Wyoming company had the right to press its case in his federal chambers. River also appointed a special master to hear testimony and to determine the facts of the suit. In the fall of 1912 both parties began taking depositions.[8]

Both sides began an increasingly expensive pursuit of their objectives. Over 7,000 pages of transcript recorded the accounts of the sugar company's witnesses. Lawyers testified to the whole murky issue of whether or not Kansas law supported the prior appropriation or riparian doctrine. The Schuylers, of course, contended that prior appropriation ruled in western Kansas. Promoters recalled the initiation and construction of the various ditch companies so that the Schuylers could establish the antecedence of the Kansas ditches. Witnesses also recounted the ill feelings among the neighbors, stemming, they said, from poor river flow in the Arkansas River. F. A. Gillespie, a stockholder in the United States Irrigating Company and the manager of the sugar factory at Garden City, gave detailed testimony on beet farming and processing and about what the lack of water did to sugar production. C. C. Hamlin of Colorado Springs, a director in the United States Sugar and Land Company, explained how the directors controlled the irrigating company as a separate Wyoming enterprise, and he related the conflicts with the water user associations of Kearny and Finney counties. If only Colorado would honor Kansas water rights, so the Schuylers intended the testimony to show, then the problems of the USS&LC would go away. By the middle of 1914 the master concluded the testimony, and both parties prepared their closing arguments.[9]

Leaving the decision in the hands of Judge River, however, made the lawyers of both parties jittery. The Arkansas Valley Ditch Association had much to lose if the judge awarded an appropriation to Kansas ditches, especially with a decree dated around 1881. Moreover, such a ruling would destroy any pretense of complete sovereignty over all stream flows originating within the state—the claim used by Colorado lawyers. On the other hand, the sugar company could not gamble everything on an award from Judge River. Even if he allowed the Great Eastern an appropriation, what would be its date? Given the dilapidated condition of the ditch from the mid-1890s to 1905, which had resulted in only minimal "beneficial" use of the river flow, the company faced the prospect of a 1905 decree, rather than 1881, for its most important ditch. The best way out for everyone was to compromise, so they entered an agreement to resolve the case.

On 19 February 1916, all parties signed a contract that avoided a court decision and averted costly defeat. Without destroying state sovereignty over water flow, the Arkansas Valley Ditch Association agreed to award the Great Eastern a right to 297 cfs, the South Side 103 cfs, the Amazon 150 cfs, and the Farmers' (if it joined the others) 150 cfs, with all water rights given a date of 27 August 1910—the day the sugar company filed its bill of complaint. The AVDA also promised not to claim any new water rights dated before 27 August 1910 on the Purgatoire River or on the Arkansas from the mouth of the Purgatoire to the state line. This in essence would ensure that no new developments in Colorado would affect river flow to Kansas irrigators. Last, the association pledged $30,000 to the sugar company, and an extra $10,000 if the Finney County association signed, plus fifty cents an acre under irrigation in addition to the court costs. In total the members of the AVDA paid about $125,000 to settle the suit.[10]

The Finney County Water Users' Association (FCWUA), the mutual stockholding company not under the sway of the Penrose's sugar company, felt cheated by the course of events and resolved to do something about it. A priority of 27 August 1910 did them no good. The sugar company could live with such a decree, because it had turned to massive pumping plants to supplement the river flow in its ditches. Besides, the sugar company had constructed a reservoir (Lake McKinney) that it filled during the nonirrigating season. Its pumping plant and reservoir storage gave it alternatives that the FCWUA lacked. When the Schuylers announced the terms of the contract, the association attempted to intervene in the case, but Judge River denied their motion. Consequently, the association's representatives refused to sign the settlement and instead initiated a new suit against the AVDA.[11]

Once again the Arkansas Valley Ditch Association braced itself for another expensive encounter with a Kansas ditch company. The attack came in the early months of 1917 when William A. Smith, the attorney for the FCWUA, filed a complaint in federal district court in Denver against the AVDA—the *Finney County Water Users' Association v. Graham Ditch Company, et al.* He noted that his clients possessed the oldest continuous operating ditch in western Kansas. He argued that they should be allowed an appropriation of 250 cfs dated 1880 (the date when the Farmers' ditch was built) against *all* "Water Users taking water directly from the Arkansas River." In this manner Smith hoped to establish the association's priority against both Colorado *and* Kansas ditches.[12]

The suit, by common consent of both parties, languished. War production took precedence over preparing for the courts. Moreover, *Wyoming v. Colorado* had already reached the United States Supreme Court, and nearly identical issues were at stake. Judge Robert E. Lewis of the federal district court in Denver wanted to await the outcome of the Supreme Court case before proceeding.[13]

Water users throughout the arid West watched with great interest the litigation of *Wyoming v. Colorado*. Wyoming irrigators had taken an active part in *Kansas v. Colorado* because they had objected to Colorado's claim to the sovereign control over the water originating within its boundaries.

Kansas v. Colorado had not completely resolved Wyoming's quandary since the suit had pitted riparian doctrine against prior appropriation. But the decision had settled one issue: Colorado did not have absolute authority over the river flows beginning within its borders. Given this interpretation, Wyoming, which also adhered to the prior appropriation doctrine, pressed Colorado for an interstate recognition of its priorities.[14]

The issue centered on the use of the Laramie River which flowed out of Colorado into southern Wyoming. Some Colorado interests had plans to divert the Laramie into other river basins, which would have depleted the volume that reached Wyoming irrigation systems. To promote growth equitably in both states, Wyoming lawyers argued that prior appropriation should apply equally across state lines along interstate rivers. In its decision, the Court ruled that the doctrine of priority covered all diverters along interstate streams in prior appropriation states. This seemed to imply that Colorado irrigators were bound to honor Wyoming's water rights.[15]

One problem emerged in extending the precedent of the Wyoming decision to the Finney County water users' suit: Was Kansas a prior appropriation state? Even though Smith and others in western Kansas still believed that the state legislature had sanctioned the prior appropriation doctrine, *Clark v. Allaman*, which seemed to endorse both the riparian and prior appropriation precepts, had cast considerable doubt on which doctrine prevailed in Kansas. Nonetheless, the Wyoming suit substantiated both the United States Irrigating Company's position in *United States Irrigating Company v. Graham Ditch Company, et al.*, and Smith's arguments in the *Finney County Water Users' Association v. Graham Ditch Company, et al*. This gave Smith great hope that he could successfully press his client's cause.

Soon after the Wyoming decision, Smith entered another complaint in Judge Lewis's chambers. In February 1923 he filed *Finney County Water Users' Association v. Coler Ditch and Reservoir Company, et al.*, bringing the same charges as in the Graham suit against an additional 150 appropriators in Colorado. All of the Colorado water users diverted from the tributaries of the Arkansas River. The complaint even included the cities of Trinidad, near Raton Pass, and Walsenburg, southwest of Pueblo. Judge J. Foster Symes, who succeeded Lewis, consolidated both cases for testimony. Smith put his witnesses on the stand, and their statements filled over 2,500 pages before Smith ended in June 1927.[16]

While Smith and the lawyers for the Arkansas Valley Ditch Association had chosen a course of conflict, Delph Carpenter, a shrewd water lawyer from Greeley, Colorado, sought cooperation. He realized that court decisions seldom resolved complex western water issues, as Justice Brewer's ruling in *Kansas v. Colorado* amply demonstrated. Carpenter had been developing an alternative to expensive high court litigation that would clear up interstate water controversies involving Colorado. He argued that states could enter into treaties—compacts—with the ratification of the United States Congress. Water lawyers and engineers of the contending states, he believed, should be the ones to work out the differences over interstate streams rather than judges untutored in western water practices.[17]

In 1921 Gov. Oliver Shoup of Colorado (who had served as secretary of the United States Sugar and Land Company) appointed Carpenter as the state's water commissioner to direct all interstate compact arbitration. In the early 1920s Carpenter played an influential role in moving the delegates of nine western states toward an agreement on the division of the Colorado River flow. He also negotiated a compact with delegates from New Mexico over the La Plata River. In Kansas Gov. Henry Allen hoped that negotiations with Carpenter might end the conflict over the Arkansas River. In 1923 the state legislature approved his appointment of George Knapp, the Kansas water commissioner, to treat with Carpenter.[18]

Beginning in June 1923 Knapp and Carpenter held meetings in order to find a way to resolve the dispute over the Arkansas River flow. Knapp summarized the situation well. He noted that for years Colorado had overappropriated the normal flow of the river. Consequently, both commissioners "felt that any attempt to merely allocate or apportion among the various users the available summer water could not solve the problem." Knapp believed that such a solution, "like a court decree, where the victorious litigant secures his water at the expense of the defeated one . . . would merely transfer the shortage from one locality to another." Therefore, a water supply for Kansas could not come from the "normal flow" of the river.[19]

The key, Knapp believed, lay in finding water that would supplement the normal flow of the Arkansas River to supply the needs in western Kansas. Two possibilities existed. Transmountain diversions could channel water into the Arkansas River, or new reservoirs could impound flood and "waste" waters for later use. Carpenter and Knapp agreed that the "constructive solution" depended on both states' cooperating to build "reservoirs to store additional water, and thus minimize the conflict, and so far as possible *to leave undisturbed the vested rights in the two states*" (emphasis added). Here Knapp and Carpenter had brought the instrumental character of engineering to full light. The commissioners ignored the excessive numbers of irrigation works and water rights in both states and focused their attention on a solution that promised to maintain both states' economic interests. Nature in the valley would have to yield more water. The commissioners picked a reservoir site in the Purgatoire River channel and wrote an agreement to regulate its administration.[20]

The main features of Knapp and Carpenter's proposed compact seemed to offer the relief that both states desired. The consultant engineers had estimated that the new Purgatoire reservoir could hold 123,000 acre-feet of water if properly constructed. Twenty years of records indicated that at its mouth the Purgatoire furnished a yearly average of 98,700 acre-feet. After deducting for transit losses, they calculated that the reservoir could deliver approximately 62,500 acre-feet annually to the state line. Reservoir releases added to regular river flow could maintain an average of 2 acre-feet of water a year per acre under irrigation in western Kansas. Kansans would assume responsibility for the cost of constructing the dam, which the commissioners placed at $720,000, and Coloradans would buy the land. The project would "relieve Colorado of any further or additional demand or claim by Kansas upon the waters of the Arkansas river within Colorado." Both commissioners considered the compact workable and equitable.[21]

Irrigators in western Kansas, however, thought the proposed compact unworkable for several reasons. First, they were not sure of the exact amount of water they would receive. The records used to compile the stream flows of the Purgatoire were incomplete. Ralph I. Meeker, one of the consulting engineers assisting Carpenter, later stated that the commissioners based their calculation on estimated quantities of Purgatoire River flow. Moreover, the reservations and restrictions in Article III could diminish the amount of water Kansans stood to receive—for example, urban water supplies for Trinidad and other towns were excluded from the Kansas supply. This constituted an indefinite allocation that Kansans would not tolerate.[22]

In addition, many irrigators around Garden City feared the compact would cost them too much. Although the Finney County Water Users' Association warmly accepted the proposed agreement as a way to supplement their weak water supplies, the other ditch companies figured the terms would provide too little in return for their investment. The Kansas state legislature would not fund the project, so the FCWUA could finance the Purgatoire dam only if it could convince every ditch company to join it in forming an irrigation district. Once established, the district could issue bonds to pay for dam construction. However, the FCWUA's past differences with the Garden City Company, formerly the United States Sugar and Land Company, blocked any chance for cooperation around Garden City on behalf of the Carpenter-Knapp compact. Besides, the Garden City Company had the 1916 contract to sustain its operations.[23]

The Arkansas Valley Ditch Association also objected to the proposal.

One member, the Fort Lyon Canal Company, hoped to develop its own reservoir in the Purgatoire River canyon. This company exerted a powerful influence in the AVDA, and any agreement that lacked its approval was doomed. Moreover, the compact essentially forbade the enterprises located below the mouth of the Purgatoire River to develop any new water rights, and none of those companies would agree to such a restriction.[24]

Carpenter and Knapp's cooperative effort failed to produce a compact because it interfered with too many property rights. Their labors, however, clarified the conditions for a successful resolution of the controversy. First, no irrigation company in either state should have to suffer any capital reduction. Second, to protect Colorado water rights, "new" water, combined with the normal flow of the Arkansas, should supply western Kansans' needs. Third, the development of additional water supplies should not conflict with other ditch companies' plans to supplement their own provisions. Fourth, the solution should be inexpensive to the irrigators in both states. In 1925, as Fred Sabin, the attorney for the Arkansas Valley Ditch Association, saw it, an agreement meeting these conditions appeared unlikely, so he worked to pursue the lawsuit against the Finney County Water Users' Association.

Fred Sabin had a long-range plan to use litigation as a means to settle the dispute between Colorado and Kansas for all time. Brewer's decision in *Kansas v. Colorado* had left the door open for repeated assaults from Kansas irrigators whenever they felt cheated of an equitable use of the river flow. Sabin wanted this loophole closed to Kansans. After consultations with H. A. Dubbs, James G. Rogers, and "Wat" McHendrie (prominent attorneys in the state associated with the Arkansas Valley Ditch Association), Sabin tried to return the case to the United States Supreme Court under the aegis of the state of Colorado. In short, the AVDA attorneys lobbied Colorado Attorney General William Boatright to file a suit of original jurisdiction in the Court. Sabin hoped for a comprehensive court decree to decide the issue as between the states rather than between private interests (that is, the AVDA and the Finney County Water Users' Association). A judgment binding the states could prohibit future suits over the same issues by any private interest in southwest Kansas. The prosecution of the suit and previous actions had taken an extreme financial toll upon the AVDA, and its members wanted relief. Some time passed, but Boatright finally agreed to Sabin's request and filed Colorado's complaint against Kansas in January 1928, thus beginning *Colorado v. Kansas*.[25]

Sabin, Rogers, and McHendrie prepared Colorado's defense. *Kansas v. Colorado*, they argued, showed that Coloradans' irrigation practices had caused Kansans little harm. Since water consumption had not increased after 1907, Coloradans could not have exceeded their share of the equitable benefits of the stream. The attorneys wanted an injunction preventing Kansas from bringing any more suits against Colorado and a ruling exonerating Colorado water users from having consumed more than their fair share of the river flow or from having caused Kansas irrigators any harm. Kansas lawyers, on the other hand, wanted a priority dated 1881 for 250 cfs for the Farmers' ditch. The attorneys also sought a guaranteed supply of river flow to the western Kansas ditches. But as Knapp already knew, Smith and the attorney general would have little hope of convincing the Court to whittle down the vested property rights of Colorado water users without the development of a water supply beyond the normal flow of the river.[26]

Michael Creed Hinderlider, the state engineer of Colorado, was hard at work trying to find the technological solution that would provide the extra water to end the Colorado-Kansas conflict. A graduate of Purdue University, he had considerable experience in hydraulic engineering. By November 1923, when he became the state engineer of Colorado, he had gained experience working for the city of Denver, the United States Geological Survey, the Reclamation Service, and as a consulting engineer. In 1923 he joined forces with the Arkansas Valley Ditch Association and began a survey to determine the best location for a dam on the Arkansas River to trap floods and high flows. Surveys led to reports in 1926 and 1927, and these in turn laid the basis for the construction of John Martin (originally, Caddoa) Dam and Reservoir and the Frying Pan Arkansas Transmountain Project.[27]

Hinderlider and the Arkansas Valley Ditch Association sought to solve two general water-supply problems. First, irrigators and municipal water users in the upper basin suffered from insufficient sources. His solution called for the development of transmountain water resources by building either a short tunnel under Tennessee Pass that could tap 17,000 acre-feet annually from the Eagle River Basin or a nine-mile tunnel near Buena Vista that would drain the Gunnison River in Taylor Park of 150,000 acre-feet a year. Second, Hinderlider observed how water users along the lower Arkansas River could not easily divert the variable tributary inflows, high flows, and freshets in that part of the basin. Hinderlider suggested building a reservoir with twice the holding capacity of any other in the state to trap these flows.[28]

The construction of Hinderlider's reservoir at Caddoa, a small town west of Las Animas, promised to alleviate a great many other problems that plagued water users in the lower basin. Hinderlider believed the reservoir could provide an additional 153,000 acre-feet to the Colorado ditch companies below Caddoa and could also supplement the supply to western Kansas ditches, thereby removing "any cause for the pending suit between ditches in the two states." The project would protect farmlands, small towns, and railroad property from any future large floods. Hinderlider thought that the terrain would hold evaporation rates to an acceptable level and that siltation could be controlled. Moreover, in conjunction with the development of transmountain systems, the dam and reservoir would "round out and stabilize all existing water rights along the main stem of the river both for municipal and irrigation purposes." The only drawback, as Hinderlider and others knew, was the estimated construction cost of $7 million.[29]

In the spring of 1926 Hinderlider and Ray McGrath, the president of the Fort Lyon Canal Company, the Arkansas Valley Ditch Association, both wrote to Hurbert Work, the secretary of interior, and requested the Bureau of Reclamation to undertake the project. Although each correspondent summarized the predicted benefits of the reservoir, Work remained unmoved. R. F. Walter, the chief engineer at the bureau, wrote that "the costs of the Caddoa reservoir would be out of proportion to the benefits obtainable therefrom." Work agreed with Walter's conclusions and also noted that the bureau's forecasted appropriations for the next ten years barely covered the completion of systems already in various stages of construction. As Work wrote to McGrath, the bureau had no immediate intention of starting new projects.[30]

While Hinderlider's and McGrath's efforts stalled, "Wat" McHendric and Fred Sabin resumed Colorado's attack in court. By late 1929 they began taking testimony. The attorneys relied exclusively on three trusted and knowledgeable engineers as witnesses—Hinderlider, Charles Patterson (consulting engineer for the Arkansas Valley Ditch Association), and Royce J. Tipton (an employee under the state engineer). In keeping with the mandate of judicial realism, there would be no credence given to farmers or hearsay evidence. Only "scientific" facts garnered by experts would be presented before the Court. Hinderlider and Patterson described the climate, geography, and geology of the Arkansas Valley and how water usage had developed in the area. The engineers explained what "overdecreed" meant and how the state engineer regulated water rights. They also attested that Colorado users had neither wasted nor increased their consumption of water.[31]

Kansas attorneys, too, had learned their lesson on judicial realism. They brought forth a formidable witness who contradicted much of what the Colorado engineers had said about water use in their state. Ralph I. Meeker, a native of Pueblo, Colorado, had received his engineering degree from the School of Mines at Golden. He had worked in the Colorado State Engineer's Office studying Colorado's river basins and, as a special deputy state engineer, had assisted Delph Carpenter with interstate negotiations from 1919 to 1928. His responsibilities gave him access to the state's water records, as well as to those of many irrigation companies, water lawyers, and the Arkansas Valley Ditch Association. In 1929 he offered to aid Kansas. He believed, as he testified, "that there was some basis for Kansas' claims and demands for Arkansas River Water." Kansas attorneys now had their own "expert" to present the "objective" and "scientific" facts that would prove their case against Colorado.[32]

In May 1932 Meeker took the witness stand to substantiate Kansas' position that water consumption had risen in Colorado since 1907 and that western Kansas lands under irrigation had suffered economic reversals as a result of inequitable apportionment of the river flow. Meeker had calculated that from 1905 to 1930 consumption in Colorado had increased from 760,000 to 1,060,000 acre-feet per year. In other words, according to him, Colorado water users in 1930 consumed approximately 85 percent of the *total* river flow and over 96 percent of the *usable* river flow. Attorneys and engineers on both sides suspected that Meeker's figures were riddled with errors.[33]

Meeker's credibility was badly shaken under McHendrie's grilling cross-examination. First the engineer validated the federal census figures that showed irrigated acreage in western Kansas increasing dramatically from 1889 to 1929. If this trend was true, then Kansas attorneys could not argue that Colorado farmers had harmed the growth of irrigation in Kearny and Finney counties. Moreover, it was claimed that Meeker relied on dubious averaging techniques that may have inflated water consumption in Colorado. Finally, he testified that Bear Creek Basin in Kansas was a possible reservoir location. Western Kansans' failure to construct there implied that they had not explored or developed all of the alternatives for solving their own problems. Yet not once did Meeker contradict this by pointing out the poor water-holding capabilities of the Bear Creek Basin soils.[34]

Kansas attorneys and George Knapp feared the effect of Meeker's performance. F. Dumont Smith, the attorney for the Finney County Water Users' Association, bitterly complained: "The more I study his figures the dizzier I get." He summarized his feelings in a letter to W. E. Stanley, another attorney for the FCWUA: "Colorado really ought to pay Meeker instead of our paying him." In the same letter he told Stanley that they should rebuild the case "on lawyers' lines and not on engineer's lines." But Knapp astutely realized that the state could not proceed along Smith's suggestions. Judges were no longer swayed by a farmer's vague recollection of facts or an attorney's biased arguments in behalf of his or her client. Given the appeal of judicial realism, they trusted cold, "objective" scientific data—the purview of engineers. Although Knapp was anxious about the challenge to Meeker's presentation, he thought a closer scrutiny of Meeker's data would still reveal rising Colorado water consumption harmful to western Kansas. Knapp also noted that McHendrie had left much of Meeker's testimony uncontested. Unless the Colorado attorneys could completely dispute Meeker's evidence, they still had a serious problem.[35]

Colorado lawyers and consulting engineers spent long hours analyzing Meeker's engineering data, criticizing and refuting it with their own calculations. Then came the unenviable task of translating their findings into language that a judge could comprehend when deciding the case. This was ticklish business given their past experience with judges unfamiliar with western water practices. An adverse ruling to Colorado could ruin the future development of the valley. McHendrie and Clarence Ireland, the attorney general of Colorado, believed the solution to the interstate fighting lay outside the courtroom with the development of Caddoa Dam and Reservoir and an agreement between the two states regulating its operation.

Kansas attorneys all along had been suspicious of making any outside deals. In 1931 Stanley clearly stated the position he held throughout the entire court proceeding. Unless Colorado presented a "plan whereby Kansas could receive its fair and reasonable share of the water," then he would not agree to any settlement. Later, in August 1933, Stanley realized that building Caddoa Dam and Reservoir could "solve the problem of Kansas ditches." He would support the project only if Colorado entered an agreement that "would allocate to Kansas *definite* flows of water during the entire growing season" (emphasis added). Stanley's demand would pose a sizable obstacle.[36]

Another considerable difficulty was finding the funds to build the dam and reservoir. The Bureau of Reclamation had already rebuffed Hinderlider's plea for Caddoa dam, but perhaps he could interest the Army Corps of Engineers in it as a flood control project with some incidental irrigation benefits. After the great Mississippi flood of 1927, Congress had authorized the surveying of the river's tributaries, including the Arkansas River, for possible flood control structures. In 1930 and 1931 Hinderlider, in conjunction with the Army Corps of Engineers, made studies in the Arkansas River basin. Discovering the key to federal support, he gained the Corps' interest in building Caddoa as a flood control project. In May 1931, following Hinderlider's suggestion, Clarence Ireland wrote to Sen. Chester Long of Kansas that Colorado lawyers were interested in settling out of court, using Caddoa as the centerpiece of the settlement. To achieve this goal, though, Long would have to organize Kansans for a joint congressional lobbying effort with Coloradans.[37]

Two tireless Colorado promoters of Caddoa had made a significant move toward realizing the project near the close of 1933. John Martin, a

CADDOA RESERVOIR PROJECT
PROJECT MAP
CADDOA ENGINEER DISTRICT
U. S ENGINEER OFFICE, CADDOA, COLO

Scale of Miles

COLORADO
BENT COUNTY

TO LAMAR
TO CHICAGO
PROWERS
1145
Graveyard Cr.
U.S. HIGHWAY NO. 50
1150
Limestone Cr.
Mud Creek
RELOCATION OF A.T.& S.F. RY.
1155
CADDOA DAM
CADDOA
CADDOA
1160
R 50 W

MAXIMUM FLOOD POOL EL. 3870
HASTY
IRRIGATION POOL EL. 3851
RIVER
1165
EXISTING A.T.& S.F. RY.
RESERVOIR
Wolf Creek
T. 23 S.
T. 24 S.
R 51 W

MAXIMUM FLOOD POOL EL. 3870
FORT LYON PROTECTIVE WORKS
ARKANSAS
R.R.
U.S.V. HOSP. FORT LYON
FORT LYON
1170
Arkansas Valley
Boise City R.R.
A.T.& S.F. RY.
1175
Purgatoire R.
NO. 101
COLO. STATE HWY.
LAS ANIMAS
TO LA JUNTA
FLOW
R 52 W

N

Reproduced by the COLORADO WATER CONSERVATION BOARD - Engineering Department

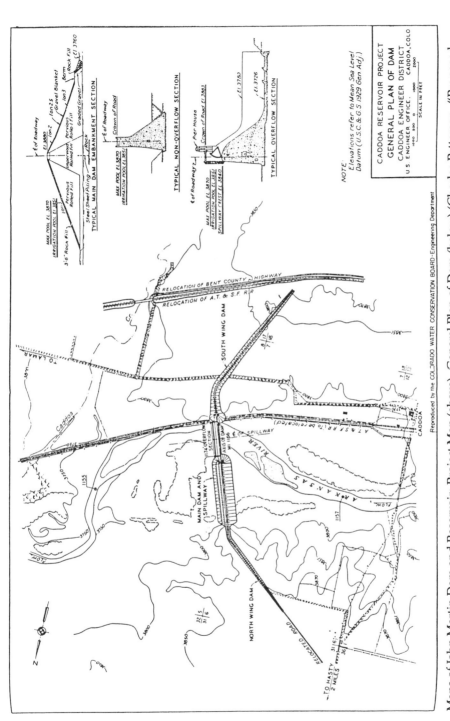

Maps of John Martin Dam and Reservoir: Project Map (above), General Plan of Dam (below) (Charles Patterson, "Proposed Consent Decree," following p. 20, file folder 295, Arkansas Valley Ditch Association Collection, Colorado Historical Society)

congressman from the district that included the Arkansas Valley, took a special interest in securing congressional support, while Vena Pointer organized the local boosters of the dam and reservoir. An unusual woman for her time, Pointer had worked as a legal secretary for Fred Sabin; read law in his office; passed her bar exam; become a partner with McHendrie; served as the secretary of the Arkansas Valley Ditch Association; organized and led the association's promotion of Caddoa; and would later serve as the valley's first representative on the Colorado Water Conservation Board, established in 1937. Irrigation farmers, state bureaucrats, engineers, and politicians, nearly all of whom were men, universally admired her knowledge of water issues and her dedication to water development in the valley. On 3 November 1933, Martin's lobbying effort in Washington, D.C., paid dividends; he wrote to Pointer that the Corps had approved Caddoa as an economically sound project. The Corps was interested, and Martin and Pointer had taken the first step toward acquiring the dam and reservoir.[38]

However, before the Corps would build Caddoa, Colorado would have to agree with Kansas on the administrative principles with which to regulate the project. By October 1933 Henry Vidal, the attorney for the Amity system who upon Fred Sabin's death had entered the case, was nearing an agreement with Stanley. One point of contention still remained. Vidal wanted to leave the supply of water entering Kansas indefinite, and Stanley would not consent to anything less than a guaranteed amount. Stanley vowed that if Colorado refused his demand, he would "have to fight the construction of the dam." Vidal's diligence to please Stanley bore fruit at the end of 1933.[39]

On 18 December 1933, the attorneys from both states signed a court-approved agreement, the "Stipulation of 1933." The agreement sought to increase the historical average of usable—that is, divertable—river flow below the planned location of the dam. Out of a potential 680,000 acre-feet capacity of the reservoir, the stipulation granted Colorado water users below the dam 160,000 acre-feet annually. Colorado, through the state engineer, promised to deliver 77,000 acre-feet to the Kansas-Colorado state line, 52,000 from October to April and 25,000 in the winter months. The 25,000 acre-feet would fill Lake McKinney, the sugar factory's reservoir near Garden City, and provide some winter irrigation supplies. The states could divide any water in excess of 237,000 acre-feet in a 50:50 ratio. In periods when the annual supply would not reach 237,000 acre-feet, the state engineer of Colorado would release 32.5 percent of the water for Kansas and 67.5 percent of it for Colorado.[40]

The project had to secure approval from the Mississippi Valley Committee, which recommended Army Corps flood control projects to Pres. Franklin D. Roosevelt's Planning Commission. The Planning Commission, composed of the cabinet members from interior, agriculture, war, and labor, had the responsibility for selecting sixty ventures for flood control, navigation, irrigation, and development of hydroelectric power. The Mississippi committee approved Caddoa as a viable project from an engineering and economic standpoint. Because it "would be largely local in character," however, the committee recommended having the local people bear part of the costs. As Carey H. Brown, the secretary of the Mississippi committee, informed Senator Long, this would include buying the land and rights-of-way, assumption of maintenance and operational costs, and probably some portion of the construction costs. Vidal wrote to Colorado Sen. Alva B. Adams that "the Caddoa situation [is] apparently hopeless, if we assume that it indicates the attitude of the administration." Nonetheless, Vena Pointer and others resolved to push ahead to gain complete federal support.[41]

Historians such as Marc Reisner, Donald Worster, and Joseph Stevens have illustrated that people of that era had an infatuation with large dams. Given the way in which Americans held these structures in awe, the government seldom faced opposition to their construction. An additional factor to consider is that the government largely undertook these projects to bail people out of the problems created when they tried to transform arid environments into something else. For example, Hoover Dam was built to remedy the mess Imperial Valley irrigators had made of the lower Colorado River. It seemed that dam lobbyists intuitively realized that once they had hooked the federal government into supporting a project, however tenuously at first, eventually the government would end up paying the entire tab.[42] This leads to a common theme in western history: Let the federal government pay the means to development, but keep control of it in private hands in the West. The history of John Martin Dam and Reservoir fully conforms to this view of western history.

Vena Pointer worked through the Caddoa Reservoir Association to obtain full federal support for the dam. Shortly after the signing of the 1933 Stipulation, Ray McGrath, Arthur C. Gordon (the lawyer for the Fort Lyon Canal Company), and Vena Pointer incorporated the association to handle the lobbying for the dam project.[43] At one mass meeting in Pueblo on 16 August 1934, the governors of the two states, along with congressmen, senators, and a whole host of interested people, publicly announced their support for the project. The meeting left Interior Secretary Harold Ickes unimpressed, and in September he wrote to Colorado Sen. Edward P. Costigan that he would not authorize the Bureau of Reclamation to build Caddoa dam. Still, this left the Army Corps of Engineers. Undaunted, supporters encouraged the state legislature to enact a bill forming a municipal conservancy district, which passed in early May

1935. The district would assume responsibility for financing the local expenses of the project (land acquisition and construction costs) and its promotion. Gov. Edwin C. Johnson appointed Arthur Dean, who was head of the Las Animas Chamber of Commerce, as president and Vena Pointer as secretary. Dean and Pointer continued to work with Congressman Martin to encourage the Corps of Engineers.[44]

Martin lobbied the Corps of Engineers hard to enlist their backing and scored some concrete successes. On 17 May he wrote Pointer that the Corps had advised him that an "informal application should be filed asking approval and construction of Caddoa Dam." By the end of June, Pointer, Dean, and Martin assured the Corps that the conservancy district would acquire the rights-of-way for the dam, which influenced the Corps to send a favorable report on the project to the National Emergency Council. The council then approved the dam for inclusion in the Emergency Relief Program as a flood control project. By April 1936 Martin had secured Caddoa's place in the Omnibus Flood Control Act, passed in May 1936.[45]

Congress, however, included no financing for construction of any of the projects. Gen. G. E. Pillsbury, acting chief of engineers, informed Dean that funding would follow when the conservancy district gave the land, rights-of-way, and easements "free of cost to the United States and was to accept responsibility for any damages arising during construction, and for the maintenance and operation of the completed structure." Major local costs involved moving several miles of Atchison, Topeka and Santa Fe railroad track and building levees to protect the hospital at Fort Lyon. This was a considerable undertaking for the district.[46]

Dean and Pointer were hard-pressed to find the money. How much could they expect from depression-ridden farmers? The Kansas ditch companies around Garden City flatly refused to pay half of the estimated $5 million of local expenses to build the dam. The Rocky Ford Ditch Company expressed opposition to the dam and any participation in its funding. Given the company's superb water rights, it had absolutely nothing to gain from its construction. Moreover, Bryon B. Blotz, a Rocky Ford businessman, claimed that silt would fill the reservoir so quickly that simple economics made the project not worth the time and expense. Tipton, who did the engineering studies for Colorado about how the reservoir should work, discounted any exchange possibilities with ditches above the site. Those ditch companies, such as the Bessemer, would not finance the project since little direct benefit would come their way. With pockets of opposition to funding the dam spreading through the valley, only the federal government was left to foot the bill.[47]

By early 1937 lobbyists from both states had begun an extensive campaign in Washington. In March, Hinderlider and Knapp, along with the senators and congressmen from both states, met with Army Corps chiefs asking if they would move the railroad tracks and build the levees to protect the Fort Lyon hospital. The Corps was not interested. The congressmen discussed the possibility of amending the Omnibus Flood Control Act to allow for complete federal financing. Meanwhile, Dean and Pointer unsuccessfully appealed to the Reconstruction Finance Corporation for a loan. A report toward the end of the year estimated that local expenses would cost farmers $3.50 per acre, whereas rental water cost between $2.00 and $2.50 an acre. Local irrigators reacted coolly to such a deal. In December 1937 R. L. Christy, treasurer of the Caddoa Dam Committee that solicited the funds to offset local expenses, reported somewhere around $8,000 in its accounts. With so little money, and lacking any financial support from western Kansans, the prospects for Caddoa appeared bleak.[48]

Active lobbying in Washington, however, hit pay dirt by the end of June 1938. Senator Adams of Colorado had kept McHendrie informed about the progress of a House bill that would have assigned to the federal government 30 percent of local expenses. Kansas and Colorado, McHendrie feared, would have to put up 70 percent before the federal government would provide the remainder. The efforts of Dean and Martin put to rest McHendrie's fears. Martin helped sponsor a House conference report that approved complete federal financing of flood control projects. Stimulated in part by the 1937 recession which many economists blamed on a lack of federal spending, the full House adopted the conference report on 14 June 1938, and the next day the Senate followed suit. The Caddoa project had become a reality.[49]

The majority of people in eastern Colorado and western Kansas cheered the development. On 20 June, Arthur Dean arrived in Las Animas, and a brass band and several hundred people welcomed him home. For his part in the successful lobbying effort the celebrants awarded him a gold watch. McHendrie visited people in Garden City where popular sentiment, so he wrote to Vidal, supported the project, despite Stanley's apprehensions that the federal government would have complete control over the water impounded in the reservoir. McHendrie noted that Clifford Hope, the representative from Kansas, had done "considerable work in connection with an effort to squelch Stanley" in order to line up public support for the project. The time was ripe, McHendrie thought, to resolve the interstate conflict with Kansas.[50]

The instrumental nature of engineering work is evident in how engineers planned the functioning of the Caddoa Dam and Reservoir. All parties in the suit between Kansas and Colorado fully realized that the dam and reservoir had the potential to ease their interstate water problems. Royce Tipton's second operational plan devised for Caddoa reservoir, dated January 1938, considered how Caddoa dam, under the provisions of the Stipulation of 1933, would have operated from 1914 to 1936. The project, he calculated, would have annually filled the average water consumption of the ditch companies below the dam, plus annually supplied an additional 56,000 acre-feet of water for each state. Only in 1932 through 1935, and less so from November 1916 to May 1921, would the irrigators below the dam have suffered any shortfall under their average consumption rates. Furthermore, the annual gross values of crops produced would have increased by $300,000. Clearly, Tipton's plans were the instruments, the tools whereby the operation of the dam along the guidelines of the 1933 stipulation could solve many of the problems between the two states.[51]

With the reality of the dam came the need for a formal agreement between Kansas and Colorado. At the beginning of 1940, McHendrie and Vidal knew some people wanted a consent decree—a legal agreement between the two states sanctioned by the United States Supreme Court—while others preferred an interstate compact negotiated outside of the Court. McHendrie and Vidal greatly favored the consent decree over a compact. With a decree the states could sidestep the Court's adjudication of the conflict, thereby avoiding a ruling by the Court that might not serve the interests of either state. Moreover, as McHendrie and Vidal noted, a decree was "at all times within the full jurisdiction and power of the Court" to enforce. In some respects, the Court would act like a police officer keeping the peace. On the other hand, any violation of a compact would require an "independent action by suit in the Supreme Court," engaging the states in time- and money-consuming litigation. In 1940 McHendrie and Vidal would begin a serious attempt to conclude the long-standing conflict between the two states with a consent decree.[52]

CHAPTER EIGHT

Quarrel and Rapport

John Martin Dam and Reservoir seemed to be the solution to five years of squabbling between Colorado and Kansas. People in both states thought the project would end the litigation, if they could agree upon how to manage the dam. For nearly a decade they would bargain, bicker, plot, and wheedle with one another on the way toward reaching the Arkansas River Compact of 1949.

The workings of water use in the valley had resulted in a dispersal of power. Irrigators, city planners, industrialists, and state and federal officials engaged in cacophonous debate over the direction of water planning in the valley. Groups of water users in the valley engaged in simultaneous tactics of conflict and cooperation as each pursued its individual agenda shaped by its goals, its institutional dynamics, and its environmental niche. Factionalization also characterized the federal government's role. The Army Corps of Engineers, the Federal Power Commission, the Bureau of Reclamation, and the Fish and Wildlife Service all had different objectives that they tried to realize in attempting to bring order to chaos, cooperation to conflict, negotiation to dissension in the valley.

The final agreement forged among all the interests reflected their values well. In essence, the Arkansas River Compact was an accounting procedure for dividing water. The river flow had such a fixed-commodity status that the water users chose to ignore growing qualitative factors of environmental degradation while they fastened their attention on solving the quantitative issues. Hence the domination of nature through John Martin Dam and Reservoir propped up market-culture values to the exclusion of anything else. This contention is well illustrated by the manner in which the water users negotiated their narrowly defined interests in the making of the Arkansas River Compact.

A renewed attempt to agree on how to manage John Martin Dam and Reservoir began at the end of 1939. William Stanley, the Finney County Water Users' Association's attorney, took a few steps toward cooperation with A. Watson "Wat" McHendrie and Henry C. Vidal, the attorneys for the Arkansas Valley Ditch Association. Stanley trusted McHendrie and Vidal and believed the time had come to enter into a consent decree with Colorado. Many factors had influenced Stanley in his decision, but most of all he feared the results of Ralph Meeker's testimony. In 1936 Charles Patterson, consulting engineer for the Arkansas Valley Ditch Association, had taken the stand and shown numerous instances where Meeker could have miscalculated stream flow in the Arkansas Basin above Pueblo. If Patterson had figured correctly, then Meeker's numbers were certainly suspect. But Patterson could not fully sustain his own computations in cross-examination. Engineers in both Colorado and Kansas, however, had raised enough questions to shake Stanley's faith in Meeker.[1]

Stanley also knew that he could not always rely on the Kansas legislature to underwrite the expenses of litigation, especially his own charges. Legislators from the eastern half of the state had little understanding of the issues at stake, and some even thought the Kansas claims were bogus. For example, in 1931, while Stanley was preparing the evidence for the Finney County Water Users' Association (FCWUA), the state legislature had nearly voted to quit funding the suit, and the governor had vetoed the appropriation. Only through the skillful maneuvering of the attorney general in the state supreme court was the veto declared unconstitutional and the appropriation restored. At other times, the state was needlessly slow in paying Stanley for his services, making him comment once that he was more of a liability to his office than an asset. In addition, the expense of the suit had weighed heavily upon his own clients, the FCWUA. He needed something to save them, and himself, from unrelenting legal costs. A consent decree negotiated with McHendrie and Vidal offered such a possibility.[2]

McHendrie and Vidal had their own worries about the prospects for successful litigation. Neither believed that the 1907 Supreme Court decision guaranteed Colorado's title to the water resources in the Arkansas River. The decision only meant that as of 1907 "even to the injury of Kansas, [Colorado] had not exceeded what Colorado was entitled to as its share of the equitable benefits of the stream."[3] Vidal feared this meant that Kansas could claim more *usable* water if it could prove that Colorado had increased its consumption since 1907. And he considered this likely; he himself wrote that Colorado had "undoubtedly" expanded its use of water since 1916. Either he or McHendrie, or both, agreed with Meeker that consumption had grown by 300,000 acre-feet since the ruling in *Kansas v. Colorado*. Vidal warned Charles Patterson (who disagreed with him) and others that Kansas was entitled "equitably to a share of the river[,] and Colorado priorities, young or old," were and always had been "subject to a determination by compact or court decree."[4] Vidal's statement, even though never made public in any brief or court argument, was a serious admission of Kansas' position.

Vidal's and McHendrie's fears about the weaknesses in Colorado's suit extended beyond their respect for Kansas' legal position. Michael Creed Hinderlider, the state engineer, criticized wasteful irrigation practices in Colorado. In October 1931 at the annual conference of the Association of Western State Engineers, Hinderlider took aim at the Colorado water appropriation system. The state district courts, he claimed, had allowed too great a volume of water to ditch decrees. In addition, the irrigators who owned the older decrees diverted more water than they needed for their crops. Engineers, especially the state engineer, had too little power to affect the administration of water usage. Hinderlider's argument essentially contradicted McHendrie and Vidal's position—that water users in Colorado had put the river flow in the Arkansas to efficient use and none remained for Kansas. Not surprisingly, after 1931 McHendrie and Vidal never used Hinderlider again as a witness for Colorado.[5]

Moreover, engineer Patterson caused problems for McHendrie and Vidal. For years McHendrie and Patterson had enjoyed a warm and personal friendship arising from their work together for the Arkansas Valley Ditch Association. All of this ended in 1937 when the state assembly created the Colorado Water Conservation Board, an institution designed to plan the state's future water development while simultaneously providing a legal bulwark to protect the state's resources. The enabling act left the administration of water rights in the hands of Hinderlider (who believed the conservation board infringed on his authority) and charged the new bureau with aiding in the protection, planning, and development of water in Colorado. Charles Patterson accepted the job as the board's chief engineer. His career choice was the wedge that separated him from McHendrie.[6]

The antagonism that grew between Patterson and McHendrie reflected the difficulty of binding together various institutions in common cause. Patterson assisted Colorado Attorney General Gail Ireland and the board's chief attorney, Jean Breitenstein. After 1941 Breitenstein and Ireland favored prosecuting the case against Kansas rather than settling it with a consent decree. They wanted no deals made with Kansas. They sought a clear vindication of Colorado's position from the United States Supreme Court justices, and they denied all along that Kansans had any right to any of the water originating within the boundaries of the state. Patterson agreed with Breitenstein and Ireland. McHendrie and Vidal, who represented the Arkansas Valley Ditch Association, preferred a court-approved agreement between the two states dividing the water originating within Colorado. After 1941 factionalism would unravel old loyalties.[7]

But at the beginning of 1940, all parties seemed to favor writing a consent decree. Vidal and McHendrie were convinced of this method's superiority for three reasons. First, the two attorneys did not trust a decision written by the Supreme Court. Second, they wanted to avoid any intervention on the part of the federal government. And last, they did not wish to incur the expense of bringing the suit before the Supreme Court. From January to March, Vidal and McHendrie corresponded with Stanley trying to schedule a conference to lay the foundation for a decree. On 25 April 1940, the governors and attorneys general of the two states met with McHendrie, Vidal, Patterson, Knapp, and Stanley, and most of them agreed to begin engineering studies to clarify the data necessary for an agreement. Stanley, who did not trust engineers anyway, viewed this as an unnecessary delay and wrote to McHendrie suggesting a meeting just between the two of them to formulate some general areas of compromise. Their conference occurred in June.[8]

Stanley presented McHendrie with a choice between two basic propositions for a consent decree. One, favored by George Knapp, the water commissioner of Kansas, would have Colorado deliver a fixed amount to the state line during the summer growing months that would guarantee Kansas farmers approximately 2 acre-feet of water per acre of land irrigated. The second, preferred by Stanley, gave both states summer amounts of water and during times of drought prorated deliveries of water, based on Colorado's summer commitment to Kansas. Stanley also wanted no more new ditches or irrigated acreage in Colorado. Any new reservoir storage should be charged against Colorado's share of its summer supply, which would have undermined the operations of the Bureau of Reclamation's plans for the Gunnison-Arkansas transmountain project. Moreover, he sought to restrain exchanges of John Martin Reservoir water with upstream users. Stanley's ideas found conditional favor with McHendrie.[9]

Soon after, many problems arose with Stanley's approach, both in Colorado and Kansas. Patterson, writing to the Colorado attorneys and engineers associated with the suit, objected to having any limitations placed on reservoir and ditch development in the state. In Kansas, Knapp resisted Stanley's concept. Stanley yielded and offered a plan, favored by Knapp, to the Coloradans in October 1940. McHendrie, Vidal, and Patterson studied the new proposition; then in December at a conference held in Denver, they met with Knapp and Stanley and hammered out the basis of a consent decree. Their plan established two control stations, one near Pueblo and the other at the mouth of the Purgatoire, to measure mountain and plains runoff. These stations were to serve as an index of all the water supply in the valley. Kansas would receive from 23 to 25 percent of the total index flow during the months of April through October. In return Coloradans could use the water in the conservation pool of John Martin Reservoir in whatever manner they desired. Moreover, Coloradans would face no restrictions on water development in the Arkansas River Valley, which would free the Bureau of Reclamation and Colorado Water Conservation Board to implement the plans for the Gunnison-Arkansas transmountain project. Vidal and McHendrie, who endorsed this approach, began drafting a formal decree embodying these principles for all parties to sign.[10]

However, McHendrie and Vidal faced many obstacles in writing an agreement that satisfied everyone. First, they encountered stiff resistance from Patterson. He thought the plan departed too radically from the Stipulation of 1933, which had not included index stations. As the decree assumed more concrete form, his opposition became entrenched. Patterson disagreed on allowing Kansans any right to water originating in the state—a legal principle, which McHendrie and Vidal thought best not left to an engineer. In addition, Patterson calculated that the decree would cause reductions in Colorado users' diversions. He figured state-line flow at a lower amount than did McHendrie, Vidal, Knapp, and Stanley—150,000 acre-feet a year. If Patterson was correct, then in times of drought those upstream from the dam would have to curtail their usage in order to guarantee Kansas its percentage of the index flow. No canal company, industry, or city would accept such a prospect, and McHendrie knew it. Under Patterson's estimates, McHendrie and Vidal could accomplish very little with the consent decree since Stanley would not accept a commitment below 25 percent of the index flow.[11]

By early summer 1941 Patterson's opinions had become so irksome that McHendrie requested a conference with him and Gov. Ralph L. Carr. During the meeting McHendrie asserted that Patterson had miscalculated the relative benefits of the decree to both Colorado and Kansas. Afterward, an aggrieved Patterson sent a letter to Governor Carr, Clifford Stone (director of the Colorado Water Conservation Board), Attorney General Ireland, McHendrie, and Vidal in which he wrote: "A confidence once lost is not so easily to be restored. For this reason I request that provision for my signature on the proposed agreement be eliminated." Without the backing of the conservation board's chief engineer, McHendrie and Vidal would find obtaining approval for their decree a difficult task.[12]

Moreover, the proposed decree failed to satisfy the Fort Lyon Canal Company—the kingpin of the Arkansas Valley Ditch Association (AVDA). Located in the vicinity of John Martin Dam and Reservoir, the Fort Lyon stood to gain significantly depending on the administrative features of the reservoir project. Arthur C. Gordon, the company's attorney, who was also an assistant attorney general during the later stages of the case, strenuously objected to the decree. He told the Fort Lyon's board of directors that the plan would bring no benefit to the company from John Martin Reservoir; that farmers would have to curtail their diversions to satisfy Kansas; that the decree would breed future litigation; and that the stockholders' lands and water rights would depreciate in value. Support among influential Colorado irrigators for McHendrie and Vidal's approach had seriously waned.[13]

In Kansas, Stanley found little support for continued negotiations. By mid March 1942 he came under heavy pressure to stop meeting with the Coloradans. He called McHendrie and informed him that Kansas Attorney General Jay Parker and Gov. Payne Ratner had flatly refused to consider the decree. They simply viewed the negotiations as an attempt by Colorado's attorneys to gain time to build a better case against Kansas. Stanley informed McHendrie that Colorado had to concede to his views, or Stanley would have to resume court proceedings. Neither side was willing to compromise, and McHendrie and Vidal's labors for an agreement stalled.[14]

Ireland and Breitenstein had consented to let the case idle during negotiations, but with the failure of McHendrie and Vidal's dealings, Ireland and Breitenstein resumed prosecution. Acting upon their request, the Supreme Court appointed a special master to hear additional testimony and to establish the facts of the case. McHendrie and many others in the case anticipated that Judge Charles Cavanah, who was seventy years old and had fifteen years experience as a federal judge in Idaho, would prove a good special master. Their optimism faded fast, and by July, after the master's first orders, attorneys and engineers from both sides agreed with Stanley's assessment: "The Judge certainly does not indicate that he knows very much about what [the case] is all about, and I question whether he ever will." For both sides conflict had taken a turn for the worse.[15]

Stanley, who truly feared leaving the suit in the hands of Judge Cavanah, renewed his efforts for a consent decree, but he was aware that an agreement had to please Patterson and Gordon. He shrewdly realized that the success of the decree rested upon Coloradans' "feeling that they are jamming these matters down our throat, and securing some material modifications." He also had to convince Knapp not to push prosecuting the case. By July he had resolved most of the sticking points with Vidal and McHendrie, but not with Knapp.[16]

George Knapp generally approved of the operating principles embodied in the consent decree, but not all of the specific provisions. He demanded that Colorado guarantee from May to September monthly quantities of water passing the state line that would supply approximately 2 acre-feet of water for every acre of irrigated farmland from the state line to Garden City, Kansas. Stanley knew that McHendrie and Vidal took a dim view of that approach, knowing that either poor engineering data or climatic changes, as revealed in the operation of the Colorado River Compact, could result in an unintended drain on Colorado water resources. In July 1942 Stanley wrote to Knapp that "there is nothing further to be done with the Decree, and it is in the ash can." He also regretted the additional time and expense that continuing the suit would entail, especially under the direction of Judge Cavanah.[17]

Stanley believed that the engineers from both states had, out of jealousy and spite, undermined what he, McHendrie, and Vidal had worked so hard to achieve. As he wrote to McHendrie in November 1942, "I feel certain that the only thing that has prevented [the decree's] ready acceptance has been a deliberate sabotage of the plan by those who were not desirous of you or Henry [Vidal] receiving the credit for it." The villain most singled out by the three attorneys was Patterson, who had his own plan to promote. Stanley, along with Vidal and McHendrie, sincerely doubted Patterson's ability to settle the respective rights of the two states to the Arkansas River.[18]

By 1942 Patterson had clearly set himself on a course counter to the designs of McHendrie and Vidal. He had, in effect, devised his own court decree and hoped to enter it into testimony. He received his chance when Judge Cavanah called for additional evidence covering the "assumed operations" of John Martin Dam and Reservoir up to 1942 (that is, how the facility would have operated had it been in place during the years studied). Although this gave Patterson his chance, it also increased the work load of all the engineers and attorneys involved in the case. Patterson refused to analyze the years beyond 1938—because higher-than-average river flow might allow Kansas to claim a greater quantity of state-line flow than the pre-1938 data would suggest—but he looked forward to disclosing his alternative for settling the dispute.[19]

In October 1942 Charles Patterson presented in testimony his ideas for a possible court decree which were embodied in his "Operations Plan F." Patterson had taken the past flow of the river, the dimensions of the dam and reservoir, and his plan of administration and had come up with the reservoir's assumed operations during the years 1907 through 1938. His plan was intended to preserve the historical operations of companies downstream from the dam. The states would have equally shared the water "conserved" in John Martin Reservoir, "water which historically was not diverted and used." During drought years when the conservation pool failed to fill, the flow into the reservoir would be prorated at roughly 60:40 for Colorado and Kansas respectively. His program also called for the elimination of winter irrigation techniques below the dam in Colorado and the maintenance of a 10,000 acre-feet reservation pool for general recreation and wildlife. In essence, Patterson had refined the Stipulation of 1933.[20]

In Colorado, McHendrie and Vidal mounted a campaign against Patterson's Operations Plan F. They adamantly stressed to Clifford Stone and Patterson that the proposal would not quiet the conflict over respective rights of the two states because it offered no "permanent" division of the basin's resources. They further disapproved of how the plan altered diversions below the dam in Colorado. They claimed that by denying winter irrigation practices in the region—in effect, preventing irrigators from using their water rights—Patterson had fundamentally changed the operation of Colorado's prior appropriation system. Since the Army Corps of Engineers was building the dam for flood control and to benefit irrigation, the two attorneys strenuously objected to a wildlife and recreational conservation pool in the reservoir.[21]

In Kansas, Stanley agreed with McHendrie and Vidal that Patterson's plan would not solve the issues between the states. Stanley wondered what would happen when silt filled the reservoir's conservation capacity—that portion of the reservoir's volume set aside to benefit irrigation. During testimony, he agitatedly accused Patterson of trying to perpetuate "the historical scarcity which has existed in Kansas." George Knapp also claimed that Colorado could operate the dam so as to exclude any flow into Kansas. He further pointed out that the benefits derived from Plan F originated solely from the water stored in the conservation pool of John Martin Reservoir. Consequently, this gave Kansas no permanent right to any "definite part of the water supply of the basin." More ominously, nothing in Plan F prevented later increases in water use upstream from the reservoir that would deplete future flows in the conservation pool.[22]

To counter Patterson's proposal, Knapp offered a substitute in closing testimony. He introduced into the court record the concept of the index stations and the derivation of state-line flow based on a percentage of the volume passing the measuring points. Knapp's plan covered the operating principles of the defunct consent decree and also explained in part Patterson's ire with McHendrie and Vidal. The lawyers had preferred Knapp's operational ideas to the exclusion of his—which the Stipulation of 1933 and Operations Plan F incorporated. Knapp reiterated for the record the basic structure of the consent decree. Two index stations would operate, one at Parkdale to gauge mountain runoff and the other at the mouth of the Purgatoire to measure plains tributary inflow to the Arkansas. The flow of the two stations would be added, and Kansas would receive at the state line a fixed percentage of the sum. In testimony Knapp arbitrarily set a figure of 50 percent of the total indexed flow as the Kansas share. A 25 percent allotment, as in the earlier draft of the consent decree, would have provided the 2 acre-feet annually per acre under irrigation that he desired. Whatever the percentage, Knapp wanted it fixed and guaranteed. In this manner he hoped to establish the respective rights of the two states for all time—a "permanent" solution to the problem.[23]

With the conclusion of testimony at the end of 1942, both sides began preparing their summation and briefs for the special master, and each worried about whether Cavanah would understand their positions. Near the end of December the strain showed on Stanley when he wrote to the Kansas assistant attorney general: "Wishing you a damned sight happier Christmas than I am having, with this thing around my neck (Masterful); and also wishing you a Happy New Year—a la Cavanah." Stanley and the others were anxious about the special master's ability to comprehend the issues.[24]

On 1 May 1943, after hearing the arguments and receiving the briefs, Charles C. Cavanah presented his report and recommendations. The judge agreed with the Kansas contention that a "material increase in the river depletion by Colorado" had occurred since the 1907 United States Supreme Court decision of *Kansas v. Colorado*. The reduction, he continued, had been injurious to the "substantial interests in Kansas." To remedy this situation, he allocated from the "dependable" 1.11 million acre-feet annual water supply 925,000 acre-feet to Colorado, or around 83 percent, and 185,000 acre-feet, or 17 percent, to Kansas. He subscribed to Knapp's plan and recommended the designation of two index stations—one at Canon City, Colorado, and the other at the mouth of the Purgatoire. The judge intended to prorate the benefits and burdens of wet and dry years in an 83:17 ratio. He also ruled that the 1933 stipulation was not binding on either state, a slap at Charles Patterson's and the Colorado Water Conservation Board's positions. With a "permanent" division of the valley's water in place, he suggested an irrevocable injunction against the Finney County Water Users' Association from further prosecution of their two pending federal district court cases.[25]

Needless to say, the lawyers and engineers working for the Colorado Water Conservation Board were dismayed by Cavanah's decree. Since his ruling had to have the approval of the Supreme Court, the injured Coloradans began an all-out effort to show the faults in Cavanah's thinking. In their briefs, the attorneys held that Cavanah should not have awarded Kansas any water because Kansas attorneys had failed to show any "injury of serious magnitude" as the result of water use in Colorado. This was the same formidable argument used in *Kansas v. Colorado*. Most damaging to the logic of the master's decree was Colorado's contention that irrigated acreage (based upon questionable federal census data) had increased in Kansas, diversions of water for irrigation had greatly risen, agricultural production had gained, and the area had experienced no reduction in population since 1907. The Coloradans thus claimed that the state's users had caused no material decrease to the water supply that reached Kansas. Based on Royce Tipton's testimony, they argued that increases in diversions for irrigation had saturated farmlands creating greater return flows that added to the river volume crossing into Kansas after 1907. Besides, if Justice David Brewer had been correct in observing in *Kansas v. Colorado* that Colorado irrigators had virtually destroyed the reliable stream flow into Kansas, then how could Colorado irrigators have reduced the flow by another 300,000 acre-feet after 1907? The lawyers further objected that Cavanah had not established the facts or defined the conditions that would make his decree workable.[26]

Kansas attorneys also found some fault with the master's conclusions, although they were generally pleased with the decree. They wanted clarification on the administrative features of the decree, and they thought Cavanah should have used greater specificity in some of his calculations. Stanley and the others assisting him summarized their position in their briefs for the justices and waited the outcome of the Supreme Court's decision.[27]

On 6 May 1943, when Justice Owen J. Roberts delivered the opinion of the United States Supreme Court in *Colorado v. Kansas*, he delighted the Coloradans and their supporters. He first noted that the master's report contained no "discussion or analysis of the proofs" of fact used in forming the decree. In other words, the Court would not approve Cavanah's decree. Roberts believed three questions had emerged in the case. First, was Colorado entitled to an injunction against further litigation by Kansas water users? Next, should Kansas irrigators receive a specific amount of the water supply in the basin? Last, had Kansas attorneys indeed proven that Colorado had "substantially and injuriously aggravated conditions which existed" at the time of the decision of *Kansas v. Colorado* in 1907?[28]

Roberts answered the questions largely to the satisfaction of the Colorado attorneys. On the first, he agreed with Cavanah that Colorado should not be subject to future litigation from Kansas irrigators. Of course, Cavanah thought that he had permanently divided the waters in the valley between the two contending states and that his division would make any future suit on the part of Kansas users unnecessary. Roberts differed completely with the rest of Cavanah's ruling, but he let this part of the decree stand. Even though Roberts rejected Colorado's notion that *Kansas v. Colorado* had established a proper allocation of the river flow between the two states, he denied Kansas' demand for an apportionment of the valley's water. Kansas attorneys, he noted, had failed to prove how additional Colorado consumption had worked injury to the water interests in Kansas. Once again, as in *Kansas v. Colorado*, the Court's decision amounted to balancing an accounting ledger. Moreover, while uphold-

Construction for John Martin Dam and Reservoir (Michael Creed Hinderlider Collection, Photographs Department, Colorado Historical Society)

ing the jurisdiction of the Court over interstate water suits, Roberts advised the states to settle any future differences through compact negotiations. Engineers and water lawyers, not Supreme Court justices, should manage the complex water issues in the valley.[29]

Justice Roberts had cleverly avoided any mention of John Martin Dam and, by so doing, was forcing the states to negotiate an accord among themselves for the administration of the project. Henry Vidal clearly realized Roberts's intention. Vidal wrote to Jean Breitenstein shortly after the decision that the dam and reservoir could and should benefit the valley's irrigators in both states, and he pointed out that Kansas irrigators had some "legitimate claim to part of those benefits." He also feared that if Kansas and Colorado could not agree on the administration of the project, the Army Corps of Engineers would "fill and discharge the Flood Plan in its own discretion," which would leave both states without any supplemental water for irrigation. Although the Court suggested devising a compact, Vidal recommended delaying until Kansans revealed their hand. He did not have long to wait.[30]

Meanwhile, the Corps had finished most of the construction of John Martin Dam and Reservoir. The relocation of the Atchison, Topeka and Santa Fe line began in December 1939, and work on the main project commenced in August 1940. In March 1943 the Corps halted construction because of the war; however, it had finished all but the installation of huge steel radial gates along the top of the dam and the protective dike around Fort Lyon. The Corps began storing water, which meant that the states had to have some agreement on operating the dam in order to receive irrigation benefits. At the end of March 1943, before the decision of the special master, Knapp and Hinderlider, who as state engineer had the responsibility for the administration of any dam in Colorado, met with Lt. Col. R. E. Cole, the district engineer for the Corps, and agreed to abide by the Stipulation of 1933 until the Court rendered its verdict.[31]

After the 1943 decision, Colonel Cole felt uncomfortable about relying on the Stipulation of 1933 and sought a firmer agreement between the states. He realized that the Finney County Water Users' Association had no intention of adhering to the stipulation or to Patterson's modification of it in Plan F. He also knew that, according to Breitenstein and Ireland, Justice Roberts's decision left the stipulation and Plan F in effect. As a result, Cole thought that it was not enough to have Hinderlider and Knapp consent to adhere to the stipulation, and he told Stone that he wanted a formal agreement between the two states. In mid March, governors John C. Vivian of Colorado and Andrew Schoeppel of Kansas met in Omaha, Nebraska, and agreed to appoint commissioners for compact negotiations. Afterwards, Breitenstein warned Governor Vivian to instruct the commissioners not to make any hard and fast promises until a federal representative (because the Corps built the project) could attend the meeting. Rather wishfully, he thought that if Colorado carefully administered the project, Kansas might not demand a formal agreement. More to the point, he needed additional time to align the Colorado irrigation interests in a united front.[32]

In late March, eleven representatives from both states and from the Corps met in Denver to write a temporary agreement on the operations of John Martin Dam and Reservoir. Kansas Attorney General A. B. Mitchell made the initial suggestion that the consent decree be used. Patterson, Breitenstein, and Ireland, however, would not discuss it, so this idea fizzled. After lengthy arguments, and upon Colorado Attorney General Ireland's recommendation, the representatives agreed to give Patterson's plan a test run, which was also amenable to the Corps.

Trouble came soon after, as the Associated Ditches of Garden City, an organization combining the five main ditch companies, completely rejected the March agreement. Roland H. Tate, the association's attorney, stated that if a settlement could not be reached, he would have Governor Schoeppel ask the Corps to discontinue conservation storage (the supplement to irrigation diversions) in John Martin Reservoir. The Corps, Tate realized, would not store water in the conservation pool for irrigation unless the states could agree on the division. And lacking an agreement, the Corps would actually dump what water there was stored for irrigation. This would deny the Colorado irrigators below the dam, especially those of the Amity system, any water from John Martin Reservoir. Letters flew between the states. Ireland noted to Mitchell that he had enough difficulties getting the Arkansas Valley Ditch Association to agree to Patterson's plan, and he hoped that in the interest of all the Garden City group would give it a try. The Kansas association, however, remained obstinate.[33]

Tate realized the Associated Ditches of Garden City could remain firm because of the fractured support in Colorado for Patterson's plan. Henry Vidal, who represented the Amity company in eastern Colorado, thoroughly detested Patterson's ideas for operating John Martin Dam and Reservoir. Neither Vidal nor his clients believed that any benefit would come to the Amity system under Patterson's plan, and Vidal knew many people around Garden City concurred. In fact, Vidal covertly approached Charles Tutt, president of the Garden City Company (which controlled the sugar factory in Garden City) and tried to arrive at some compromise with him. Vidal vaguely hinted at an arrangement modeled on his formerly rejected consent decree. Word of this reached George Knapp and the governor of Kansas, and naturally, both found Vidal's proposal interesting. Before acting, however, they decided to wait and see just how strong Vidal's hand was.[34]

Vidal's intrigues against Patterson remained unknown to Ireland, who did his best to bridge troubled waters. In June he sent Mitchell a lengthy statement detailing how Patterson's plan would benefit Kansas. However, by the end of that month, Tate decided he had seen enough. He and George Knapp were now convinced that the releases made from the dam supplemented only the irrigators in District No. 67, the portion of the valley in Colorado below the dam, leaving Kansas ditches with just the accretions to the channel. On 11 July 1944, Mitchell informed Ireland that unless Kansas received one-half of the releases from the conservation pool, Governor Schoeppel would make a formal complaint to the Corps—which he did on the twenty-fourth. Soon after, Lieutenant Colonel Cole informed both governors that on 1 August he would begin releasing the conservation pool in amounts not to exceed the flood capacity of the channel. Governor Vivian sent an urgent request to Governor Schoeppel asking him to halt his action. Schoeppel agreed, and both planned another meeting in Omaha to try again to resolve the situation.[35]

The governors and their advisers agreed to a temporary solution in early August. Of the remaining water in storage, Kansas would receive at the state line one-half of any release made for Colorado ditches. George Knapp asked Roland Tate to consider this new proposition. Tate later transmitted to Governor Schoeppel the Associated Ditches' agreement with the accord and thanked him and Knapp for their support. For the moment, the governors had temporarily controlled the situation, and they hoped future compact negotiations would permanently settle the issue.[36]

By the end of February 1945, Governor Vivian had appointed the delegates of the Colorado commission. He selected as chairman Henry C. Vidal, who represented the Arkansas Valley Ditch Association and the Colorado ditch companies below the dam. To speak for the Colorado Water Conservation Board and to perform the engineering work, he chose Charles Patterson. To voice the views of those irrigators around Rocky Ford who had opposed the construction of John Martin Dam and Reservoir, the governor named Harry C. Mendenhall. Mendenhall operated a bank at Rocky Ford and served as the president of the Rocky Ford Ditch Company. Gail Ireland, as the attorney general of Colorado, had an automatic seat on the commission.[37]

By the first week in March Governor Schoeppel had made his appointments. George Knapp, the chairman and guiding force of the Kansas delegation, served as the engineering expert. Roland Tate, the attorney for the Associated Ditches of Garden City, and William E. Leavitt, the manager of the Garden City Company, represented interests in western Kansas. Mitchell, as the attorney general for Kansas, rounded out the membership. The commissioners' task was relatively simple: Devise a compact that protected the irrigation enterprises around Garden City, and secure some water from John Martin Dam and Reservoir. United by a common goal, very little discord marked the Kansas commission throughout the negotiations. Their counterparts in Colorado, however, were deeply divided.[38]

Each irrigation company in Colorado, uniquely conditioned by its niche, wanted something different from the negotiations. The commission had to make sure that the compact would not damage the operations of ditches above the project, such as the Bessemer and the Rocky Ford. Of course, Mendenhall would see to that. More difficult to please was Arthur Gordon, the attorney for the Fort Lyon Canal Company. The company shareholders, hoping to gain extra water, had taken an active role in promoting John Martin Reservoir, and these irrigators did not relish the idea of sharing with Kansas farmers. Gordon, who fully reflected their view, thought the project should only guarantee the water that Kansas had "historically received and used." Beyond this, Gordon remained unconvinced that Kansas should receive any additional benefit.[39]

The commissioners also were also faced with the concerns of Harold Christy, the chief engineer of the Colorado Fuel and Iron Corporation. Christy would be carefully watching the compact negotiations. Not only did he have the water interest of the steel company to protect, he wanted to reserve the future benefits arising from the Gunnison-Arkansas transmountain project solely for Colorado. He was a member of the Board of Directors of the Water Development Association of Southeastern Colorado—the agency responsible for coordinating with the federal government the plans for the Gunnison-Arkansas project. The Bureau of Reclamation had estimated that the enterprise would provide water for future urban and industrial growth, as well as for increases in irrigated acreage. Christy wanted to ensure that the compact would not interfere with this prospect. Moreover, the city managers in both Pueblo and Colorado Springs began assuming a larger role in the negotiation for water resources in the valley. The managers predicted huge population growth in the aftermath of World War II; they also wanted to save the transmountain water for themselves, not Kansans.

The commissioners also had to consider Colorado bureaucrats—especially state engineer Hinderlider. Hinderlider had spent years assisting in the construction of the dam and reservoir, and it was his duty to administer the irrigation benefits (the Corps being solely responsible for flood protection). The commissioners could not entirely overlook his views, nor could they avoid the Colorado Water Conservation Board. Patterson and Stone stood squarely behind the concepts embodied in Operations Plan F, and they would not be happy until the compact incorporated the plan. The conservation board had to approve any proposal, which meant that the commissioners would listen carefully to Patterson and Stone.

In March 1945 the commissioners from both states met in Lamar, Colorado, to reach an agreement on administration of the dam for that year's irrigation season. They amicably arrived at terms roughly equivalent to those that prevailed in 1944. The provisions allowed for fifteen days of releases at 500 cubic feet of water per second (cfs) for District No. 67 and 250 cfs at the state line for Kansas beginning on 1 April. Afterward, Hinderlider had to match the state-line river flow to any discharges made for District No. 67 in Colorado. Hinderlider would direct the ditch calls through the Corps' district engineer at Albuquerque, New Mexico. The governors agreed, and the commissioners passed their first test.[40]

The federal government came slowly into the negotiations. In April 1945 Congress passed legislation granting Colorado and Kansas the right to negotiate a compact regulating the operations of the dam and reservoir. Pres. Harry Truman waited until November 1945 before appointing Hans Kramer, retired brigadier general of the United States Army, as the federal government's representative. General Kramer had served with the Army Corps of Engineers and had participated in the building of John Martin Dam and Reservoir. Wishing to see his project operative, he took a keen interest in the success of the negotiations. For this reason, and because of his connections within the Corps and to other federal bureaus, the commissioners elected him as the permanent chairman of the commission.[41]

The Army Corps of Engineers demonstrated its ability to lead the commissioners toward cooperation in early 1946. In March negotiations broke down when the commissioners undertook to devise a temporary procedure for the 1946 growing season. Several Colorado ditch companies—for example, the Bessemer—had deemed the 1945 agreement overly generous to Kansas. As a result, Colorado commissioners sought substantive changes to the former accord that the Associated Ditches of Garden City refused to consider. The association instructed Leavitt that they would consent to one more year under the 1945 agreement, and nothing else. Consequently, the commissioners failed to strike any bargain, and in May Lieutenant Colonel Cole drained the conservation pool. All parties considered this a terrible waste, and Col. Henry F. Hannis, Cole's replacement, wrote the commission asking for a temporary plan that he could implement.[42]

In late August, during the fourth compact meeting, the commissioners took up the issue of Hannis's letter. They requested that the governors of Colorado and Kansas appoint Mendenhall and Leavitt, respectively, as negotiators and advisers; those two would then formulate an interim interstate agreement governing the operations of the dam and reservoir until such time as the commissioners had concluded writing the compact. The governors complied, and by the first week in November Leavitt and Mendenhall had reached an understanding (through mutual respect and common sense) that laid the basis for the compact. Essentially, their one-page resolution assigned Colorado 60 percent of the conservation benefits and Kansas 40 percent. The governors approved the agreement, thereby giving Colonel Hannis a guide for regulating dam operations.[43]

Mendenhall and Leavitt, the only two nonexperts on the commission, succeeded where the water lawyers and hydrologists failed. These two businessmen, both associated with the sugar-beet industry, simply viewed water as resource to be divided. They understood better than the others the dollars-and-cents aspects of water regulation. The reservoir was the bank, and the inflows were the deposits. They divided the account so that nobody felt cheated and established the guidelines for an agreement.

Besides prorating the conservation benefits of the reservoir, the commissioners had to settle issues that involved the extent of the federal government's rights in the compact. The Federal Power Commission (FPC) gave the negotiators the most problems. The FPC wanted a clear expression of principle included in the compact that would not restrict their right to develop hydroelectric power plants. During the first meetings the commissioners favored copying Articles X and XI from the Republican River Compact, thus incorporating the "paramountcy clause." Section (b) of Article XI specified that "the United States . . . shall recognize . . . that *beneficial consumptive use* of the waters within the Basin is of *paramount* importance to the development of the Basin" (emphasis added). The FPC warned that it would not tolerate this phrasing.[44]

The federal bureau had opposed the paramountcy clause when it first emerged in the drafting of the initial Republican River Compact. Commissioners Hinderlider (for Colorado), Knapp (for Kansas), and Wardner G. Scott (for Nebraska) had written into Article I that the Republican River and its tributaries were not navigable (by which they hoped to deny any federal control over the Republican River) and that "consumptive" applications of water constituted paramount use (which would protect irrigators, then and in the future, from any water losses resulting from subsequent federal projects). The Federal Power Commission strenuously objected to this language, fearing it could not build under such restrictions. Although it lobbied against the compact in the House and Senate, Congress approved it without change. However, President Roosevelt listened to the FPC and vetoed the act on 2 April 1942. Congress then granted permission for the three states to devise a modified compact and also appointed a commissioner, G. L. Parker, the chief hydraulic engineer of the Geological Survey, to represent the federal government. These men wrote Articles X and XI for the revised version. Again, the FPC objected, but the most obnoxious phrasing that had declared the river nonnavigable had been eliminated. Consequently, with considerable pressure on the president applied by western interests, the second attempt to secure the passage of the compact succeeded.[45]

Still, the paramountcy clause could restrict the Federal Power Commission's building plans. As Willard D. Gatchell, the principal attorney for the FPC, explained to Arkansas River commissioners, the "paramount" right of the federal government to control "navigable" rivers lay in the commerce clause of the Constitution. Gatchell argued that even when the FPC built hydroelectric plants, the dams assumed some role, real or imagined, in the control of navigation. The right of federal regulation over navigable rivers was thus clear, but not so when it came to nonnavigable streams. The New River case, *United States v. Appalachian Electric Power Company* (1940), gave the federal government control over nonnavigable tributaries to navigable rivers in the belief that the former needed regulation in order to maintain the latter. Therefore, Gatchell questioned the authority of the commissioners to exclude federal control over a stream simply because it was nonnavigable. Moreover, the Constitution gave compacts the same standing as international treaties. If a compact declared beneficial consumptive use paramount and Congress ratified the agreement, then how was the federal government's paramount right over navigable streams protected? In the case of the Republican River, the issue was entirely hypothetical because the stream did not join a navigable river. But the Arkansas River did, and the FPC stood its ground in the assertion that the phrasing constituted a bad precedent.[46]

The commissioners needed a compromise that would please the Federal Power Commission and westerners. To people such as Clifford Stone, the federal government's involvement in the navigability of rivers in the arid regions was nothing more than a ploy to deprive the states of their rights. Stone, no friend to federal control over any western river, resolved the impasse. He recommended, consonant with a suggestion made earlier by Gatchell, deleting the paramountcy clause since the Congressional Flood Control Act of 1944 and the Rivers and Harbors Act of 1946 both protected beneficial consumptive use of water west of the 98th meridian from "navigation and power uses" east of the line. The issue of paramountcy had been eliminated, and power development could occur as long as it was not at the expense of irrigation. The commissioners accepted the proposal, and the FPC welcomed it with open arms. The commissioners had satisfied one federal agency, but others still awaited their due.[47]

The debate over qualitative factors versus quantitative ones came fully before the commissioners when the Fish and Wildlife Service (FWS) presented its views. Except for Patterson, the commissioners simply did not accord any merit to the potential recreational and wildlife benefits of John Martin Dam and Reservoir. The FWS wanted a 10,000 acre-feet permanent conservation pool established for fish, wildlife, boating, and hunting. The central flyway passed over eastern Colorado, and a waterfowl refuge at John Martin Reservoir made perfect sense. R. A. Schmidt, the regional director of the FWS, made the most telling appeal to the commissioners for a recreational reserve. The commissioners, however, concluded that maintaining such a pool would deplete the water stored for irrigation. Besides, Colorado prior appropriation laws recognized no beneficial uses of water for wildlife. Water that allowed another real-estate subdivision to be built in Colorado Springs was fine, but to provide migrating mallards or Canadian geese with water was wasteful and unconstitutional. In that light, the commissioners refused to consider a permanent reservoir.[48]

Schmidt also asked the commissioners to take into account Cheyenne Bottoms—a large wetland basin just northeast of Great Bend, Kansas. The federal government, in conjunction with the Kansas Forestry, Fish and Game Commission, planned to develop the area as a wildlife refuge and hunting ground. Since the Arkansas River provided the water supply, Schmidt did not want the agreement to reduce the quantity reaching Cheyenne Bottoms. In reply, Knapp pointed out that the compact only allocated water supplies to the state line; hence, from that point on the affair was in Kansas' hands. The compact was not obliged to consider the issue.[49]

Even if the commissioners could easily disregard wildlife, they could not ignore the growing environmental problems affecting the very nature of the river channel. The riverbed had filled with silt over the years; amounting to both an environmental and economic challenge. After the 1942 flood, J. B. Marcellus, an engineer-appraiser who worked for the Federal Land Bank of Wichita, Kansas, wrote to Vena Pointer about channel changes that had affected the property values of lands upon which the agency made loans. He noted that the riverbed had filled in with sand and become flatter and that this interfered with canal drainage and caused extensive property damage during times of high flows. He also observed the growth of the salt cedar all along the flood plain, which had worsened the problem. Marcellus asked Pointer, acting on behalf of the Arkansas Valley Ditch Association, to petition the Corps to make surveys of the river channel, noting the problem areas and laying plans to "improve" the valley.[50]

The Army Corps of Engineers were also aware of the channel's deterioration. Colonel Hannis wrote the commissioners that the river below the dam had narrowed from a capacity of 10,000 to 5,000 cfs since 1936. Consequently, he wanted to increase the flood storage of the reservoir to provide better property protection. Hannis's move, however, would have cut into the volume set aside in the reservoir for irrigation. Quickly, George Knapp produced studies revealing that the narrowed areas of the river were largely in Kansas. Moreover, cities such as Garden City and Dodge City had already constructed levees for flood protection. Based on these findings, both the commissioners and Kansas Governor Schoeppel persuaded Hannis to abandon his position. George Knapp had preserved the conservation benefits—the quantitative nature—of the reservoir.[51]

Although in this instance Knapp had protected the quantity of water in the reservoir, he could not prevent a decline in its quality. He voiced his concern that the development of the Bureau of Reclamation's Gunnison-Arkansas project would increase the salinity levels in the river. The clear water transported into the Arkansas River Valley would remove more minerals from the farmlands in the western end of the basin and concentrate them in the lower end. Already, irrigators in Colorado and in western Kansas had troubles dealing with the use of saline water. The salt-laden river flows reduced crop yields and left the land worthless for dry-land farming practices. The Gunnison-Arkansas transmountain, however, was not yet a reality. Since this problem lay in the future, the commissioners ignored it; the more important struggle was dividing the quantity of river flow that each state should receive, not considering its quality.[52]

Complex issues affected the division of water between the two states. Clifford Stone had further confused matters in the way he drafted the bill that Congress passed approving the compact proceedings. Stone's bill, modeled on the enabling legislation of the Republican River Compact, had charged the commissioners with the task of equitably dividing the waters of the Arkansas River and all its tributaries. He had included no geographical limitations. Conceivably, the commissioners could write a compact regulating the river not only in Colorado and Kansas but also in Oklahoma and Arkansas. This problem the commissioners resolved by simply defining the region affected in the compact.[53]

More important, Stone's bill neglected to clarify exactly what water the commissioners would divide. At times, as McHendrie had previously feared would happen, the commissioners had difficulty determining whether they were dividing *only* the water stored in John Martin Dam and Reservoir, or whether they were attempting a division of *all* of the Arkansas Valley water supply. To Breitenstein, Ireland, Hinderlider, and Patterson, the Supreme Court had twice ruled that Kansas had failed to establish a right to the Arkansas River flow. Regardless of how Stone's enabling bill read, they denied that it gave Kansas any pretense for making a claim to the normal river flow.[54]

The Kansas commissioners took a clear position: They opposed any compact not guaranteeing them some *permanent* benefit. Again, the bank account analogy seems appropriate. If they accepted a division of the water deposited in the conservation-pool "bank" and if they relinquished their demand for a defined percentage of the limited water supply in the Arkansas River Valley, then they had to protect their "deposits" coming into the reservoir against any future depletions of the valley's supply caused by developments in Colorado. Without such protection, it was entirely possible that the inflow to the reservoir would decline as projects upstream multiplied. Kansas' bank account, reckoned as a percentage of the conservation pool, had to be saved from potential exhaustion. Knapp saw little good coming from a fixed percentage of a decreasing supply and drafted a clause prohibiting any future developments in Colorado from depleting the averaged historical river flow into the reservoir. Interests from Colorado and the federal government, however, objected to this provision.

Protests in Colorado came from three major fronts—Harold Christy of the Colorado Fuel and Iron Corporation, Arthur Gordon of the Fort Lyon Canal Company, and C. H. Hoper, the city manager of Colorado Springs. Christy also represented the association that would be working with the Bureau of Reclamation on the Gunnison-Arkansas transmountain project, and he thought that the nondepletion clause of the compact would deny the feasibility of the bureau's plans. The bureau's proposed reservoir west of Pueblo could store both transmountain and basin water, which could lower the river flow into John Martin Reservoir below the historical average. In fact, Christy wanted to stop the negotiations altogether in the interest of preserving the future of the Gunnison-Arkansas undertaking. Christy viewed it as the "valley's last chance of future expansion. . . . The cities . . . cannot grow and industry cannot expand without the benefits of this project." Gordon, representing the views of the shareholders of the Fort Lyon Canal Company, concurred in Christy's position. Gordon believed his company would not gain from the John Martin project as once thought, so he turned to the bureau hoping for more water. The city of Colorado Springs also wanted the bureau's future work protected. The nondepletion clause of the compact, as Hoper saw it, prevented the city from any further development of water in the valley.[55]

The Bureau of Reclamation worried about how the compact would affect its ventures in the valley. J. W. Dixon, the director of branch project planning, told the commissioners that the bureau could not be restricted in its plans for future water development in Colorado. The commissioners all wanted more dams and stored water to supply economic growth. Moreover, proposed dams along the upper Purgatoire near Trinidad and at Pueblo could extend the life of John Martin Reservoir by reducing its rate of siltation.[56]

The bureau and the commissioners needed a compromise that allowed future development in Colorado while "permanently" protecting the benefits of John Martin Reservoir to Kansas. The commissioners recognized that return flows from cities were greater than from agriculture. They realized (regardless of the 1922 Colorado River Compact's prohibition on any Colorado River basin water passing to any noncompact state like Kansas) that some transmountain water would accumulate in John Martin Reservoir as return flows and pass on to Kansas. They sought economic growth and knew that growth would result in some depletion of the river flow. Therefore, in what became Article IV, section D, of the compact, the commissioners inserted but left undefined the word "materially." The key provision then read that the waters of the Arkansas River as defined in the compact "shall not be materially depleted in usable quantity or availability" for use in Kansas and Colorado by future development and construction. No one, however, knew exactly what that meant, nor did they apparently want to know. Only McHendrie defined an amount (a 10,000 to 12,000 acre-feet increase in the appropriation of floodwater) that he thought would deprive Kansas of its rights, but he was not a commissioner. Knapp and Kramer noted that "materially" could signify anything, which is why the commissioners used it. They all could define "materially" as they wished and believe that they had protected their interests.[57]

The last bothersome issue of the negotiations concerned the actual division of the water in the reservoir, or the bank account itself. If Article IV was a concession to Knapp's desire for a permanent resolution of the conflict, then Article V recognized the principles of Patterson's plan as adopted in the Leavitt-Mendenhall agreement. The states would share a sixty-forty split of the water stored in the conservation pool. The commissioners simplified the compact: they eliminated any sophisticated bookkeeping needs by prohibiting shortages or overages in deliveries to either state from being carried over into the next year of operation. This scheme would work well as long as water was in the conservation pool. But how would the project preserve the 1943 status quo between the states when it held no supplies, or when storage water existed but irrigators only demanded river flow? The commissioners had to struggle to resolve these two questions.[58]

How to regulate an empty reservoir might not seem to be a tricky problem: Colorado ditches below the dam, and those in Kansas, could simply operate as if no dam or compact existed. Hinderlider would administer Colorado water rights as he had before the Corps had built the dam. When enough water accumulated in the conservation pool, Hinderlider would manage water rights under the provisions of the compact. As the commissioners understood it, an empty reservoir would only occur during times of severe drought. However, Vidal in particular wanted to preserve a ten-day water supply for the companies below the dam for periods of emergency, which would have worked especially well for his client, the Amity system. The commissioners concocted a scheme that when the reservoir reached 20,000 acre-feet in storage, it would be declared "empty."[59]

This "cushion" provision met with opposition from all water users upstream from the dam. Conceivably, the upstream ditches might have to forego water diversions in order to fulfill downstream senior ditch rights when water was still in the reservoir. Arthur Gordon summarized the problem. Already the Fort Lyon and other upstream ditch companies had lost the exchange possibilities of John Martin Reservoir. The only benefit left to upstream companies derived from the storage of flood and "waste" waters used to supply downstream companies. The upstream companies could divert a greater amount from the normal flow while these stored waste waters supplied downstream rights. The "cushion" clause threatened to deprive upstream companies of even that meager advantage. So overpowering was the chorus of complaint that the commissioners deleted the provision, and the reservoir became empty when it was actually empty. Moreover, whenever water existed in the conservation pool, the compact would not require upstream companies to stop diverting in order to supply any senior rights below the dam.[60]

The commissioners' second problem concerning water division was how to satisfy companies in District No. 67 and in Kansas when all they wanted were releases equivalent to the river inflow to the reservoir. The commissioners attempted to fix the status quo as of 1943 to determine the operational procedure. Studies by Knapp, Patterson, and Kramer concluded that a release of 750 cfs could sustain the current operations in both states. Their plan gave Colorado irrigators a right to demand the first 500 cfs, if river flow at that amount was entering the reservoir. Kansans could call for any amount between 500 and 750 cfs, so long as the river flow into the reservoir equaled their demand. This provision also gave Kansas irrigators something Coloradans had always denied them—a right to the *normal* flow of the river whenever its flows measured between 500 and 750s cfs into the reservoir.[61]

Where to measure the Colorado and Kansas releases complicated the negotiations. The Colorado commissioners first wanted to gauge Colorado runs at the headgates of the ditches in District No. 67 and at the Kansas state line. The Kansas commissioners, however, foresaw disadvantages in this approach. They argued that, after factoring in transit loss, it would take more than a 500 cfs release to provide the same amount at the headgates in Colorado. If the compact restricted Kansas to the volume of river flow between 500 and 750 cfs, then its irrigators could never achieve their demands if Coloradans in District No. 67 were fully diverting, since transit loss would come out of the Kansas share. The Colorado negotiators relinquished enumeration at the headgates and accepted it at the dam outlets. As far as Kansans were concerned, this procedure approximated the status quo of 1943.[62]

Two side issues gave the commissioners headaches as they attempted to protect the 1943 status quo. To solve one problem they placed a major restriction on the ditch companies in District No. 67 and in Kansas. These enterprises could not increase their capacities or sell their water rights with a change of diversion to above the dam without the approval of the compact administration. The other thorny question centered on the Frontier ditch, because it diverted water inside Colorado and applied it in Kansas. The Kansas commissioners accepted jurisdiction of the enterprise and also considered any water that it carried a part of the state-line flow rather than a credit to District No. 67.[63]

The commissioners had concluded the difficult portion of the negotiations once they had divided the reservoir water and had protected each state's share of the conservation pool. They easily resolved the other issues pertaining to administrative concerns, and they affixed their signatures to the final version on 14 December 1948. The negotiations, however, had taken a heavy personal toll. Charles Patterson became ill and resigned his post in February 1948. In March 1949 Mendenhall wrote to Clifford Stone that Roland Tate had had a "complete breakdown." Vidal often suffered from ill health, which the compact disputes seemed to aggravate. Mendenhall wrote that there was "something about the Compact that gets [the commissioners] down." Nevertheless, they had produced an agreement that they hoped would silence over sixty years of conflict.[64]

The commissioners' work received some harsh criticism. Oakely Wade, the Colorado state representative of Bent and Kiowa counties, led the fight in the state assembly against the compact, or, as he called it, the "damnable proposal." He recommended bringing in Hinderlider, Fred Farrar (general counsel for the Colorado Fuel and Iron Corporation), Arthur Gordon, W. I. Sanford (president of the Bessemer Irrigating Ditch Company), and E. B. Debler (a consulting engineer for Colorado Springs) to testify against the agreement.[65]

Hinderlider's statement before the Irrigation and Water Resources Committee of the Colorado assembly represented the general thinking of the critics. He believed the compact provisions were "overly generous" to Kansas. He did not like the idea of Kansans receiving any of the natural flow of the Arkansas River into the reservoir. He thought a seventy-thirty division of the conservation water between the states was a better ratio than the sixty-forty in the compact. In particular, he detested the clause forbidding "material depletion," given "the almost desperate needs of municipalities and irrigation interests for additional water supplies." How would growth occur if not for the depletion of the river flow?[66]

The assembly chose to ignore Hinderlider and gave more weight to Clifford Stone's assessment of the compact and to the Arkansas Valley Ditch Association's approval of the agreement. Stone summarized the main attraction of the compact before both the Colorado state assembly and the United States Congress. He testified that the compact represented the equitable quieting of long-standing conflict between Kansas and Colorado. The legislature of Colorado agreed, and Gov. Lee Knous signed it on 19 February 1949. The compact met with no recorded opposition in Kansas; the Kansas legislature approved it, and Gov. Frank Carlson later signed it on 7 March 1949. No one testified against the compact before congressional committees, and the bill to ratify the compact sailed through Congress, with President Truman signing it on 31 May 1949. The compact had become part of the law of the nation.[67]

In framing the compact, the commissioners overcame tremendous odds. Considering the myriad interests that they had to please, their ability to write an accord that nearly all could accept attested to their political acumen. Aside from reflecting their negotiating talents, the terms of the compact also revealed much about the cultural values they represented and how these related to the environment. The compact was like a charter that mirrored the interests of shareholders—that is, water users in Colorado and Kansas. The commissioners devised a bookkeeping system that fixed the rules of deposits and withdrawals. To attach some degree of permanence to the benefits that Kansas would receive, the commissioners included Article IV. This allowed for future development of water resources above the dam and reservoir and also guaranteed Kansas no "material" depletions of its rights.

The negotiations, however, sidestepped qualitative issues. The commissioners knew that environmental degradation in the valley had and would occur and that the dam and reservoir would further exacerbate those problems. Their commitment to growth simply did not allow for any alternatives. In an area of limited resources, nature would have to yield more water for larger cities, new industries, and increases in agricultural acreage. John Martin Dam and Reservoir constituted one piece of the technology that would make such goals partially feasible. The commissioners knew that the dam and reservoir could provide both states with more water, and they hoped their compact would make for a future of harmonious interstate relations. Still, other components for growth were needed—a dam on the Purgatoire, the Gunnison-Arkansas transmountain and the Blue River projects, increased pumping of groundwater, and flood levees in Kansas, to mention only a few. These projects promised the continuation of growth and of environmental breakdown. The one question nobody would ask was, how long could market-culture values continue at the expense of the valley's environment?

CHAPTER NINE

False Expectations

When white settlers first moved into the Arkansas River Valley, they dreamed of transforming the region through the conquest of nature. They hoped to remove any vestige of the short-grass plains by putting the water in the basin to "useful" purposes. Their vision included mutual stockholding irrigation companies, well supplied with water and raising profitable crops; populous cities marked by tree-lined boulevards, with business sections protected from fire by well-placed street hydrants and homes surrounded by green lawns; and growing factories free from any constraints because of a lack of water. In such a setting, the prosperous inhabitants would live peacefully and contentedly with one another, and their social and economic institutions—schools, churches, banks, and cooperatives—would flourish.

This dream held powerful sway over the first settlers and those who followed them. During his career as the state engineer, Michael Creed Hinderlider, a man schooled in science and rationality, reached rapturous heights when discussing the possible future of the valley. In the 1920s and 1930s, Hinderlider preached that water could be made the "untiring slave" of people, turning the wheels of industry and filling the needs of farmers and city dwellers. A transmountain water project and the creation of a reservoir at Caddoa would, he believed, create a continuous urban community stretching eastward from Pueblo to the state line. The projects would also supply over 60,000 *additional* acres of irrigated farms in the state and would settle for all time the interstate conflict with Kansas. Ultimately, the development of these water projects would unite all the people in cooperative and prosperous enterprise. Hinderlider could not have made a clearer statement of dominating nature for market-culture values. This utopia, however, never materialized.[1]

In the first place, the valley's people never won the battle with nature. They considered nature something to own, exploit, and control. Their thinking, fully captured by Hinderlider, gave little regard to water's place in the natural environment. The tenacious adherence to market-culture values made water a commodity governed in its use by the prior appropriation doctrine. In Colorado, the state affirmed a person's right to use water in "beneficial" pursuits—development for domestic (urban), farm, and industrial functions. This placed a distinctly utilitarian mark on the proper use of water. The state assembly did not regard the use of water for recreation, or for stream protection, beneficial until the late 1960s and early 1970s. The same held true for the laws passed by state legislators of Kansas, whose legislation also made surface and ground-water a commodity to develop.[2]

The conquest of the Arkansas River remained incomplete. People battled nature armed with a false preconception—that nature would yield to their technology. The building of dams, reservoirs, and trans-mountain projects would supply water to formerly worthless junior wa-ter rights; more land would come under cultivation, cities would grow, and interstate feuding over scant supplies would end. Applied hydraulic engineering would solve the problem of supporting market-culture val-ues in a region of limited water supplies.

Only when smallness of scale was practiced did "conquest" work. The Rocky Ford Ditch Company is a good example of this. The small ditch system watered lands well suited for irrigation. The company owned sound water rights which always supplied its irrigators with wa-ter. In comparison to other companies, the Rocky Ford irrigators found little need for costly technological improvements employed in the more extensive Fort Lyon and Bessemer systems. In many respects, the Rocky Ford ditch is a testimony to E. F. Schumacher's concepts in *Small Is Beau-tiful*. Still, the Rocky Ford irrigators never achieved full dominion over their environment, as their experiences with floods, siltation, and phreatophytes showed.[3]

Indeed, over the years, nature increasingly reacted against its subju-gation as its would-be conquerors built more dams, irrigation systems, and municipal water facilities. Unwanted plants, such as the salt cedar, flourished as irrigators turned the river flow saline. Dams could lessen the intensity of floods and freshets, but silt settled behind and upstream from the structures. Below the dam riverbanks narrowed, salinity rose, and phreatophytes thrived. The inundation of irrigated farmland with saline water made it nearly impossible to convert the fields to dry-land farming. Agriculture helped produce high levels of sedimentation that, along with the natural silt load in the river, buried diversion dams and ir-rigation headworks. The Frying Pan Arkansas project undoubtedly ben-efited Colorado Springs and supplemented the agricultural water rights in the valley. Yet neither it nor John Martin Dam and Reservoir nor Trini-dad Dam and Lake have added one new acre of farmland to the valley. People's expectations exceeded reality.

When their aspirations fell short and their water systems failed, as was wont to happen during drought, the road to conflict opened. Occa-sionally people fought one another with guns, as had the angry people of Victor who took back "their" water from the citizens of Colorado Springs. Far more often, people responded with hired assailants or protectors (depending on their relative position in litigation) called water lawyers. The attorneys took to court the questions concerning the equitable distribution of water flow. As users claimed more rights to the river flow than the stream could ever normally supply, and as urban, industrial, and agricultural demands continued apace, water lawyers multiplied with the rise of inevitable conflict.

The court system could not ensure the demands of growth in a changing environment. Consequently, lawsuits could never permanently settle any disputes over water resources in the valley. Legal decisions sidestepped the root causes of the litigation—market-culture values realized through the domination of nature. Rather, the judges, who shared the basic values of the people filing the suits, produced rulings focused on the equitable distribution of the economic returns rendered through the development of water. In essence, these decisions benefited the people who had spent the most to apply water in "beneficial" pursuits. As Harold Christy, the crusty engineer of the Colorado Fuel and Iron Corporation, once noted, "As has been proven in history many times, beneficial use in the actual application of the water is the best title [to it] you can get."[4] If you did not use water in some economic pursuit, then you had no right to it. This application of water helped establish the rule of equity. Lawyers, however, never felt comfortable about judges' abilities to understand or arbitrate the complex problems of water use in the arid West. As exemplified by the 1897 federal court ruling awarding the Great Eastern ditch in Kansas ten times the water it was capable of diverting, lawyers could never depend on judges to distribute a limited supply of water equitably. Besides, litigation was expensive and time-consuming for companies and states.

Cooperation through interstate water compacts promised a legal alternative to unpredictable courtroom decisions that were the result of conflict. In 1904 Frederick Newell, the first commissioner of the Reclamation Service, testified for the federal government during *Kansas v. Colorado* and suggested compact negotiations by experts as a way to unravel complex water problems. Later, the canny Colorado water lawyer, Delph Carpenter, perfected Newell's thinking, and his labors paved the path toward the Colorado River Compact of 1922. Engineers, lawyers, and state and federal bureaucrats negotiated a division of the Colorado River flow among nine western states. This set a precedent for resolving future interstate water fights.

Still, the results of compact negotiations, as shown in the commissioners' bargaining in the Arkansas River Compact, focused simply on dividing resources. They ignored such environmental considerations as wildlife, rising salinity levels, and changes in the river channel. The final draft of the Arkansas River Compact was simply an accounting procedure. A bank clerk could have understood the terms written into the agreement just as easily as the average irrigation farmer in the valley. Compacts merely expressed one other way in which people had made water a commodity.

The Arkansas River Compact negotiations also reveal the role of the federal government in water development in the valley. The nationalistic designs of federal bureaus had to adjust to regional situations. There is no reason to doubt Donald Worster's persuasive argument that the federal government supplied the means for powerful economic interests, as in the case of Sunkist, to hold sway over the economy and society in the Central and Imperial valleys. But as other historians—for example, Richard Lowitt and Gilbert Fite—have observed, California is not a useful model for the West as a whole.[5] In the Arkansas River Valley, the federal government behaved more like a parent bringing squabbling siblings to terms over the division of candy. The Army Corps of Engineers built the dam that stored enough "waste" water to guarantee (in most seasons) the irrigation operations of eastern Coloradans and western Kansans. The Corps directors used the project as leverage to steer the contentious states toward the formation of the compact.

However, the Corps' successes in coaxing water users toward agreement did not spell its endorsement of a power elite's hegemony over the water in the valley. In fact, the water users in the valley feared centralized federal power and could unite to exclude unwanted governmental intrusions. During the compact negotiations of the 1940s, the representatives from the Bureau of Reclamation, the Federal Power Commission, and the Federal Wildlife Service lobbied for their respective agencies. Yet the compact commissioners showed great adroitness in getting their way against the wishes of federal agencies.

Moreover, the economic power structure in the valley was too splintered for any one company, sugar factory, steel factory, city, or union of interests to rule over all the others. No marketing combines existed in the valley, such as they did in California, that could pull, push, or induce all water users in the valley toward common goals through economic rewards or reprisals. The existence of the mutual stockholding company may account for the lack of centralized power in the valley. Each company, constrained by its niche, water rights, and individual responses to historical economic, social, and climatic trends, guided itself. They could unite to fight a common foe, as did the members of the Arkansas Valley Ditch Association. They could unite to lobby the federal government for flood control or reclamation projects. But no single company possessed enough economic clout to control the others. Even the Arkansas Valley

Ditch Association was so divided between downstream and upstream water users that only substantive mutual harm or gain could bind the parts as one. Moreover, the association had to contend with state bureaucracies, such as the State Engineer's Office and the Colorado Water Conservation Board, that seldom worked in concert. In retrospect, it is amazing that the diverse interests in the valley and the states could agree on anything.

Nonetheless, people found cooperation with the federal government most helpful in developing their water systems. The Colorado Fuel and Iron Company acquired Sugar Loaf Reservoir. Colorado Springs secured the Pikes Peak watershed to supply urban development. In the 1930s the Public Works Administration contributed to the construction of the north slope reservoir system for Colorado Springs, and the military greatly stimulated the city's economy during World War II. Yet when the Bureau of Reclamation's interests conflicted with the city's over the development of the Blue River project, the city promptly and successfully argued its position in court. Similarly, in western Kansas, federal reclamation spurred economic growth around 1910. But the service failed to have a long-lasting influence there because the local farmers refused to follow the direction of Frederick Newell.

Still, by 1950 the federal government had made it possible for irrigators, city planners, and industrialists to believe their troubles were behind them. The Arkansas River Compact administered John Martin Dam and Reservoir in the interest of both Colorado and Kansas irrigators. Later, the Corps would build a reservoir near Trinidad on the Purgatoire River that would help prolong the life of John Martin Dam and Reservoir. In 1963 Pres. John Kennedy signed the legislation that initiated the construction of the Frying Pan Arkansas transmountain project (the partial fulfillment of the Gunnison-Arkansas plan). In the early 1980s the Bureau of Reclamation completed the project and began operating the system in support of agriculture and cities in Colorado.

The decline of sugar beets, however, led to problems and conflict in Colorado. Before 1950 the industry was in serious trouble, and by 1980 all the factories in the valley had closed their doors. In 1979 the American Crystal Sugar Company at Rocky Ford found it more lucrative to sell its rights to cities than to rent them to farmers. The irrigators of the Rocky Ford Ditch Company protested vehemently about the sale because they saw it threatening their water supply.[6]

The passing of the sugar-beet industry has been compounded, beginning in the 1970s, by a depressed agricultural economy that has further hurt irrigators. Consequently, many of the Bessemer and Fort Lyon shareholders have wanted to sell their rights, thereby splitting the companies into contending groups: those that want to sell and those that desire to continue farming. The Fort Lyon has encountered such hard times that the board even entertained the notion of consolidating with its nemesis—the Amity system. The two companies could combine their rights and systems for their mutual benefit. However, several factors make any future union very unlikely: Some Amity shareholders want to sell their water rights to cities; the administrative body of John Martin Dam and Reservoir would have to approve the merger; and residual animosities linger between the shareholders of the two companies.[7]

In the 1970s the CF&I Steel Corporation also faced a changing economic milieu that caused its managers to reconsider their administration of the company's water rights. A depressed international market for steel made in the United States led to curtailments in production. With less tonnage, the corporation reorganized its operations. Its streamlined plant production consumed less water, so the company placed some of its rights on the regional market. The plant managers found takers among the growing urban centers along the Front Range.[8]

The purchase by Colorado Springs and Denver of water rights might help offset the worsening economic conditions experienced by farmers and industrialists and alleviate some anticipated urban water-supply obstacles to future expansion. Urban purchases, however, come with environmental costs and conflict. Beginning in 1985 Colorado Springs began tapping the Frying Pan Arkansas project, but that supply could not support predicted growth. The city planned a new transmountain project that environmentalists feared would threaten the wilderness ecology around Holy Cross Mountain. They strongly opposed the development, and both sides began tedious litigation. In the valley, where irrigators have sold their rights to cities, the land has become desolate and supports only salt-tolerant weeds. Moreover, no one has been certain about the effect that changing diversion points from canal to city would have on the river flow. Consulting engineers and water lawyers have profited handsomely as irrigators, environmentalists, and city planners battle over water.[9]

Irrigators in western Kansas have also experienced difficult times since the signing of the compact. The failure of the sugar-beet industry caused the closing of the Garden City company in 1955. An important and profitable part of the Garden City economy disappeared. The company, though, retained its water rights and farmland and simply rented both to tenants. Deep-well drilling has threatened the Ogallala Aquifer with complete depletion by the year 2000. Some people have even blamed the drying out of Cheyenne Bottoms northeast of Great Bend, Kansas (a situation feared by R. A. Schmidt of the Fish and Wildlife Service in 1948), on increasing water usage in Kansas and Colorado. During the 1970s, drought, the expansion of groundwater pumping in Colorado, and one state's general distrust of the other provoked Kansans to such an extent that the state filed another complaint in the United States Supreme Court in 1985. The suit argued that Colorado had "materially" depleted the river flow and that the administrators of the Arkansas River Compact had not supplied Kansans with their fair share of the water.[10]

The valley's residents face serious problems, and they have taken some steps to resolve their mess. City planners have started cooperating with the Soil Conservation Service and horticulturalists from Colorado State University in trying to find ways to convert formerly irrigated farmlands to either native or exotic grasses (so far with little success). The United States Geological Survey and the Colorado Water Conservation Board jointly and routinely conduct studies of the river. Both agencies hope to discover methods of cleaning and of conserving water. Perhaps, albeit doubtfully, the United States Supreme Court will produce a ruling that will permanently settle the rights of Colorado and Kansas to the river flow.[11]

Still, as of the late 1980s the people of the Arkansas River Valley have far to go before fully solving their problems. As one engineer from Colorado Springs noted, trends in the valley have not spoken well about the people's "stewardship" of water. The point is, people in the Arkansas River Valley have seldom observed "stewardship," with its implication of caring for something that one does not own. Rather, they have thought in terms of the commodity value of the stream and of how the domination of the river, especially through engineering, could increase the value of their vested property rights.

The history of conflict in the valley shows that technology alone will not solve its people's problems. The Army Corps of Engineers and the Bureau of Reclamation have already developed all of the large dam sites in the valley, and the possibilities of additional transmountain projects diminish as available locations become scarcer and the costs of building and litigation mount. People's faith in technology to overcome the problems of supplying growing urban, farm, and industrial economies has blinded them to a maxim in Andre Gorz's *Ecology as Politics*: "Physical growth has physical limits, and any attempt to push them back only pushes the problem around."[12] The inhabitants of the Arkansas River Basin must learn the lesson they have avoided for the last hundred years: They must blend their economic ambitions to nature's reality for a valley of content to emerge.

NOTES

ABBREVIATIONS USED

AVDA	Arkansas Valley Ditch Association Collection
BPWW	Board of Pueblo Water Works
CF&IC	Colorado Fuel and Iron Company Collection
CHS	Colorado Historical Society, Denver
CSA	Colorado State Archives, Denver
CWCB	Colorado Water Conservation Board
DWR	Division of Water Resources
FRCD	Federal Record Center, Denver
ff	file folder
KAG	Kansas Attorney General
KSBA	Kansas State Board of Agriculture
KSHS	Kansas State Historical Society
MCHC	Michael Creed Hinderlider Collection
PUOCS	Public Utilities Office, Colorado Springs
UCLL	University of Colorado Law Library
WDCS	Water Department, Colorado Springs
WHC/DPL	Western History Collections, Denver Public Library
RG	Record Group

CHAPTER ONE. DISCORD IN THE VALLEY OF CONTENT

1. For an excellent essay discussing the current historiography of western water history, see Donald J. Pisani, "Deep and Troubled Waters: A New Field of Western History?" *New Mexico Historical Review* 63 (October 1988): 311-31. See also William Smythe, *The Conquest of Arid America*, with an introduction by Lawrence B. Lee (Seattle: University of Washington Press, 1969; reprint, Seattle: Americana Library, 1970); and Arthur Maass and Raymond Anderson, . . . *and the Desert Shall Rejoice* (Cambridge: MIT Press, 1978).

2. The critical theory school of philosophy centered its discussion on the domination of nature. The concept had its most fruitful elaboration in the works of Max Horkheimer, Theodore Adorno, Herbert Marcuse, and Jürgen Habermas. A student of Marcuse, William Leiss, has written the best comprehensive study of the theme, *The Domination of Nature* (New York: George Braziller, 1972). For the

most part, these writers have stressed how modern technology resulted not only in the control of nature but also in control over people by the few who directed the conquest. The ultimate result, they argued, is the revolt of people against technology and its proponents.

Karl Wittfogel was associated with the critical school, and his *Oriental Despotism: A Comparative Study of Total Power* (New Haven, Conn.: Yale University Press, 1957) is his most recognized work. Donald Worster, in "Hydraulic Society in California: An Ecological Interpretation," *Agricultural History* 56 (July 1982): 503–15, and *Rivers of Empire: Water, Aridity and the Growth of the American West* (New York: Pantheon Books, 1985), shows the distinct influence of Wittfogel. Although both authors' works have merit, they have focused attention too exclusively on irrigation as a technology that results in centralized bureaucratic despotism over people and nature. The reality of irrigation in the Arkansas River Valley is more complex and does not fit neatly into their model. For further discussions on irrigation, consult Theodore Downing and Gibson McGuire, eds., *Irrigation's Impact on Society* (Tucson: University of Arizona Press, 1974); Donald Worster, "Irrigation and Democracy in California: The Early Promise," *Pacific Historian* 27 (Spring 1983): 30–35; idem, "History as Natural History: An Essay on Theory and Method," *Pacific Historical Review* 53 (February 1984): 1–19; idem, "New West, True West: Interpreting the Region's History," *Western Historical Quarterly* 18 (April 1987): 141–56; and Marc Reisner, *Cadillac Desert: The American West and Its Disappearing Water* (New York: Viking Penguin, 1986).

There are also other ways to study irrigation. The best of the econometric studies is by Maurice M. Kelso, E. Martin William, and Lawrence E. Mack, *Water Supplies and Economic Growth in an Arid Environment: An Arizona Case Study* (Tucson: University of Arizona Press, 1973). The foremost works on the political, institutional, and legal side of irrigation are Ira Clark, *Water in New Mexico* (Albuquerque: University of New Mexico Press, 1988); Robert G. Dunbar, *Forging New Rights in Western Waters* (Lincoln: University of Nebraska Press, 1983); Norris Hundley, Jr., *Water and the West: The Colorado River Compact and the Politics of Water in the American West* (Berkeley and Los Angeles: University of California Press, 1966); Donald J. Pisani, *From Family Farm to Agribusiness: The Irrigation Crusade in California and the West, 1850–1931* (Berkeley and Los Angeles: University of California Press, 1984); and idem, "Enterprise and Equity: A Critique of Western Water Law in the Nineteenth Century," *Western Historical Quarterly* 18 (January 1987): 15–37. Also see F. Lee Brown and Helen M. Ingram, *Water and Poverty in the Southwest* (Tucson: University of Arizona Press, 1987); and Ernest A. Engelbert and Ann Foley Scheuring, eds., *Water Scarcity: Impacts on Western Agriculture* (Berkeley and Los Angeles: University of California Press, 1984). A good bibliography to consult for additional works is in Lawrence B. Lee's *Reclaiming the American West: An Historiography and Guide* (Santa Barbara, Calif.: ABC-Clio, 1980).

3. Richard White, "American Environmental History: The Development of a New Historical Field," *Pacific Historical Review* 54 (August 1985): 334–35.

4. The social theory of conflict and cooperation provides a useful tool for interpreting the historical development of irrigation in the Arkansas River Valley. Analyzing the environment and the social factors that have given rise to cooperation and/or conflict in the large community of water users in the valley does much to explain the historical reality of irrigation. For a good introduction to social theory, see Don Harrison Doyle, "Social Theory and New Communities in Nineteenth-Century America," *Western Historical Quarterly* 8 (April 1977): 151–65.

5. Donald Worster, *Dust Bowl: The Southern Plains in the 1930s* (New York: Oxford University Press, 1979), 6.

6. Leiss, *Domination of Nature*, 164, noted in passing that external nature itself has shown signs in both past and present of not accepting the dominion of people. Even though Leiss did not elaborate, nature in a variety of ways can react against its subjugation.

7. Richard White, *Land Use, Environment, and Social Change: The Shaping of Island County, Washington* (Seattle: University of Washington Press, 1980), 74; and Arthur F. McEvoy, *The Fisherman's Problem: Ecology and Law in the California Fisheries, 1850–1980* (New York: Cambridge University Press, 1986), 13–14.

8. James Willard Hurst, "Legal Elements in United States History," in *Perspectives in American History,* vol. 5 of *Law in American History* (Cambridge: Harvard University Press, 1971), 68 and 73. See also James Willard Hurst, *Law and Economic Growth: The Legal History of the Lumber Industry in Wisconsin, 1836–1915* (Cambridge: Harvard University Press, 1964); Harry N. Scheiber, "At the Borderland of Law and Economic History: The Contributions of Willard Hurst," *American Historical Review* 75 (February 1970): 744–56; idem, "American Constitutional History and the New Legal History: Complementary Themes in Two Modes," *Journal of American History* 68 (September 1981): 337–50; Stephen Diamond, "Legal Realism and Historical Method: J. Willard Hurst and American Legal History," *Michigan Law Review* 77 (January–March 1979): 784–94; David H. Flaherty, "An Approach to American History: Willard Hurst as Legal Historian," *American Journal of Legal History* 14 (1970): 222–34; Kermit L. Hall, "The 'Magic Mirror' and the Promise of Western Legal History at the Bicentennial of the Constitution," *Western Historical Quarterly* 18 (October 1987): 429–35; James Willard Hurst, *Law and the Conditions of Freedom in Nineteenth-Century United States* (Madison: University of Wisconsin Press, 1966); and Lawrence M. Friedman and Harry N. Scheiber, eds., *American Law and the Constitutional Order: Historical Perspectives* (Cambridge: Harvard University Press, 1978).

9. P. O. Abbott, *Descriptions of Water-Systems Operations in the Arkansas River Basin, Colorado*, Water Resources Investigations Report 85-4092 (Lakewood, Colo.: U.S. Geological Survey, 1985), 11, 31–32.

10. The Colorado company went through many reorganizations and name changes: Colorado Coal and Iron Company, 1880–92; Colorado Fuel and Iron Company, 1892–1936; Colorado Fuel and Iron Corporation, 1936–69; CF&I Steel Corporation, 1969–present. The name used in the text corresponds as closely as possible to the time period discussed.

11. For a discussion of privatism see Samuel Hays, "The Politics of Reform in Municipal Government in the Progressive Era," *Pacific Northwest Quarterly* 55 (October 1964): 159–65; and Sam Bass Warner, Jr., *The Private City: Philadelphia in Three Periods of Its Growth* (Philadelphia: University of Pennsylvania Press, 1968), x. For an introduction to instrumentalism and the role of the engineer see James E. Sherow, "The Chimerical Vision: Michael Creed Hinderlider and Progressive Engineering in Colorado," *Essays and Monographs in Colorado History* No. 9 (1989): 37–59.

12. I have used several different sources for the Supreme Court case, *Kansas v. Colorado* (1907). The verbatim testimony is found in both the Colorado State Archives and in the Kansas State Historical Society. All of the briefs and the abstracted transcript of the testimony are on microfiche cards in the University of Colorado Law Library and can be found in most law libraries either on microfiche cards or in microfilm. The early briefs of all the participants, along with the ab-

stracted testimony, were published in two volumes by Judd & Detweiler of Washington, D.C., in 1905. Throughout the footnotes, the variances in the citations reflect the specific source used.

CHAPTER TWO. THE EMERGENCE OF THE
MUTUAL STOCKHOLDING IRRIGATION
COMPANY, 1870–1900

1. *The State of Kansas v. The State of Colorado, et al.*, United States Supreme Court, October Term, 1901, No. 3, Original, Testimony and Proceedings in the Above Entitled Cause before Special Commissioner Granville A. Richardson, Defendant Colorado's Evidence, O. P. Wiggins's testimony, vol. 5, 2500–2510, location #47936, CSA.

2. U.S. Congress, House, *Report of Exploration for a Route for the Pacific Railroad, by Capt. J. W. Gunnison, Topographical Engineers, near the 38th and 39th Parallels of North Latitude, from the Mouth of the Kansas River, Mo., to the Sevier Lake, in the Great Basin*, by Lt. E. G. Beckwith, H. Doc. 91, 33d Cong., 2d sess., 1855, 25–28; and *Kansas v. Colorado*, Testimony and Proceedings, O. P. Wiggins's testimony, vol. 6, 2680.

3. Janet Lecompte, *Pueblo, Hardscrabble, Greenhorn: The Upper Arkansas, 1832–1856* (Norman: University of Oklahoma Press, 1978), 108.

4. Robert Follansbee and Edward E. Jones, *The Arkansas River Flood of June 3–5, 1921*, Water Supply Paper 487 (Washington, D.C.: Government Printing Office, 1922), 35–36; and Lecompte, *Pueblo, Hardscrabble, Greenhorn*, 108.

5. U.S. Congress, Senate, *Report of an Expedition Led by Lieutenant Abert, on the Upper Arkansas through the Country of the Camanche Indians*, by J. W. Abert, S. Doc. 483, 29th Cong., 1st sess., 1846, 438–39.

6. Worster, *Dust Bowl*, 6.

7. G. E. Radosevich, K. C. Nobe, D. Allardice, and C. Kirkwood, *Evolution and Administration of Colorado Water Law: 1876–1976* (Littleton, Colo.: Water Resources Publication, 1976), 9–12, 56–60.

8. According to James Willard Hurst, in the nineteenth century one function of law was to provide the "organization through which entrepreneurs could better mobilize and release economic energy." See his *Law and the Conditions of Freedom in the Nineteenth-Century United States* (Madison: University of Wisconsin Press, 1966), 17.

9. Charles W. Bowman, "History of Bent County," in *History of the Arkansas Valley, Colorado* (Chicago: O. L. Baskin & Co., 1881), 847, 886–87; and *Kansas v. Colorado*, Testimony and Proceedings, George Swink's testimony, vol. 7, 3243–44, CSA.

10. *Kansas v. Colorado*, Testimony and Proceedings, Swink's testimony, vol. 7, 3243–45, CSA; and Mr. and Mrs. James R. Harvey, "Rocky Ford Melons," *Colorado Magazine* 26 (January 1949): 26–28.

11. Joseph O. Van Hook, "Development of Irrigation in the Arkansas Valley," *Colorado Magazine* 10 (January 1933): 10; "New Corporation," *Rocky Mountain News*, 28 July 1882, 2; and In the District Court of the Third Judicial District of the State of Colorado, in and for the county of Bent: In the Matter of the Priorities to the Use of Water in District No. 17, *The Rocky-Ford Ditch*, #4954, location # 39098, CSA.

12. In the Matter of the Priorities to *The Rocky-Ford Ditch*, #4954, location # 39098, CSA. A good general discussion of Colorado's prior appropriation system is by Robert G. Dunbar, "The Origins of the Colorado System of Water-Right Control," *Colorado Magazine* 27 (October 1950): 241–62; and Radosevich et al., *Evolution and Administration of Colorado Water Law.*

13. Harvey, "Rocky Ford Melons," 29.

14. The information concerning Swink's development of the Rocky Ford Netted Gem cantaloupe, honey production, and alfalfa comes from *Kansas v. Colorado*, Testimony and Proceedings, Swink's testimony, vol. 7, 3246–54, CSA. Swink probably overrated the importance of honey bees in pollination. The first flowers of cantaloupes are mostly male flowers which continue to fall off. The female blossoms do not appear in large numbers until about a week later. See H. N. Griffin, *Cantaloupes*, Colorado Agricultural Experiment Station Bulletin 62 (Fort Collins, April 1901), 15–16.

15. The information regarding Swink's role in the valley's sugar-beet industry comes from *Kansas v. Colorado*, Testimony and Proceedings, Swink's testimony, vol. 7, 3254–61; and John E. Frost, "Story of Irrigation: The Beet Sugar Industry in the Arkansas River Valley of Eastern Colorado," *Irrigation Age* 17 (January 1902): 5–11.

16. T. L. Lyon's name shows up as Lunn in Swink's testimony. A check at the University of Nebraska revealed that no one by the name of Lunn had taught there around the turn of the twentieth century. At the same time, however, several articles on sugar beets appeared by T. L. Lyon in University of Nebraska publications. Either the court reporter had confused Swink's pronunciation of Lyon, or Swink had confused Lyon's name during testimony.

17. James D. Schuyler, "Report on the Property of the Fort Lyon Canal Company, Colorado, Its Water Supply, Its Present Physical Condition, and the Betterments Needed to Complete the Irrigation System, 1910," typewritten, 3–4, Record Vault, Fort Lyon Canal Office Building, Las Animas, Colorado; U.S. Department of Interior, Office of Indian Affairs, *Report of the Secretary of the Interior, for the Fiscal Year Ended 30 June 1865*, 387, 393–95; and U.S. Department of Interior, Bureau of Indian Affairs, *Letters Received by the Office of Indian Affairs, 1824–81*, M234, roll 878 (Henry Fosdick to Gov. John Evans, 29 May 1864), and M234, roll 879 (J. Haynes to D. N. Cooley, commissioner of Indian affairs, 28 May 1866).

18. "What It Means," *Pueblo Chieftain*, 11 March 1884, 2; and Schuyler, "Report on the Property of the Fort Lyon Canal Company," 4–6.

19. "Father of Western Irrigation Is Dead," *Rocky Mountain News*, 3 February 1914, 1; *Kansas v. Colorado*, T. C. Henry's Testimony, vol. 5, 2365–69, CSA; and CWCB, *A Hundred Years of Irrigation in Colorado: 100 Years of Organized and Continuous Irrigation, 1852–1952* (Denver: CWCB; and Fort Collins: Colorado Agricultural and Mechanical College, 1952), 86.

20. M. F. Hockemeyer, "Irrigation Company Dramas Unfold," *Arkansas Valley Journal*, 29 August 1983, 1 and 3; and "Early Construction Methods and Problems," in handwritten manuscript titled "Water: The Sustainer of Life," by M. C. Hinderlider, 1–3, ff 453, MCHC, CHS.

21. "Early Construction Methods and Problems," by M. C. Hinderlider, 1–3, ff 453, MCHC, CHS.

22. Schuyler, "Report on the Property of the Fort Lyon Canal Company," 6–7.

23. Don Miles, in *Salinity in the Arkansas Valley of Colorado* (Denver: Environ-

mental Protection Agency, 1977), 6–7, noted that water rights before 1887 are "usually very undependable" and that during an "extremely dry period, only water rights senior to 1875 can be fully exercised."

24. See Pisani, "Enterprise and Equity," 15–37; William Lilley II and Lewis L. Gould, "The Western Irrigation Movement, 1878–1902: A Reappraisal," in *The American West: A Reorientation*, ed. Gene M. Gressley (Laramie: University of Wyoming, 1966), 63; and Worster, *Rivers of Empire*, 87–96.

25. Schuyler, "Report on the Property of the Fort Lyon Canal Company," 6–12; and Brief in Support of Motion of the Fort Lyon Canal Company, *The La Junta and Lamar Canal Co. v. Hess* (#3768), 31 Colo. 1 (1903), 6–8, and 283–87, location # 38903, CSA; and *To the Owners of Rights to Water from the La Junta and Lamar Canal* (Las Animas, Colo.: n.p., 10 June 1897, pamphlet submitted as evidence in *The La Junta and Lamar Canal Co. v. Hess* (#3768), 31 Colo. 1 (1903), location #38903, CSA.

26. Brief in Support of Motion of the Fort Lyon Canal Company, 11–18, and Bill of Complaint, 7–39, *The Arkansas Valley Sugar Beet and Irrigated Land Company v. The Fort Lyon Canal Company* (D. Colo.) (#7902), box 325, RG 21, FRCD.

27. *The La Junta and Lamar Canal Co. v. Hess* (#3768), 25 Colo. 513 (1898); dismissed for errors and resubmitted as *The La Junta and Lamar Canal Company v. Hess* (1903); *The La Junta and Lamar Canal Company v. The Fort Lyon Canal Company* (#3996), 31 Colo. 1 (1903); and *Blakely v. The Fort Lyon Canal Company* (#4204), 31 Colo. 224 (1903).

28. Robert Athearn, *The Denver and Rio Grande Western Railroad* (Lincoln: University of Nebraska Press, 1962), 9.

29. Central Colorado Improvement Company, *Second Report of the Board of Directors to the Stockholders and Bondholders*, 1874 (Colorado Springs, Colo.: "Out West" Printing and Publishing Co., 1875), 8–10, ff 3, CF&IC, CHS.

30. Central Colorado Improvement Company, *Third Report of the Board of Directors*, 1875, 6–8; and Central Colorado Improvement Company, *Fourth Report of the Board of Directors*, 1876–77, 4–7.

31. Colorado Fuel and Iron Company, "Predecessor Companies of the Colorado Coal & Iron Co.—The Central Colorado Improvement Co., The Southern Colorado Coal & Town Co., The Colorado Coal & Steel Works Co., and The Colorado Coal and Iron Company," typewritten report c. 1923, 205–6, ff 202, CF&IC, CHS.

32. Ibid., 207; and H. Lee Scamehorn, *Pioneer Steelmaker in the West: The Colorado Fuel and Iron Company, 1872–1903*, (Boulder, Colo.: Pruett Publishing Co., 1976), 51–54.

33. Colorado Coal and Iron Company, *Seventh Annual Report of the Colorado Coal and Iron Co.*, December 31, 1885 (New York: Evening Post Job Printing Office, 1886), ff 3, CF&IC, CHS.

34. *Eighth Annual Report of the Colorado Coal and Iron Co.* 1888, 16; and *Eleventh Annual Report of the Colorado Coal and Iron Co.* 1889, 15–16, ff 19.

35. Colorado Coal and Iron Company, Minutes, 16 August 1888, ff 41, CF&IC, CHS.

36. *Eleventh Annual Report of the Colorado Coal and Iron Co.*, 1889, 16–17, ff 19.

37. State Engineer, Southeastern Colorado Water Conservancy District, *Tabulation of Ditch and Reservoir Decrees, Main Stem Arkansas River, Colorado: Water District 11, 12, 14, 17 and 67 (Tributary Decrees Not Included)* (n.p., n.d.); and interview by author with William Mullin, superintendent of the Bessemer Irrigating Ditch Company, Pueblo, Colorado, July 1985.

38. Colorado Fuel and Iron Company, "Predecessor Companies," 30, 35–36; Colorado Coal and Iron Company, Minutes, 7 April 1890, ff 43; Colorado Coal and Iron Company, Minutes, 25 September 1891, ff 43; and Scamehorn, *Pioneer Steelmaker in the West*, 68.

39. Colorado Fuel and Iron Company, "Predecessor Companies," 35–36.

40. Colorado Coal and Iron Company, Minutes, 25 August 1892, 277–78, ff 43; and Scamehorn, *Pioneer Steelmaker in the West*, 99.

41. M. F. Hockemeyer, "Bessemer Ditch Incorporated in 1888," *Arkansas Valley Journal*, 31 October 1983, 1–2; "1921 Flood Damages Bessemer Canal," ibid., 7 November 1983, 1; and Certificate of Incorporation of the Bessemer Irrigating Ditch Company, 25 July 1894, CSA.

CHAPTER THREE. THE INCOMPLETE CONQUEST

1. Doug Cain, *Quality of the Arkansas River and Irrigation-Return Flows in the Lower Arkansas River Valley, Colorado*, Water Resources Investigations Report 84-4273 (Lakewood, Colo.: U.S. Geological Survey, 1985), 1–2.

2. Don Miles, "Recharge: Its Role in Total Water Management, Arkansas Valley of Colorado" (Paper presented to the Great Plains Council Groundwater Management Seminar, Denver, Colorado, April 1974), 1–2; *Kansas v. Colorado*, W. M. Wiley's Testimony, vol. 11, 5463–64; and S. W. Cressy's Testimony, vol. 9, 3174, location #47936, CSA.

3. *Kansas v. Colorado*, R. E. Edwards's Testimony, vol. 3, 1099, CSA.

4. Miles, *Salinity in the Arkansas Valley*, 12; and Thomas H. Means, "Report on Effect of Sediment in Caddoa Reservoir, Colorado, upon Relocation of the Atchison, Topeka and Santa Fe Railroad," February 1939, ff 139, MCHC, CHS.

5. M. F. Hockemeyer, "Key Men Help Ft. Lyon Survive," *Arkansas Valley Journal*, 24 October 1983, 1.

6. Newspaper clipping, "Communities along Stream Making Valuable Suggestions," 14 April 1944, in "Pueblo Water Works—General," ff 1, WDCS.

7. Miles, *Salinity in the Arkansas Valley*, 10, reported that between Lamar and Granada, Colorado, the salinity level in the Arkansas River averaged over 4,000 parts per million (ppm) of total dissolved solids (tds).

8. Charles E. Kellogg, *The Soils That Support Us* (New York: Macmillan, 1943), 123–29; Miles, *Salinity in the Arkansas Valley*, 17–18; Milton Fireman and H. E. Hayward, "Irrigation Water and Saline and Alkali Soils," in *Water: The Yearbook of Agriculture* (Washington, D.C.: Government Printing Office, 1955), 321–27; and "An Irrigation Problem Solved: The Valley of the Arkansas," *Colorado Chieftain*, 15 July 1875, 1.

9. G. K. Gilbert, "The Underground Water of the Arkansas Valley in Eastern Colorado," in *Seventeenth Annual Report of the United States Geological Survey*, 1895–96, part 2 (Washington, D.C.: Government Printing Office, 1896), 601.

10. Ivo E. Lindauer, in his *A Survey of the Woody Phreatophytes in the Lower Arkansas River Valley of Colorado* (Fort Collins: Department of Botany and Plant Pathology, Colorado State University, 1968), ii, defines phreatophytes as "the name generally given to plants that extend their roots into the water table or the capillary fringe just above it to obtain their water supply." See also T. W. Robinson, *Introduction, Spread, and Areal Extent of Saltcedar (Tamarix) in the Western States*, U.S. Geological Survey Professional Paper 491-A (Washington, D.C.: Government

Printing Office, 1965), A3–A4; and Ivo E. Lindauer, "A Comparison of the Plant Communities of the South Platte and Arkansas River Drainages in Eastern Colorado," *Southwestern Naturalist* 28 (August 1983): 249–58; and Miles, *Salinity in the Arkansas Valley*, 34.

11. Schuyler, "Report on the Property of the Fort Lyon Canal Company," 22–23; *Kansas v. Colorado*, R. E. Edward's Testimony, vol. 3), 1099, CSA; Bessemer Irrigating Ditch Company, Pueblo, Colorado, Minutes of Board of Directors meeting, (hereafter Bessemer company Minutes) 8 January 1923; and *Kansas v. Colorado*, Frederick F. Newell's Testimony, vol. 10, 4923, CSA.

12. *Kansas v. Colorado*, L. G. Carpenter's Testimony, vol. 5, 2137–58, CSA.

13. *Daily Democrat*, 12 January 1924, 5.

14. M. F. Hockemeyer, "1921 Flood Damages Bessemer Canal," *Arkansas Valley Journal*, 7 November 1983, 1; and Bessemer company Minutes, 9 June, 17 July, and 20 August 1921.

15. Bessemer company Minutes, 5 and 13 September 1921.

16. Bessemer Irrigating Ditch Company, Pueblo, Colorado, *Annual Report*, 19 January 1943.

17. Statement of Facts, *The Fort Lyon Canal Company v. The Arkansas Valley Sugar Beet and Irrigated Land Company* (C.C.D. Colo.) (No. 319), 9–22, box 26, RG 21, FRCD; Bill of Complaint, *The Arkansas Valley Sugar Beet and Irrigated Land Company v. The Fort Lyon Canal Company*, 41–52; and M. F. Hockemeyer, "Litigation: Way of Life for Ft. Lyon," *Arkansas Valley Journal*, 17 October 1983, 1; and M. F. Hockemeyer and Joanne McIntyre, "Court Fight Creates Amity Mutual," *Arkansas Valley Journal*, 5 December 1983, 1.

18. *Annual Report of the Fort Lyon Canal Company* (1915), 11, Record Vault, Fort Lyon Canal Company, Las Animas, Colorado.

19. Ibid. (1916), 8.

20. E. R. Chew, "Annual Report Division Engineer, Division No. 2—1917," in *Nineteenth Biennial Report of the State Engineer, Colorado*, 1917–18 (Denver: State Printers, 1918), 84.

21. Interview with Paul Converse, former superintendent of the Fort Lyon Canal Company, Las Animas, Colorado, 5 April 1983.

22. By 1905 the state of Colorado had approved ditch decrees amounting to 4,200 cfs in the Arkansas River Valley with the Arkansas River's averaged flow at Canon City measuring 750 cfs. With such figures, the importance of return flow use and the relative dates of water decrees becomes clearer. See *Kansas v. Colorado*, No. 3, Original, 27 Sup. Ct. Report, 671 (1906).

23. James Sherow, "Discord in the 'Valley of Content': Strife over Natural Resources in a Changing Environment on the Arkansas River Valley of the High Plains" (Ph.D. dissertation, University of Colorado, 1987), 462–64.

24. Ibid.

25. Ibid., 465–67; and Hockemeyer, "Key Men Help Ft. Lyon Survive," *Arkansas Valley Journal*, 24 October 1983, 1.

26. *Annual Report of Fort Lyon Canal Company* (1932), 3–6.

27. Ibid. (1934), 4–7.

28. Ibid. (1932), 4; and (1934), 6.

29. Bessemer company, Minutes, 2 March 1931, 4 January 1932, 5 September 1932, 5 December 1932, and 2 April 1934; and *Annual Report*, 15 January 1935.

30. The sugar beet industry was heavily subsidized by the federal government during the Great Depression. See Richard Lowitt, *The New Deal and the West* (Bloomington: Indiana University Press, 1984), 95–98.

31. "Sugar Factory Doubly Assured," *Rocky Ford Enterprise*, 7 December 1899, 2; "The American Beet Sugar Co. Goes Steadily Forward," *Rocky Ford Enterprise*, 4 January 1900, 2; "Rocky Ford's Water Threatened," *Denver Post*, 12 June 1983, 6c.

32. Interview with Edward Kidder, irrigation farmer under the Rocky Ford Ditch Company, Rocky Ford, Colorado, July 1985.

33. Roy J. Larsen, Donald R. Martin, and M. Bruce McCullough, *Soil Survey of Otero County, Colorado* (Washington, D.C.: Government Printing Office, 1971), 32 and 59.

34. Sherow, "Discord in the 'Valley of Content,' " 431–32.

35. Ibid.

36. Hockemeyer, "1921 Flood Damages Bessemer Canal," *Arkansas Valley Journal*, 7 November 1983, 1; and Bessemer company Minutes, 6 September and 5 October 1920.

37. Bessemer company Minutes, 1 October 1923.

38. M. F. Hockemeyer, "Bessemer Fights Clear Water Problem," *Arkansas Valley Journal*, 21 November 1983, 2; and Bessemer company Minutes, 6 July 1926 and 21 January 1936.

39. *Middelkamp v. Bessemer Irrigating [Ditch] Company*, #5402, 46 Colo. 102–25 (1909); *Barnum v. Bessemer Irrigating [Ditch] Company*, #5403, 46 Colo. 125–6 (1909); *Brown v. Bessemer Irrigating [Ditch] Company*, #5404, 46 Colo. 126 (1909); *Patry v. Bessemer Irrigating [Ditch] Company*, #5405, 46 Colo. 127 (1909); and *Vail et al. v. Bessemer Irrigating [Ditch] Company*, #5406, 46 Colo. 128 (1909).

40. Bessemer company Minutes, 5 November 1934, and Bessemer Company, *Annual Report*, 19 January 1937.

41. Sherow, "Discord in the 'Valley of Content,' " 431–34.

42. Schuyler, "Report on the Property of the Fort Lyon Canal Company," 20–22; Interview with Paul Converse; and Larsen, Martin, and McCullough, *Soil Survey of Otero County*, 25, 32, and 33.

43. James Pannell, Roy J. Larsen, M. Bruce McCullough, Ronald E. Moreland, and Stanley Woodyard *Soil Survey of Powers County, Colorado* (Washington, D.C.: Government Printing Office, 1966), 32 and 39.

44. Interview with Paul Converse, 5 April 1983; and interview with George Reyher, irrigation farmer, Bent County, Colorado, 5 April 1983.

45. Sherow, "Discord in the 'Valley of Content,' " 435–37.

46. *Annual Report of Fort Lyon Canal Company* (1941), 3; and (1944), 3–5.

CHAPTER FOUR. URBAN AND INDUSTRIAL WATER USES AND POLICIES, 1870–1950

1. "Water: History of the Schemes for Obtaining a Supply for Our City," *Colorado Chieftain*, 12 November 1874, 3.

2. *Colorado Chieftain*, 16 February 1871, 3; "Water Works," 17 October 1872, 2; 24 April 1873, 4; "A Great Public Work," 12 June 1873, 3; "The Big Ditch: A Success," 24 July 1873, 1; 7 August 1873, 3; and "The Ditch Question," 12 March 1874, 1.

3. *Colorado Chieftain*, "Waterworks," 19 March 1874, 1; and "Water Works Meeting" 2 April 1874, 4.

4. *Colorado Chieftain*, "Aqueous," 15 October 1874, 3, and "Water," 12 November 1874,3; and Frank Hall, *History of the State of Colorado*, vol. 3 (Chicago: Blakely Printing Co., 1895), 459.

5. Hall, *History of the State of Colorado*, 3:469; L. A. Henry, "Water: The Second of a Series of Studies Sponsored by the Pueblo, Colorado, Chamber of Commerce under the Direction of L. A. Henry, Consultant, Little Rock, Arkansas," typewritten report, March 1946, 13, folder no. 1, James W. Preston Files, BPWW; and "History of the Pueblo Water Supply," BPWW.

6. Central Colorado Improvement Company, *Second Report of the Board of Directors to the Stockholders and Bondholders*, 1874 (Colorado Springs, Colo.: "Out West" Printing and Publishing Co., 1875), 3 and 8–10, ff 3, CF&IC, CHS; and Colorado Fuel and Iron Company, "Predecessor Companies of the Colorado Coal & Iron Company," 2, ff 202, CF&IC, CHS.

7. Central Colorado Improvement Company, *Third Report*, 1876, 6; Central Colorado Improvement Company, Fourth Report, 1876–77, 8; and Scamehorn, *Pioneer Steelmaker in the West*, 18–19.

8. *First Report of the Colorado Coal and Iron Co. comprising the Sixth Report of the Central Colorado Improvement Co. and the Second Report of the Southern Colorado Coal and Town Co.*, 1879, 11.

9. *Second Annual Report of the Colorado Coal and Iron Co.*, 31 December 1880, 14; *Third Annual Report of the Colorado Coal and Iron Co.*, 31 December 1881, 21–22; *Fourth Annual Report of the Colorado Coal and Iron Co.*, 31 December 1882, 16; *Pueblo Daily Chieftain*, 22 October 1885, 1; *Ninth Annual Report of the Colorado Coal and Iron Co.*, 31 December 1887, 15; and "History of the Pueblo Water Supply," BPWW.

10. "History of the Pueblo Water Supply," BPWW.

11. Sherow, "Discord in the 'Valley of Content,' " 468–70.

12. See ibid., 444–45; and "The Water Works," *Pueblo Daily Chieftain*, 8 April 1890, 2.

13. "Water Trustees 'Good Showing,' " 1 January 1901, 19; "Progress of Pueblo Water Co.," 1 January 1903, 10; and "Water Works Vastly Improved," 1 January 1901, 24—all in *Pueblo Daily Chieftain*.

14. Sherow, "Discord in the 'Valley of Content,' " 470–71; and Henry, "Water," 46–49.

15. See Sherow, "Discord in the 'Valley of Content,' " p. 449; "Flow of Arkansas at Lowest Ebb in Recorded History," *Pueblo Daily Chieftain*, 7 July 1934, 1; and "Arkansas River Goes Dry, Second Time in History," ibid., 24 March 1935, 2.

16. Preliminary Report on Wurtz Ditch, folder no. 8H, James W. Preston Files, BPWW; and *Baker et al. v. City of Pueblo et al.*, #12171, 87 Colo. 489–97 (1930).

17. James W. Preston to Trustees of the Pueblo Water Works, 27 June 1938, folder no. 8H; and A. W. McHendrie to James W. Preston, 9 November 1935, folder no. 8H; Charles Patterson, "Report on the Wurtz Ditch to the Trustees of the Pueblo Water Works," 6 September 1937, 3–8, folder no. 8H, James W. Preston Files, BPWW.

18. Patterson, "Report on the Wurtz Ditch," 3–8, folder no. 8H; Minutes of meeting of Tennessee Pass Water Association and the Trustees of the Pueblo Water Works, 26 January 1938, folder no. 8H; Certificate from the city clerk of Pueblo, 1 April 1938, folder no. 8H, James W. Preston Files, BPWW.

19. Follansbee and Jones, *Arkansas River Flood of June 3–5, 1921*, 7–9.

20. Trustees of the Pueblo Water Works to Lt. Col. R. E. Cole, 1 April 1944, folder no. 1, James W. Preston Files, BPWW.

21. Dana E. Depner, "Report on an Investigation of the Pollution of the Arkansas River above Pueblo, Colorado, 1928", folder no. 1; T. Storer to C. G. Nikick, 29 April 1929, folder no. 1; and "Memorandum: Suit Brought against the Colorado Zinc and Lead Company to Prevent Pollution of the Arkansas River," 7 September 1928, folder no. 1, James W. Preston Files, BPWW.

22. Henry, "Water," 16–17, 26–27, folder no. 1; and Dana E. Depner, "Report on the Sanitation of the Public Water Supply at Pueblo, Colorado, 1928," folder no. 1, James W. Preston Files, BPWW.

23. Henry, "Water," 18.

24. "Filtered Water Comes Too High," *Pueblo Daily Chieftain*, 9 May 1901, 4; and "Fountain Underflow Project Means Pure Water for Pueblo," ibid., 1 January 1908, 15.

25. *Pueblo Daily Chieftain*, 7 January 1908, 2.

26. "Fountain Underflow to Be Turned Off to Await Chance for a Better Test," *Pueblo Daily Chieftain*, 11 January 1908, 1; "At Big Mass Meeting Water Trustees Pass Resolution to Shut Off the Fountain Underflow from City Mains," ibid., 12 January 1908, 1; and Henry, "Water," 16.

27. Henry, "Water," 51–53; 59–66, folder no. 1; and Trustees of the Pueblo Water Works and Board of Directors of Public Water Works District No. 2 of the City of Pueblo to Harold H. Christy and Charles J. Beise, 13 July 1949, folder no. 1, James W. Preston Files, BPWW.

28. Marshall Sprague, *Newport in the Rockies* (Denver: Sage Books, 1961), 29–31.

29. *Colorado Springs Weekly Gazette*, 2 January 1875, 2; "Water Supply Overtakes, Forges Ahead City Needs," 27 December 1936, scrapbook (June 1935 to 12 October 1937), PUOCS. The scrapbooks contain clippings mostly from the *Colorado Springs Weekly Gazette, Evening Telegraph*, and *Colorado Springs Gazette-Telegraph* and cover issues relating to water, gas, electric, and sewage services.

30. *Colorado Springs Weekly Gazette*, 13 November 1875, 2; and 4 December 1875, 2.

31. "54 Years Ago C. S. Got First Water Supply," December 1932, scrapbook (1932–38), PUOCS; from the *Colorado Springs Weekly Gazette*: "The Water Question," 12 January 1878, 2; 19 January 1878, 2; "The Water Question," 26 January 1878, 2; "The Water Question," 2 February 1878, 2; 6 April 1878, 2; and "Supplement," 20 April 1878, 1.

32. "Aqua Pura," 10 December 1878, 4; "At Last—Water! Water! Water!" 5 December 1878, 4; and "The Water Works" 3 December 1878, 4—all from *Colorado Springs Weekly Gazette*.

33. H. I. Reid, "The Water-Works of Colorado Springs and the Strickler Tunnel," *Engineering News* 36 (27 August 1896): 131–34; "History of Water System—Colorado Springs," 27 January 1961, file "Historical," Board of Public Utilities, WDCS; and "Our Mountain Water System," *Colorado Springs Daily Gazette*, 31 December 1899, 1.

34. Reid, "Water-Works of Colorado Springs and the Strickler Tunnel," 132; and *Strickler v. City of Colorado Springs*, #2863, 16 Colo. 61–75 (1891).

35. "Millions of Gallons of Water Are Stolen by Daring Masked Men," file "Historical," Board of Public Utilities, WDCS; "Victor Steals 25,000,000 Gallons," *Colorado Springs Daily Gazette* 24 June 1909, 1; "Victor," ibid., 26 June 1909, 1; and "Victor to Be Given Water," ibid., 24 July 1909, 5.

36. "Committee Reports on Water Situation," *Colorado Springs Daily Gazette*, 14 July 1908, 1 and 2.

37. Ibid.; "Water Reports Are Approved," *Colorado Springs Daily Gazette*, 15 August 1908, 1 and 3; and "Citizens Call Mass Meeting," ibid., 13 August 1908, 1.

38. "City Officials Are Requested to Resign," *Colorado Springs Daily Gazette*, 17 July 1908, 1; and "Competent Engineer to Go Over Water System," ibid., 14 July 1916, 6.

39. "Water Supply Is Adequate; Additions to Cost $720,000 Recommended by Engineer," *Colorado Springs Daily Gazette*, 13 December 1916, 1 and 6; and "Anderson Presents Results of His Recent Survey Here and Outlines Vast Project," ibid., 9 December 1919, 1 and 2.

40. For a discussion of instrumentalism see Max Horkheimer's *The Eclipse of Reason* (New York: Oxford University Press, 1947), esp. chap. 3, "The Revolt of Nature"; Leiss, *Domination of Nature*; and Donald Worster, "Preface to New Edition" in his *Nature's Economy* (San Francisco: Sierra Club Books, 1977; reprint, New York: Cambridge University Press, 1985), vii–xii; and idem, "Taxonomy: The Flow of Power in History," in *Rivers of Empire*, 19–60.

41. See Sherow, "Discord in the 'Valley of Content,' " 444–45, 471–73; and E. C. Davis, "Report of Water Commissioner," in *City of Colorado Springs: Town Incorporation, City Organization and Reorganization, also Classification as City of the First Class* (Colorado Springs: City Council, 1902), 142–144.

42. "Water Reserve Situation Now Getting Worse," 8 July 1932, and "Water Violators Fined $15 Each," 22 July 1932, scrapbook (1932–38); " 'Conserve Water' Plea of Officials," 15 June 1934, and "1934 Driest Year City Has Ever Known," 1 January 1935, scrapbook (23 April 1934 to 1 June 1935); "Lack of Data on City's Cost Delays Water Case," 2 February 1950, scrapbook (1949–51)—all at PUOCS.

43. "Development North Slope Watershed Began in 1908," 28 November 1932, scrapbook (17 August 1932 to 24 March 1933), PUOCS.

44. "North Slope Water Job Blocked by F. F. Schreiber," 10 September 1933, and "City Girds for Battle for North Slope Project," 13 February 1934, scrapbook (29 August 1933 to 20 April 1934), PUOCS; and *Town of Green Mountain Falls v. Colorado Springs*, #13494, 97 Colo. 420–21 (1935).

45. "Water Project Grant is Okayed Today at Capital," 13 October 1933, and "U.S. to Ignore Ute Pass Protest," 10 March 1934, scrapbook (29 August 1933 to 20 April 1934); "To Dedicate $2,000,000 North Slope Project Today," 12 September 1937, scrapbook (June 1935 to 12 October 1937), PUOCS.

46. "Lack of Data on City's Cost Delays Water Case," 2 February 1950, scrapbook (1949–51); and "Army Camp Touching Many People in Many Ways and Is Only the Beginning," 22 February 1942, scrapbook (December 1940 to December 1943), PUOCS.

47. "Pipeline Cost Is $4,000,000," 7 December 1944; "City to Take 'Gamble' on Blue River," 11 August 1948; "City Will Spend 16 Million If All Projects Materialize," 17 February 1949; "Springs' Long-Range Water Outlay Figured at $24,750,000," 13 July 1949—all in scrapbook (1944–49), PUOCS; and "Colorado Springs in Water Quest," 2 December 1951, scrapbook (1951–52), PUOCS.

48. "City Begins Project to Stake Claim for Blue River Waters," September 1948; "City to Purchase Northfield Co.," 13 April 1949; "Northfield Purchase Clears State PUC [Public Utility Commission]," 4 June 1949—scrapbook (1944–49), PUOCS.

49. "Carr Maps City's Last Stand Against U.S. Water Grab," 7 July 1949,

scrapbook (1944–49); "City to Present Its Side of Water Case This Week," 11 December 1949, scrapbook (1949–51), PUOCS.

50. "Growth of Springs Linked to Future of Water Supplies," 31 January 1950; "Lack of Data on City's Cost Delays Water Case," 2 February 1950; "City Battles Federal Claim to Blue River in U.S. Court," 2 July 1950—scrapbook (1949–50); and "Blue River Water Flows Thru Hoosier Pass Bore," 2 August 1951, scrapbook (1951–52), PUOCS.

51. "Water Decision in City's Favor," 30 November 1951, scrapbook (1951–52), PUOCS.

52. B. B. McReynolds to the Cresson Construction Co., 24 June 1918, file "Historical," WDCS.

53. Burton Lourther, "A Report on the Sanitation on the Municipal Water Shed of Colorado Springs, Colorado," typewritten, 1927, file "Historical"; "History of Water System—Colorado Springs," file "Historical"; and "Report upon the Water Collecting System of Colorado Springs, Colorado, by the Committee Appointed by the Chamber of Commerce of this City," 15 January 1912, file "Historical," WDCS; "Grants Restrain City's Use of Watershed for Recreation," 18 May 1948, scrapbook (1944–49); "Anti-Fishing Ordinance, Fence on Watershed Planned by City," 18 October 1950, and "City Begins Building Fences on Pikes Peak Watershed," 20 October 1950, scrapbook (1949–50) PUOCS.

54. Henry, "Water," 19–20.

55. Scamehorn, *Pioneer Steelmaker in the West*, 46–47.

56. *Second Annual Report of the Colorado Coal and Iron Co.*, 31 December 1880, 14; and *Third Annual Report of the Colorado Coal and Iron Co.*, 31 December 1881, 21–22.

57. Scamehorn, *Pioneer Steelmaker in the West*, 51–54.

58. Ibid., 66–67; and "Present Status of C.F.&I. Water Supply," 1, ff 183, CF&IC, CHS.

59. *Twelfth Annual Report of the Colorado Coal and Iron Co.*, 31 December 1890, 18; and Scamehorn, *Pioneer Steelmaker in the West*, 68.

60. Scamehorn, *Pioneer Steelmaker in the West*, 91–105.

61. "Present Status of C.F.&I. Water Supply," 5; and "Methods of Utilizing the Arkansas River Water Rights Considered," 3, ff 183, CF&IC, CHS.

62. Ralph W. Adkins, "Water Supply for an Integrated Steel Plant at High Altitude" (Paper presented at San Francisco Regional Technical Meeting of American Iron and Steel Institute, 9 November 1962), 8.

63. "Colorado Fuel and Iron Company Water Rights," part 1, chap. 1, 2–4, box 11, CF&IC; and Devine & Dubbs to Cass E. Herrington, 20 January 1905, ff 183, CF&IC, CHS.

64. Ibid.

65. John Birkinbine, *Report on the Water Supply of the Minnequa Works at Pueblo, Colo.* (Philadelphia, Pa.: Smith-Brooks Press, 1906), 8–9, ff 185, CF&IC, CHS; Devin & Dubbs to Cass E. Herrington, 20 January 1905, ff 183, CF&IC, CHS.

66. Untitled estimates of the Arkansas Valley conduit, ff 184, CF&IC, CHS; and Birkinbine, *Report on the Water Supply of the Minnequa Works*, 9–11, ff 185, CF&IC, CHS.

67. *Kansas v. Colorado*, D. C. Beaman's Testimony, vol. 5, 2463–82.

68. R. M. Hosea, "Minnequa Steel Works Water Supply," *Camp and Plant* 2 (29 November 1902): 514; *Kansas v. Colorado*, Testimony and Proceedings, 2464–67; and Sherow, "Discord in the 'Valley of Content,' " pp. 474–75.

69. Radosevich et al., *Evolution and Administration of Colorado Water Law*, 16–

19; and Charles L. Patterson, "Preliminary Report: Disposal of Water Used for Industrial Purposes at Steel Plant of C.F.&I. Corp., Pueblo, Colo., June 1942," location #20019, administrative files, CWCB, CSA.

70. Adkins, "Water Supply for an Integrated Steel Plant," 3; and interview with Harold Christy conducted by Dr. H. Lee Scamehorn, Pueblo, Colorado, 29 and 30 June 1982.

71. Interview with Harold Christy.

72. Ibid.; and Adkins, "Water Supply for an Integrated Steel Plant," 2–8.

73. Interview with Ralph D. Adkins, Pueblo, Colorado, 9 July 1986; "Colorado Fuel and Iron Company Water Rights," part 1, chap. 4, 164–66, box 11, CF&IC, CHS; and Sherow, "Discord in the 'Valley of Content,' " p. 474.

CHAPTER FIVE. IRRIGATION IN SOUTHWESTERN KANSAS, 1870–1950

1. *The State of Colorado, Complainant, v. The State of Kansas, and The Finney County Water Users' Association, a Corporation, Defendants,* United States Supreme Court, October Term, 1928, No. 14, Original, Transcript of Evidence, C. L. Patterson's Testimony, vol. 4, 510–21, DWR, KSBA.

2. *Kansas v. Colorado,* R. E. Edward's Testimony, vol. 3, 1099–1100, and Robert Wright's Testimony, 1208–9, and A. E. Pyle's Testimony, vol. 4, 1852, CSA.

3. See Sherow, "Discord in the 'Valley of Content,' " pp. 450–51.

4. Kenneth H. Sallee, Vernon L. Hamilton, Charles W. McBee, and Edward L. Fleming, *Soil Survey of Kearny County, Kansas* (Washington, D.C.: Government Printing Office, 1963), 4–5, 14, and 42–43.

5. *Colorado v. Kansas,* C. L. Patterson's Testimony, vol. 4, 521–25, DWR, KSBA.

6. Richard Pfister, *Water Resources and Irrigation,* Economic Development in Southwestern Kansas, part 4 (Lawrence: University of Kansas Press, 1955), 7–24.

7. Ibid.

8. Richard J. Hinton, "Irrigation in the Arid West," *Harper's Weekly* 32 (22 September 1888): 729, Subject Collection, Agriculture—Insects—Irrigation in Colorado, CHS.

9. "Birth of Irrigation in Kansas," *Irrigation Age* 6 (March 1894): 95; and F. Dumont Smith, "Cross Examination of R. I. Meeker: Notes by F. Dumont Smith," 9, file 1932, "*Kansas v. Colorado,* 1931–32," KAG, KSHS.

10. Anne M. Marvin, "The Fertile Domain: Irrigation as Adaptation in the Garden City, Kansas, Area, 1880–1910" (Ph.D. dissertation, University of Kansas, 1985), 58–59.

11. Marvin, "The Fertile Domain," 60–61.

12. *Colorado v. Kansas,* C. L. Patterson's Testimony, vol. 21, 3468–69, DWR, KSBA; and Marvin, "The Fertile Domain," 64 and 69.

13. *Colorado v. Kansas,* C. L. Patterson's Testimony, vol. 21, 3469–71, DWR, KSBA; Marvin, "The Fertile Domain," 91–94, 144–47; and *United States Irrigating Company v. Graham Ditch Company, et al.* (C.C.D. Colo.) (#5578), C. J. Jones's Testimony, vol. 11, 5084, location #48000, CSA.

14. *Colorado v. Kansas,* C. L. Patterson's Testimony, vol. 21, 3494–96, 3501,

DWR, KSBA; Marvin, "The Fertile Domain," 225–26, 255–57, and 258–59; and *United States Irrigating Company v. Graham Ditch Company*, George Garrettson's Testimony, vol. 8, 3561–62, 3566, and 3894.

15. *Colorado v. Kansas*, C. L. Patterson's Testimony, vol. 21, 3501–5, DWR, KSBA.

16. Ibid., C. L. Patterson's Testimony, vol. 20, 3465–68, and vol. 21, 3501–5, DWR, KSBA; and Marvin, "The Fertile Domain," 63, 67, 70, 87–88, 91, 226, and 262.

17. *Colorado v. Kansas*, C. L. Patterson's Testimony, vol. 20, 3471–73, DWR, KSBA; and Marvin, "The Fertile Domain," 64, 69, 74, 98, 228, and 262.

18. *Colorado v. Kansas*, C. L. Patterson's Testimony, vol. 20, 3473–74, DWR, KSBA; and *United States Irrigating Company v. Graham Ditch Company*, C. J. Jones's Testimony, vol. 11, 5099–5102.

19. Marvin, "The Fertile Domain," 167–69, 226–29, 259–60, 262, and 263; and *Colorado v. Kansas*, C. L. Patterson's Testimony, vol. 20, 3474, and vol. 21, 3496, DWR, KSBA.

20. "Kansas," *Irrigation Age* 2 (June 1893): 26; G. D. Buchanan, "The Water Supply for Western Kansas," *Irrigation Age* 8 (March 1895): 118; J. W. Gregory, "Irrigation in Southwest Kansas: Experience Teaches Practicability of Pump Irrigation," *Irrigation Age* 8 (January 1895): 13–17; and Marvin, "The Fertile Domain," 248–51 and 263–67.

21. F. B. Nichols, "Pumping Irrigation in Kansas," *Irrigation Age* 31 (January 1916): 42; and Marvin, "The Fertile Domain," 345.

22. R. H. Faxon, "Garden City, Kansas, and Vicinity," *Irrigation Age* 24 (January 1909): 85–86; Marvin, "The Fertile Domain," 227–28; and George B. Harrison, "The Beet-Sugar Industry in Kansas," in *Fifteenth Biennial Report of the State Board of Agriculture*, 1905–6 (Topeka: State Printer, 1907), 921–22.

23. *Colorado v. Kansas*, C. L. Patterson's Testimony, vol. 21, 3508–10, DWR, KSBA; and Marvin, "The Fertile Domain," 320–21.

24. Ibid.

25. *United States Irrigating Company v. Graham Ditch Company*, C. J. Jones's Testimony, vol. 11, 5180–81, 5186, and 5211.

26. Ibid., 5195. William George, an officer of the Arkansas Valley Beet, Land and Irrigation Company, stated in his testimony that the investors made a profit of over $100,000 in cash and $50,000 in United States Irrigation Company stock.

27. Ibid., F. A. Gillespie's Testimony, vol. 12, 5970, and vol. 13, 6343–63. Also see Eugene Stoeckly, "A Company and Factory," n.d., and Barbara Oringderff, "A Short History of the United States Sugar and Land Company, Now Called the Garden City Company," n.d., Garden City Company files, for additional information on the sugar factory.

28. R. H. Faxon, "Garden City, Kansas, and Vicinity," *Irrigation Age* 24 (January 1909): 85; and idem, "Garden City, Kansas, and Vicinity," *Irrigation Age* 24 (July 1909): 347.

29. Marvin, "The Fertile Domain," 199–208.

30. U.S. Congress, Senate, *Report of the Special Committee on the Irrigation and Reclamation of Arid Lands*, S. Rep. 928, 51st Cong., 1st sess., 27, 69–73, 88–89, and 183–91.

31. Conner Sorensen, "Federal Reclamation on the High Plains: The Garden City Project," *Great Plains Journal* 15 (Spring 1976): 114–33; and Marvin, "The Fertile Domain," 330–44. The Reclamation Service, which was created by the Newlands Act of 1902, became the Bureau of Reclamation in 1923.

32. *United States Irrigating Company v. Graham Ditch Company*, F. A. Gillespie's Testimony, vol. 13, 6061–64.

33. Sorensen, "Federal Reclamation on the High Plains," 129–30.

34. R. H. Faxon, "Garden City, Kansas, and Vicinity," *Irrigation Age* 24 (February 1909): 116; and idem, "Garden City, Kansas, and Vicinity," *Irrigation Age* 24 (April 1909): 175–76.

35. Pfister, *Water Resources and Irrigation*, 30–31.

36. Ibid., 31–32.

37. Ibid., 32–35; and Wells A. Hutchins, R. V. Smrha, and Robert L. Smith, *The Kansas Law of Water Rights* (Topeka, Kans.: State Board of Agriculture, 1957), 43–44.

38. Pfister, *Water Resources and Irrigation*, 35–44; Hutchins et al., *Kansas Law of Water Rights*, 44–48; and R. V. Smrha, "George Knapp and the Kansas Water Rights Act," *Kansas Water News* 9 (April 1966): 3–4.

39. *United States Irrigating Company v. Graham Ditch Company*, James Craig's Testimony, vol. 8, 3796–3852, and C. J. Jones's Testimony, vol. 11, 5099–5115.

40. *Colorado v. Kansas*, C. L. Patterson's Testimony, vol. 21, 3496–3501, DWR, KSBA.

41. Ibid., 3530–37.

42. Ibid.

43. Ibid., 3515; and *United States Irrigating Company v. Graham Ditch Company*, F. A. Gillespie's Testimony, vol. 12, 5969–72, 5974–76, and 5980–81.

44. *United States Irrigating Company v. Graham Ditch Company*, Clarence C. Hamlin's Testimony, vol. 13, 6359–63; and *Colorado v. Kansas*, C. L. Patterson's Testimony, vol. 21, 3515–17, DWR, KSBA.

45. *United States Irrigating Company v. Graham Ditch Company*, F. A. Gillespie's Testimony, vol. 12, 5980–81 and 6152–55.

46. See Sherow, "Discord in the 'Valley of Content,' " 422.

47. See ibid., 477.

48. See ibid., 478.

49. Melvin Scanlan to George Knapp, 26 May 1942, and George Knapp to Melvin Scanlan, 29 May 1942, file "General Correspondence," box 10, Water Resources Division, KSBA; Smith, "Cross Examination of R. I. Meeker: Notes," 9, file 1932, "*Kansas v. Colorado*, 1931–32," KAG, KSHS; *Colorado v. Kansas*, T. E. Grable's Testimony, vol. 7, 1021–26, and George Knapp's Testimony, vol. 39, 7058–59, DWR, KSBA; and Sherow, "Discord in the 'Valley of Content,' " 460–61.

50. See Sherow, "Discord in the 'Valley of Content,' " 479–85; and Knapp to Scanlan, 29 May 1942.

51. Pfister, *Water Resources and Irrigation*, 69–79; and memorandum, "October 14, 1929, Colorado vs. Kansas, et al.," file 1929, "Kansas v. Colorado, 1927–1930," KAG, KSHS.

52. Pfister, *Water Resources and Irrigation*, 76–77; and W. James Foreman and Robert S. Eckley, *Agriculture*, Economic Development in Southwestern Kansas, part 5 (Lawrence: University of Kansas Press, 1955), 76–77, 102–3, and 106–10.

53. Pfister, *Water Resources and Irrigation*, 69; and U.S. Department of Commerce, Bureau of the Census, *Seventeenth Census of the United States, 1950: Irrigation of Agricultural Lands* (Washington, D.C.: Government Printing Office, 1950), 7:20–21.

54. Abstracts of the Minutes of the Colorado-Kansas Arkansas River Compact Commission, meeting no. 5, 20–21, Hill and Robbins Law Firm, Denver,

Colorado; and Kansas Water Resources Board, *State Water Plan Studies*, part A, *Preliminary Appraisal of Kansas Water Problems: Section II. Upper Arkansas Unit* (Topeka: State Printing Office, 1962), 48–53.

55. Kansas Water Resources Board, *State Water Plan Studies*, part A, *Preliminary Appraisal*, 54–64; and Pfister, *Water Resources and Irrigation*, 7–44.

56. Robinson, *Introduction, Spread, and Areal Extent of Saltcedar*, A7–A10.

CHAPTER SIX. THE CONTEST FOR THE "NILE OF AMERICA": *KANSAS V. COLORADO*, 1890–1910

1. The case was decided in the October 1906 session of the Supreme Court and thus appears in the 1906 volume of the court reports. The decision was announced on 13 May 1907, however, so the case is conventionally dated 1907.

2. Hurst, *Law and Social Order in the United States*, 42–47; for a notable achievement in this direction, see Arthur F. McEvoy, "Toward an Interactive Theory of Nature and Culture: Ecology, Production, and Cognition in the California Fishing Industry," in *The Ends of the Earth: Perspectives on Modern Environmental History*, ed. Donald Worster (Cambridge: Cambridge University Press, 1988), 211–29.

3. Worster, *Dust Bowl*, 6.

4. White, *Land Use, Environment, and Social Change*, 14; and McEvoy, *The Fisherman's Problem*, 14. For a discussion of how the prior appropriation doctrine has been used as a tool for furthering economic growth, see Lilley and Gould, "The Western Irrigation Movement, 1878–1902," in *American West*, ed. Gene Greeley, 63; Pisani, "Enterprise and Equity," 15–37; and Worster, *Rivers of Empire*, 83–96.

5. Transcript, *Kansas v. Colorado*, Oral Arguments of Counsel on Final Hearing, 17–20 December 1906, Oral Argument of Nelson H. Loomis for Complainant, 41; and Oral Argument of David C. Beaman, Solicitor for Defendant the Colorado Fuel and Iron Company, 61–64, microfiche card 55, UCLL. (Hereafter, "Transcript, *Kansas v. Colorado*," denotes the use of the microfiche collection at UCLL.)

6. Transcript, *Kansas v. Colorado*, Oral Arguments of Counsel on Final Hearing, 17–20 December 1906, Oral Argument of A. C. Campbell for Intervenor, 91–92, microfiche card 56, UCLL.

7. *Kansas v. Colorado*, R. E. Lawrence's Testimony, vol. 1, 388, 471–72, location #47932, CSA; and H. Craig Miner, *Wichita: The Early Years, 1865–80* (Lincoln: University of Nebraska Press, 1982), 149–50.

8. Walter H. Schowe, "The Geography of Kansas: Hydrogeography," *Transactions of the Kansas Academy of Science* 56 (June 1953): 175.

9. *United States Irrigating Company v. Graham Ditch Company*, C. J. Jones's Testimony, vol. 11, 5108, CSA.

10. Senate *Report of the Special Committee on the Irrigation and Reclamation of Arid Lands*, S. Rep. 928, 51st Cong., 1st sess., 186, 201–2.

11. Ibid., 112.

12. Wallace Stegner, *Beyond the Hundredth Meridian: John Wesley Powell and the Second Opening of the West* (Lincoln: University of Nebraska Press, 1953), 202–38; Orren Donaldson, "Irrigation and State Boundaries: A Problem of the Arid West and Its Solution," *Irrigation Age* 8 (February 1895): 47–53; and Elwood Mead, "An

Unsolved Western Problem: The Division of the Waters of Inter-State Streams,"
Irrigation Age 7 (July 1894): 15.

13. Miner, *Wichita*, 149–51; *Kansas v. Colorado*, vol. 1, R. E. Lawrence's Testimony, 388, 471–72, and 569–70, and Marshall Murdock's Testimony, vol. 1, 9–10; and Transcript, *Kansas v. Colorado*, Oral Arguments of Counsel on Final Hearing, 17–20 December 1906, Argument of S. S. Ashbaugh, 24, microfiche card 55, UCLL.

14. *Kansas v. Colorado*, Marshall Murdock's Testimony, vol. 1, 9–10; Hutchins et al., *Kansas Law of Water Rights*, 38–48; and "The Original Jurisdiction of the United States Supreme Court," *Stanford Law Review* 2 (July 1959): 669, 681–83

15. U.S. Supreme Court, *The State of Kansas, Complainant, vs. The State of Colorado et al., and the United States, Intervenor. In Equity. Transcript of Record.* October Term, 1905. No. 7, Original. Vol. 1, "The State of Kansas, Complainant, vs. The State of Colorado, Defendant. Bill in Equity." (Washington, D.C.: Judd & Detweiler, 1905), 6–19 (hereafter referred to as *Transcript of Record*); and Transcript, *Kansas v. Colorado*, Brief of Complainant on Final Hearing, microfiche card 28, UCLL.

16. *Transcript of Record*, "The State of Kansas, Complainant, vs. The State of Colorado et al., Defendants. Amended Bill in Equity," 62–75.

17. *Transcript of Record*, "The State of Kansas, Plaintiff, vs. The State of Colorado, Defendant. Demurrer to Bill," 23–25; and "The State of Kansas, Complainant, vs. The State of Colorado, Defendant. The Answer of the State of Colorado, Defendant, to the Bill of Complaint of the State of Kansas, Complainant," 46–57; and Transcript, *Kansas v. Colorado*, Brief on Behalf of the State of Colorado on Final Hearing, microfiche cards 46–49, and Brief of the State of Colorado in Reply to Brief of Intervenor, microfiche card 52, UCLL. On the Harmon Doctrine, see Robert D. Scott, "Kansas v. Colorado Revisited," *American Journal of International Law* 52 (July 1958): 432.

18. *Transcript of Record*, "The State of Kansas, Complainant, vs. The State of Colorado et al., Defendants. Answer of the Colorado Fuel and Iron Company to Amended Bill," 190–208; and Transcript, *Kansas v. Colorado*, Brief of Counsel for the Arkansas Valley Sugar Beet and Irrigated Land Company and other Individual Defendants, in Support of their Motion to Dismiss the Bill of Complaint Herein, microfiche card 45, UCLL.

19. Francis K. Carey to N. C. Miller, 16 October 1903, attorney general, general correspondence, location #18348, CSA.

20. Donald J. Pisani, "State vs. Nation: Federal Reclamation and Water Rights in the Progressive Era," *Pacific Historical Review* 51 (August 1982): 276.

21. *Transcript of Record*, "The State of Kansas, Complainant, v. The State of Colorado et al., Defendants. Petition of Intervention on Behalf of the United States," 235–40; Transcript, *Kansas v. Colorado*, Brief for the United States on Final Hearing, microfiche cards 34–35; Summary of Solicitor General's Oral Argument Filed by Leave of Court with Some Additional Considerations, 1–23, microfiche card 39; Brief for the United States on Final Hearing, microfiche card 56, UCLL.

22. Transcript, *Kansas v. Colorado*, Summary of Solicitor General's Oral Argument Filed by Leave of Court with Some Additional Considerations," 10–11, microfiche card 39; Oral Arguments of Counsel on Final Hearing, 17–20 December 1906, Argument of A. C. Campbell, 119–20, microfiche card 56, UCLL. See also Lucien Hugh Alexander, "James Wilson, Patriot, and the Wilson Doctrine," *North American Review* 183 (16 November 1906): 971–89.

23. C. C. Coleman to N. C. Miller, 4 May 1904, and summary of testimony

(untitled), n.d., attorney general, general correspondence, location #18348, CSA; and Transcript, *Kansas v. Colorado*, State of Complainant in Support of Motion for a Rule to Assign the Case for Hearing, 1–3, microfiche card 28, UCLL; "Original Jurisdiction of the United States Supreme Court," 688.

24. C. C. Coleman to Morris Bien, 10 January 1907, enclosed "copy of C. C. Coleman's argument before the Supreme Court," 7, U.S. Department of Interior, Reclamation Service, correspondence re *Kansas vs. Colorado*, RG 115, File 665.

25. *Kansas v. Colorado*, Louis G. Carpenter's Testimony, vol. 5, 2260–65.

26. D. C. Beaman summarized the lack of specificity in the Kansans' testimonies as to the exact nature of the Arkansas River flow. See Transcript, *Kansas v. Colorado*, Brief for Defendant, the Colorado Fuel and Iron Company, on Final Hearing, 47–59, microfiche card 51, UCLL.

27. *Kansas v. Colorado*, Louis G. Carpenter's Testimony, vol. 5, 2259–87, location #47936, CSA. Carpenter even quoted findings from geologists associated with the colleges in Kansas to prove his points about the "underflow," witnesses whom Kansas attorneys never had testify. See also Charles S. Slichter's Testimony, vol. 11, 5141–5228; and Charles S. Slichter, *The Underflow in Arkansas Valley in Western Kansas*, U.S. Geological Survey Water Supply and Irrigation Paper 153 (Washington, D.C.: Government Printing Office, 1906).

28. *Kansas v. Colorado*, Frederick H. Newell's Testimony, vol. 10, 4876–77, location #47961, CSA.

29. Ira G. Clark, "The Elephant Butte Controversy: A Chapter in the Emergence of Federal Water Law," *Journal of American History* 61 (March 1975): 1006–33.

30. *Kansas v. Colorado*, Louis G. Carpenter's Testimony, vol. 5, 2068–70, location #47936, CSA.

31. *Kansas v. Colorado*, Frederick Newell's Testimony, vol. 10, 4854, 4870–76, and 4903; and Elwood Mead's Testimony, vol. 11, 5275.

32. *Transcript of Record*, vol. 1, J. A. Van Orsdel's abstracted testimony, 1055–61.

33. Ibid., vol. 2, B. F. Stock's abstracted testimony, 1475–91.

34. J. R. Mulvane to N. C. Miller, 2 May 1903; J. R. Sites to Charles Hayt, 27 September 1904; and L. A. Young to N. C. Miller, 13 July 1904 and 18 July 1904, attorney general, general correspondence, location #18348, CSA.

35. "Spread It Out," (Topeka, Kansas) *Journal*, 11 August 1903, L. G. Carpenter Scrapbooks, vol. 1, WHC/DPL; N. C. Miller to William A. Hill, 13 April 1903, attorney general, letterpress book, location #19101, CSA.

36. D. C. Beaman to N. C. Miller, 3 August 1904, attorney general, general correspondence, location #18384, CSA; Francis K. Carey to N. C. Miller, 16 October 1903, attorney general, general correspondence, location #18384, CSA; and "Denver Post Makes Vicious Attack on Prof. Carpenter," *Republican*, 8 June 1905.

37. D. C. Beaman to Charles D. Walcott, 11 November 1903; and Morris Bien to A. E. Chandler, 22 December 1906, U.S. Department of Interior, Reclamation Service, correspondence re *Kansas v. Colorado*, RG 115, file 665.

38. *State of Kansas, Complainant, v. State of Colorado et al., Defendants, The United States of America, Intervenor*, 206 U.S. 672–76; and Transcript, *Kansas v. Colorado*, Oral Argument of Nelson H. Loomis, 58–60, microfiche card 55, UCLL.

39. *Kansas v. Colorado*, 206 U.S. 672–76; and Mark J. Wagner, "The Parting of the Waters—The Dispute between Colorado and Kansas over the Arkansas River," *Washburn Law Journal* 24 (1984): 101–2.

40. *Kansas v. Colorado*, 206 U.S. 653–67.

41. Pisani, "State vs. Nation," 276–82; A. L. Fellows to Morris Bien, 1 June 1907, and Morris Bien to A. L. Fellows, 5 June 1907, RG 115, file 665; and *Fort Collins Evening Courier*, 9 July 1907, L. G. Carpenter scrapbooks, vol. 1, WHC/DPL.

42. "Colorado Wins Out in Famous Water Case," *Daily Chieftain*, 14 May 1907, 1 and 7.

43. *United States Irrigating Company v. Graham Ditch Company, et al.*, Transcript of Evidence, C. J. Jones's Testimony, vol. 11, 5108–15.

44. The creation of prior appropriation as a means of economic development rather than environmental adaptation is ably argued by Donald Pisani, in "Enterprise and Equity."

CHAPTER SEVEN. INCREASING THE WATER SUPPLY FOR ALL, 1910–1939

1. U.S. Congress, Senate, *The Effect upon Certain Rivers in Colorado of the Diversion of Water for Irrigation*, by J. W. Powell, Sen. Ex. Doc. 120, vol. 3, 50th Cong., 2d sess., 1889. On Powell's instrumentalism, see Worster, *Rivers of Empire*, 133–35.

2. *United States Irrigating Company v. Graham Ditch Company*, William George's Testimony, vol. 11, 5180–86 and 5211, location #48000, CSA.

3. For future reference, it would be helpful to note here the reorganizations of the United States Sugar and Land Company—which became the Garden City Sugar and Land Company in 1913, the Garden City Company in 1920, and The Garden City Company in 1930.

4. *United States Irrigating Company v. Graham Ditch Company*, Clarence C. Hamlin's Testimony, vol. 13, 6342–44 and 6350, location #48000, CSA.

5. Ibid., 6359–63.

6. *United States Irrigating Company v. Graham Ditch Company*, Bill of Complaint, filed 27 August 1910, box 1028, RG 21, FRCD.

7. Ibid., Brief of Defendants in Support of Their Several Demurrers to the Bill of Complaint, filed 1 May 1911.

8. Ibid., Memorandum of Ruling on Exceptions to Answer, filed 19 March 1912.

9. *United States Irrigating Company v. Graham Ditch Company*, vols. 7–13. See F. A. Gillespie's Testimony, 5937–99, and 6007–6205; and Clarence C. Hamlin's Testimony, 6330–6434.

10. "Contract of the United States Irrigating Company, the Finney County Water Users' Association, the Kearny County Farmers' Irrigation Association, and the Garden City Irrigation Association with the Graham Ditch Company, et al., 1916," file "Miscellaneous Documents, *Kansas v. Colorado*," KAG, KSHS.

11. *United States Irrigating Company v. Graham Ditch Company, et al.*, Motion of Finney County Water Users' Association for Leave to Intervene; and Order: Denying Motion of Finney County Water Users' Association (C.C.D. Colo.) (#5578), RG21, FRCD; and F. Dumont Smith to William A. Smith, 14 December 1927, file 1927, "Kansas v. Colorado, 1927–30," KAG, KSHS.

12. F. Dumont Smith to William A. Smith, 14 December 1927, file 1927, "Kansas v. Colorado, 1927–30," KAG, KSHS.

13. Ibid.; and A. W. McHendrie, "[History of Caddoa Reservoir District]," n.d., 9–10, ff 307; and Vena Pointer, "Report to the Colorado Water Conservation Board concerning Irrigation and Water Problems of the Arkansas Valley, Colorado," 1937, 2, ff 305, AVDA, CHS.

14. Clarence T. Johnson, state engineer of Wyoming, abstracted testimony, 1022–34; Nellis E. Corthell, attorney from Laramie, Wyoming, 1034–44, S. C. Downing, secretary of the Wyoming Central Land and Improvement Company, 1045–46; Gibson Clark, attorney in Cheyenne, Wyoming, and a former state supreme court justice, 1047–54; and J. A. Van Orsdel, attorney general of Wyoming, 1055–61—all in *Transcript of Record*, vol. 1.

15. Hundley, *Water and the West*, 76–78, 177–80; and Dunbar, *Forging New Rights in Western Waters*, 136–37.

16. F. Dumont Smith to William A. Smith, 14 December 1927, file 1927, "Kansas v. Colorado, 1927–30," KAG, KSHS.

17. Delph E. Carpenter, "Brief on Law of Interstate Compacts," in *Report of the State Irrigation Commissioner to the Kansas State Board of Agriculture*, 1 July 1924 to 30 June 1926 (Topeka: State Printer, 1926), 25–26.

18. George Knapp, "The Kansas-Colorado Water Controversy," in *Report of the State Irrigation Commissioner to the Kansas State Board of Agriculture*, 16 June 1919 to 30 June 1920 (Topeka: State Printer, 1920), 18–20; and idem, "The Proposed Arkansas River Compact," in *Report of the State Irrigation Commissioner to the Kansas State Board of Agriculture*, 1 July 1924 to 30 June 1926 (Topeka: State Printer, 1926), 13–24.

19. Knapp, "The Proposed Arkansas River Compact," 13–14.

20. Ibid., 13.

21. Ibid., 13–24.

22. *Colorado v. Kansas*, R. I. Meeker's Testimony, vol. 11, 1759–75, and vol. 13, 2127–32, DWR, KSBA; F. Dumont Smith to John G. Egan, Kansas assistant attorney general, 3 December 1932, file 1932, "Kansas v. Colorado, 1931–32," KAG, KSHS.

23. Smith to Egan, 3 December 1932, file 1932, "Kansas v. Colorado, 1931–32," KAG, KSHS.

24. *Colorado v. Kansas*, George Knapp's Testimony, vol. 30, 5279–89, DWR, KSBA.

25. Vena Pointer, "Report to the Colorado Water Conservation Board concerning Irrigation and Water Problems of the Arkansas Valley, Colorado," 1937, 3–4, ff 305, AVDA, CHS.

26. *State of Colorado, Complainant, v. the State of Kansas and Finney County Water Users' Association*, Brief of Complaint in Equity, vol. 802, 45–50, CWCB; and F. Dumont Smith to William A. Smith, 14 December 1927, file 1927, "Kansas v. Colorado, 1927–30," KAG, KSHS.

27. *Colorado v. Kansas*, M. C. Hinderlider's Testimony, vol 1, 61–64, DWR, KSBA.

28. M. C. Hinderlider, "Trans-Mountain Diversions," in *Twenty-Third Biennial Report of the State Engineer, Colorado*, 1925–26 (Denver: State Printers, 1926), 41; and "Investigations" and "Additional Water Supplies for the Arkansas Valley," in *Twenty-Fourth Biennial Report of the State Engineer, Colorado*, 1927–28 (Denver: State Printers, 1928), 32 and 33–35, respectively. For a description from the Army Corps of Engineers' perspective of the events leading to the construction of John Martin Dam and Reservoir see Michael Welsh, *U.S. Army Corps of Engi-*

neers: Albuquerque District, 1935-1985 (Albuquerque: University of New Mexico Press, 1987), 53-70.

29. Hinderlider, "Additional Water," 33-35.

30. Ray McGrath to Hurbert Work, 27 April 1926; Hurbert Work to W. S. Partridge, 20 August 1927; and R. F. Walter to the commissioner of the Bureau of Reclamation, 8 May 1926—ff 136, AVDA, CHS.

31. *Colorado v. Kansas,* M. C. Hinderlider's Testimony and C. L. Patterson's Testimony, vols. 1-6, 1-920, DWR, KSBA.

32. *Colorado v. Kansas,* R. I. Meeker's Testimony, vol. 9, 1345-52; and vol. 15, 2532, DWR, KSBA.

33. Ibid., vol. 10, 1563-69 and 1574-78.

34. F. Dumont Smith to William Stanley, with enclosure, "Cross-Examination of R. I. Meeker, Notes by F. Dumont Smith," 29 September 1932, file 1932, "Kansas v. Colorado, 1931-32," KAG, KSHS.

35. Ibid.; and George Knapp to John G. Egan, with enclosure, "Notes on the Cross-Examination of R. I. Meeker," 17 October 1932, file 1932, "Kansas v. Colorado, 1931-32," KAG, KSHS.

36. W. E. Stanley to John G. Egan, 24 April 1931, file 1931, "Kansas v. Colorado, 1931-32,"; and W. E. Stanley to John G. Egan, 12 August 1933, file 1933, "Kansas v. Colorado, 1933-44," KAG, KSHS.

37. The results of this joint study can be found in R. J. Tipton, "General Conclusions and Conclusions re the proposed Caddoa Reservoir from Report on 'Arkansas River Water Resources Survey' Dated July 1, 1931," State Engineering Department, Denver, Colorado, ff 283, AVDA, CHS. They became the basis for the Army Corps of Engineers' conclusions on Caddoa included in U.S. House, *Arkansas River and Tributaries. Letter from the Secretary of War Transmitting a Letter from the Chief of Engineers, U.S. Army, Dated July 26, 1935, Submitting a Report, together with Accompanying Papers and Illustrations, Containing a General Plan for the Improvement of Arkansas River and Tributaries, for the Purposes of Navigation and Efficient Development of Its Water Power, the Control of Floods, and the Needs of Irrigation,* 3 vols., H. Doc. 308, 74th Cong., 1st sess. (Washington, D.C.: Government Printing Office, 1936). See also A. W. McHendrie, "[History of Caddoa Reservoir District]," n.d., 3-4, ff 307, AVDA, CHS; John G. Egan to F. Dumont Smith, 23 April 1931, file 1931, "Kansas v. Colorado, 1931-32," KAG, KSHS. For a good general survey of how the Army Corps of Engineers became involved in western water projects, see Arthur E. Morgan, *Dams and Other Disasters: A Century of the Army Corps of Engineers in Civil Works* (Boston: Porter Sargent, 1971), 252-309; and Reisner, *Cadillac Desert,* 176-221.

38. Interview with Douglas McHendrie, 7 February 1986, Denver, Colorado; and interview with Ralph Adkins, 9 July 1986, Pueblo, Colorado. See also John A. Martin to Vena Pointer, 3 November 1933, ff 156, AVDA, CHS.

39. W. E. Stanley to John G. Egan, 25 October 1933, file 1933, "Kansas v. Colorado, 1933-44," KAG, KSHS.

40. A. W. McHendrie, "[History of Caddoa Reservoir District]," n.d., 11-12, ff 307, AVDA, CHS.

41. "Memorandum of Conference between Major Carey H. Brown, Secretary of the Mississippi Valley Committee, M. C. Hinderlider, Colorado State Engineer, and Chester I. Long, Held in Major Brown's Office on March 14, 1934," file 1934, "Kansas v. Colorado, 1933-44," KAG, KSHS. See also Carey H. Brown to Chester I. Long, 24 February 1934, and Henry C. Vidal to Alva B. Adams, 2 March 1934, ff 159, AVDA, CHS.

42. Joseph E. Stevens, *Hoover Dam: An American Adventure* (Norman: University of Oklahoma Press, 1988), vii–viii and 10–35; Reisner, *Cadillac Desert*, 393–451; and Worster, *Rivers of Empire*, 262–76.

43. A. W. McHendrie, "[History of Caddoa Reservoir District]," 4.

44. Dean's and Pointer's letters to all the invitees can be found in ff 164 and 165, AVDA, CHS. On the meeting itself, see *Pueblo Daily Chieftain*, 17 August 1934, 1. See also Harold L. Ickes to Edward P. Costigan, 21 September 1934, ff 169; and A. W. McHendrie, "[History of Caddoa Reservoir District]," 1–2, ff 307, AVDA, CHS.

45. John A. Martin to Vena Pointer, 17 May 1935, ff 176; Maj. Gen. E. M. Markham to M. C. Hinderlider, 12 June 1935, telegram from C. C. Heezmalhalch to M. C. Hinderlider, 17 June 1936, ff 177; Franklin D. Roosevelt to Alva B. Adams, n.d., ff 180; Elwood Mead to John A. Martin, 6 December 1935, ff 144; and John A. Martin to Arthur S. Dean, 29 April 1936, ff 187—AVDA, CHS.

46. Brig. Gen. G. E. Pillsbury to Arthur Dean, 12 June 1936, ff 189, AVDA, CHS.

47. W. E. Stanley to John G. Egan, 12 August 1933, file 1933, "Kansas v. Colorado, 1933–44," KAG, KSHS. Also, Bryon B. Blotz to A. W. McHendrie, 15 December 1934, ff 171; Henry C. Vidal to Arthur Dean, 4 January 1937, ff 194; G. A. Blotz to Lt. Col. E. Reybold, 8 January 1937, ff 194—AVDA, CHS. However, Hinderlider's studies refuted the Blotzes' notions of a projected sedimentation rate for Caddoa reservoir. See "Sedimentation, Caddoa Reservoir: Notes on Conference in the U.S. Engineer Office, Little Rock, Arkansas, 21 March 1939," ff 142, MCHC, CHS.

48. M. C. Hinderlider to Arthur Dean, 2 March 1937, ff 196; and R. L. Christy to Vena Pointer, 16 December 1937, ff 203, AVDA, CHS; memorandum to Clarence V. Beck, Kansas attorney general, from J. S. Parker, Kansas assistant attorney general, file 1937, "Kansas v. Colorado, 1933–44," KAG, KSHS.

49. Alva B. Adams to A. W. McHendrie, 28 May 1938, ff 208; and John Martin to A. W. McHendrie, 14 June 1938 and 15 June 1938, ff 209, AVDA, CHS.

50. Vena Pointer to Lt. Col. E. Reybold, 20 June 1938, ff 209; and A. W. McHendrie to Henry C. Vidal, 20 July 1938, ff 210, AVDA, CHS.

51. Royce J. Tipton, "Caddoa Reservoir Study: Summary of Assumed Operation No. 2," 1–5, ff 287, AVDA, CHS.

52. Bryon G. Rogers, H. C. Vidal, and A. W. McHendrie to Col. S. L. Scott, 16 February 1939, ff 214, AVDA, CHS.

CHAPTER EIGHT. QUARREL AND RAPPORT

1. *Colorado v. Kansas*, Royce J. Tipton's Testimony, vol. 19, 3117–3217, and Charles Patterson's Testimony, vol. 4, 4868–4900, DWR, KSBA.

2. F. Dumont Smith to John G. Egan, attorney general, 15 February 1931; Egan to William E. Stanley, 14 March 1931; Egan to Stanley, 18 March 1931; Egan to Stanley, 26 March 1931; and Egan to Smith, 3 July 1931—file 1931, "Kansas v. Colorado Water Controversy, 1931–32," KAG, KSHS.

3. Henry C. Vidal, "Comments on Patterson's Report of September 1941 concerning Draft of Consent Decree in Colorado v. Kansas," 4, ff 44, AVDA, CHS.

4. Ibid., 6; and n.a., "Memo for Statement at La Junta Meeting, January 24, 1942," containing "Memorandum of Negotiations in re Consent Decree," 14, ff 44, AVDA, CHS.

5. George S. Knapp to John G. Egan, 17 February 1932, file 1932, "Kansas v. Colorado Water Controversy, 1931–32," KAG, KSHS.

6. *Water Conservation, Laws Passed* (1937) 265:1300–1308.

7. Henry C. Vidal to Watson McHendrie, 1 October 1942, ff 43, AVDA, CHS.

8. "Memorandum of Negotiations in re Consent Decree," 6–7, ff 44, AVDA, CHS.

9. Ibid; and Charles L. Patterson, "Confidential Memoranda Supplementing 'Summary of Basic Data,' 12 July 1940," 2–3, ff 44, AVDA, CHS.

10. "Memorandum of Negotiations in re Consent Decree," 8–10, ff 44, AVDA, CHS.

11. Charles Patterson, "Proposed Consent Decree, Case of Colorado v. Kansas, Arkansas River–Caddoa Reservoir, Confidential," 1–66, ff 295; and Vidal, "Comments on Patterson's Report of September 1941 concerning Draft of Consent Decree in Colorado v. Kansas," 1–17, ff 44, AVDA, CHS.

12. Charles Patterson to Gov. Ralph Carr, Atty. Gen. Gail Ireland, Wat McHendrie, Henry Vidal, and Clifford Stone, 13 July 1941, Attorney General, ff "Water Conservation Board, 1941–42," location #19046, CSA.

13. *Annual Report of the Officers of the Fort Lyon Canal Co.*, 1941, 6.

14. Henry Vidal to Gov. Ralph Carr and Atty. Gen. Gail Ireland, 24 March 1942, ff 42, AVDA, CHS.

15. Wat McHendrie to Henry Vidal, 5 May 1942, ff 42, AVDA, CHS; and William Stanley to Atty. Gen. Jay S. Parker, 17 July 1942, file 1942, "Kansas v. Colorado Water Controversy, 1933–44," KAG, KSHS.

16. Stanley to Parker, 17 June and 17 July 1942, file 1942, "Kansas v. Colorado Water Controversy, 1933–44," KAG, KSHS.

17. William Stanley to George Knapp, 25 July 1942, file 1942; and George Knapp to William Stanley, 24 December 1942, file 1943, "Kansas v. Colorado Water Controversy, 1933–44," KAG, KSHS.

18. Wat McHendrie to William Stanley, "Personal and Confidential," 11 November 1942; and William Stanley to Wat McHendrie, 12 November 1942, ff 43, AVDA, CHS.

19. Wat McHendrie to Henry Vidal, 1 September 1942, ff 43, AVDA, CHS.

20. Henry C. Vidal to Wat McHendrie, 1 October 1942, ff 43, AVDA, CHS; *Colorado v. Kansas*, Charles Patterson's Testimony, vol. 38, 6690–6750, DWR, KSBA; and Charles Patterson, "Caddoa Reservoir Study, Operations Plan F, Assumed Administrative Regulations," 5 November 1942, ff 44, AVDA, CHS.

21. Wat McHendrie to William Stanley, "Personal and Confidential," 11 November 1942; and William Stanley to Wat McHendrie, 12 November 1942; McHendrie to Vidal, 15 September 1942; and Vidal to McHendrie, 16 September 1942—ff 43, AVDA, CHS.

22. *Colorado v. Kansas*, Charles Patterson's Testimony, vol. 38, 6714–16; and George Knapp's Testimony, vol. 38, 7010–16, DWR, KSBA.

23. *Colorado v. Kansas*, George Knapp's Testimony, vol. 38, 7010–25 and 7054–73, DWR, KSBA.

24. William Stanley to Asst. Atty. Gen. Eldon Wallingford, 22 December 1942, file 1942, "Kansas v. Colorado Water Controversy, 1933–44," KAG, KSHS.

25. "Report and Recommendations of the Special Master," vol. 804, CWCB, CSA.

26. "Exceptions of Complainant to Report of Special Master," vol. 804, CWCB, CSA.

27. "Brief of Defendant," vol. 806, 34–40, CWCB, CSA.

28. *State of Colorado, Complainant, v. The State of Kansas, et al., Defendants,* 320 U.S. 386.

29. Ibid, 386–92.

30. Vidal to Ireland, 10 December 1943, J. S. Breitenstein Correspondence, 1941–53, CWCB, CSA.

31. Lt. Col. Cole to the Chief of Engineers, 16 June 1943, Kramer Collection, Hill and Robbins Law Firm, Denver, Colorado.

32. Lt. Col. Cole to Stone, 28 January 1944; and Breitenstein to Gov. Vivian, 16 March 1944, J. S. Breitenstein Correspondence, 1941–53, CWCB, CSA.

33. "Record of Proceedings of Kansas-Colorado meeting (27 and 28 March 1944, Denver, Colorado) concerning Temporary Plan of Administration of Water of Arkansas River"; and Roland Tate to Knapp, 4 April 1944, Governor Schoeppel, correspondence, general file, box 18, ff 9 ("Caddoa Res."), KSHS; Ireland to Mitchell, 17 April 1944, J. S. Breitenstein Correspondence, 1941–53, CWCB, CSA.

34. Roland Tate to George Knapp, 2 May 1944, Governor Schoeppel, correspondence, general file, box 18, ff 9 ("Caddoa Res."), KSHS.

35. "Statement re Interstate Relations under Plan of Operation of Caddoa Reservoir and Administration of Rights in Arkansas River," 12 June 1944; Ireland to Mitchell, 11 July 1944; Gov. Schoeppel to Lt. Col. Cole, 24 July 1944; Lt. Col. Cole to Gov. Schoeppel, 28 July 1944; and Gov. Vivian to Lt. Col. Cole, 31 July 1944—Governor Schoeppel, correspondence, general file, box 18, ff 9 ("Caddoa Res."), KSHS.

36. Knapp to Tate, 7 August 1944; and Tate to Gov. Schoeppel, 9 August 1944, Governor Schoeppel, correspondence, general file, box 18, ff 9 ("Caddoa Res."), KSHS.

37. Clifford Stone to Knapp, 27 February 1945, Governor Schoeppel, correspondence, general file, box 31, ff 9 ("Caddoa Res."), KSHS.

38. Knapp to Tate, 9 March 1945, Governor Schoeppel, correspondence, general file, box 31, ff 9 ("Caddoa Res."), KSHS.

39. Gordon to Ireland, 24 March 1944, J. S. Breitenstein Correspondence, 1941–53, CWCB, CSA.

40. Gov. Vivian to Gov. Schoeppel, 13 April 1945; Mitchell to Gov. Schoeppel, 17 April 1945; and Gov. Schoeppel to Gov. Vivian, 18 April 1945, Governor Schoeppel, correspondence, general file, box 31, ff 9 ("Caddoa Res."), KSHS.

41. Pres. Harry Truman to Gov. Schoeppel, 20 November 1945; Gov. Schoeppel to Gov. Vivian, 18 April 1945, Governor Schoeppel, correspondence, general file, box 31, ff 9 ("Caddoa Res."), KSHS.

42. "Record of First Meeting, Colorado-Kansas Arkansas River Compact Commission, Denver, Colorado, 7 January 1946," 1:9–11; and "Record of Second Meeting, Colorado-Kansas Compact Commission, Topeka, Kansas, 25–26 March 1946," 2:2, Hill and Robbins Law Firm, Denver, Colorado. This is a bound volume of the abstracted minutes of the commissioners' seventeen meetings. A verbatim copy of the minutes also exists, but unless otherwise noted, the citations herein are drawn from the abstracted minutes. Three other copies of the abstracted minutes exist. One is in General Kramer's collection, another in the A. Watson McHendrie Collection (CHS), and the last in the Colorado Supreme Court library. The only copy of the verbatim minutes is in General Kramer's col-

lection. The attorneys of the Hill and Robbins Law Firm have been kind enough to allow me to use their copies of the abstracted minutes as well as the verbatim minutes.

Knapp to Vidal, 3 April 1946; Lt. Col. Cole to Gov. Schoeppel, 9 May 1946; Gov. Schoeppel to Gov. Vivian, 18 April 1945; and Col. Henry Hannis to Gov. Schoeppel, 16 August 1946, Governor Schoeppel, correspondence, general file, box 45, ff 18 ("Kansas & Colorado Compact"), KSHS.

43. "Record of Fourth Meeting, Colorado-Kansas Compact Commission, Denver, Colorado, 28–29 August 1946," 4:16–20; and "Record of Sixth Meeting, Colorado-Kansas Compact Commission, Denver, Colorado, 25–26 November 1946," 6:41–42; Gov. Schoeppel to Leavitt, 19 December 1946, Governor Schoeppel, correspondence, general file, box 45, ff 18 ("Kansas & Colorado Compact"), KSHS.

44. For a copy of the Republican River Compact, see George E. Radosevich, ed., *Colorado Water Laws: A Compilation of Statutes, Regulations, Compacts, and Selected Cases*, 5th ed. (Fort Collins: Colorado State University, 1983), 1:123–29.

45. "Republican River Compact, 1942," in manuscript titled "Water the Sustainer of Life," 1–3, MCHC, CHS; M. C. Hinderlider, "Interstate Negotiations for River Compacts: Republican River," in *Thirty-First Biennial Report of the State Engineer, Colorado*, 1941–42 (Denver: State Printers, 1942), 30–42. Leland Olds to G. L. Parker, 30 November 1942; and Knapp to Gov. Ratner, 18 December 1942, file 1943, "Kansas v. Colorado, 1933–44," KAG, KSHS. Clifford H. Stone to CWCB, "Memorandum: Republican River Compact Legislation," 20 February 1942; Gov. Carr to Ireland, 2 April 1942; and Stone to CWCB, "Memorandum: Republican River Compact," 15 December 1942, location #19046, ff "Republican River Compact," CSA. For a general discussion of the Federal Power Commission and western water rights see Betsy Vencill, "The Federal Power Act and Western Water Law—Can States Maintain Their Own Water Use Priorities?" *Natural Resources Journal* 27 (Winter 1987): 213–34.

46. "Record of Seventh Meeting, Colorado-Kansas Compact Commission, Topeka, Kansas, 22–23 January 1947," 7:24–39.

47. "Record of Twelfth Meeting, Colorado-Kansas Compact Commission, Denver, Colorado, 3–5 February 1948," 12:22–25; and "Record of Sixteenth Meeting, Colorado-Kansas Compact Commission, Denver, Colorado, 8–10 November 1948," 16:11.

48. "Record of Eighth Meeting, Colorado-Kansas Compact Commission, Denver, Colorado, 10–11 April 1947," 8:43–58; and the verbatim minutes, "Record of Fifth Meeting, Colorado-Kansas Compact Commission, Topeka, Kansas, 23–24 October 1946," 21–23.

49. "Record of Eighth Meeting, Colorado-Kansas Compact Commission, Denver, Colorado, 10–11 April 1947," 43–49.

50. Marcellus to Pointer, 2 June 1942, ff 230, AVDA, CHS.

51. "Record of Fifth Meeting, Colorado-Kansas Compact Commission, Topeka, Kansas, 23–24 October 1946," 5:5–7 and 20–25; and "Record of Seventh Meeting, Colorado-Kansas Compact Commission, Topeka, Kansas, 22–23 January 1947," 7:14–19.

52. Verbatim minutes, "Record of Eighth Meeting, Colorado-Kansas Compact Commission, Denver, Colorado, 10–11 April 1947," 77–78.

53. McHendrie to Vidal, 30 December 1944, J. S. Breitenstein Correspondence, 1941–53, CWCB, CSA.

54. Ibid.

55. Christy to McHendrie, 5 November 1948; Christy to Vidal, Ireland, and Mendenhall, 5 November 1948; Gordon to Vidal, 14 August 1948; and Vidal to Ireland and Mendenhall, 15 November 1948—ff 121, AVDA, CHS.

56. "Record of Thirteenth Meeting, Colorado-Kansas Compact Commission, Denver, Colorado, 30 June–3 July 1948," 13:97–120.

57. "Record of Seventeenth Meeting, Colorado-Kansas Compact Commission, Colorado Springs, Colorado, 13–14 December 1948," 17:32–36; McHendrie to Christy, 26 March 1948, ff 119, AVDA, CHS.

58. McHendrie to Vidal, 26 December 1947; McHendrie to Vidal, 30 January 1948; McHendrie to Vidal, 17 March 1948; and McHendrie to Vidal, 20 August 1948—ff 119, AVDA, CHS. "Record of Fourteenth Meeting, Colorado-Kansas Compact Commission, Denver, Colorado, 29–31 July 1948," 14:62–70 and 82–84.

59. "Record of Fourteenth Meeting, Colorado-Kansas Compact Commission, Denver, Colorado, 29–31 July 1948," 14:79–80.

60. Gordon to Vidal, 27 July 1948; Gordon to Vidal, 14 August 1948; McHendrie to Vidal, 20 August 1948; McHendrie to Vidal, 10 September 1948; McHendrie to Ireland, 25 October 1948; and Christy to Vidal, Ireland, and Mendenhall, 5 November 1948—ff 121, AVDA, CHS. "Record of Sixteenth Meeting, Colorado-Kansas Compact Commission, Denver, Colorado, 8–10 November 1948," 16:54–55; and "Record of Seventeenth Meeting, Colorado-Kansas Compact Commission, Colorado Springs, Colorado, 13–14 December 1948," 17:78–80 and 85–96.

61. "Record of Fourteenth Meeting, Colorado-Kansas Compact Commission, Denver, Colorado, 29–31 July 1948," 14:22–65.

62. Ibid.

63. Ibid., 14:92–96; "Record of Fifteenth Meeting, Colorado-Kansas Compact Commission, Colorado Springs, Colorado, 13–16 September 1948," 15:10–17 and 72–73; and "Record of Seventeenth Meeting, Colorado-Kansas Compact Commission, Denver, Colorado, 13–14 December 1948," 17:62–70 and 82–85. McHendrie to Vidal, 20 August 1948; and Royce Tipton to Vidal, Mendenhall, and Ireland, 24 November 1948—ff 121, AVDA, CHS.

64. Stone to Kramer, 1 March 1949, J. S. Breitenstein Correspondence, 1941–53, CWCB, CSA.

65. T. H. Dameron to M. C. Hinderlider, 31 January 1949, ff 37, MCHC, CHS.

66. M. C. Hinderlider, "Statement before Committee of the Legislature, Irrigation and Water Resources, 3 February 1949: On Provisions of the Proposed Colorado-Kansas Compact on the Arkansas River," ff 86, MCHC, CHS.

67. U.S. Congress, Senate, Committee on Interior and Insular Affairs, *Arkansas River Compact, Hearing before the Committee on Interior and Insular Affairs on S. 1448*, 81st Cong., 1st sess., 1949, 8–9 and 18–19.

CHAPTER NINE. FALSE EXPECTATIONS

1. U.S. Department of Interior, Bureau of Reclamation, *Gunnison-Arkansas Project, Colorado: A Potential Transmountain Diversion Project*, June 1948, ff 89, and *Gunnison-Arkansas Project: Appendix A: General Discussion*, June 1948, ff 90, A Watson McHendrie Collection, CHS; and M. C. Hinderlider, "Discussion of Supplemental Water Supply Possibilities for Arkansas Valley," November 1927, ff 290, MCHC, CHS.

2. Radosevich, et al., *Evolution and Administration of Colorado Water Law*, 51–60.

3. E. F. Schumacher, *Small Is Beautiful: Economics As If People Mattered* (New York: Harper & Row, 1973).

4. DuVoid Burris, interviewer, "Fourteen Statements: History of Fryingpan-Arkansas Project and Southeastern Colorado Water Conservancy District" (sponsored by the Southeastern Colorado Water Conservancy District, [1976?]), 47.

5. Gilbert C. Fite, *The Farmers' Frontier, 1865–1900* (Albuquerque: University of New Mexico Press, 1974), 156–74; and Lowitt, *The New Deal and the West*, 81–99 and 175–88.

6. Dena S. Markoff, "A Bittersweet Saga: The Arkansas Valley Beet Sugar Industry, 1900–1979," *Colorado Magazine* 56 (1979): 161–78; CWCB, "Rocky Ford Ditch to Pueblo Reservoir, Transfer Proceeding," case #283CW18; and "Rocky Ford's Water Threatened," *Denver Post*, 12 June 1983, 1C.

7. In the last decade newspapers in the valley have been replete with articles about companies selling their rights to cities. For example, see "Amity Conducting Own Survey on Sale Interest," *Arkansas Valley Journal*, 14 March 1985; "Bessemer Ditch Shareholders Want Answers before Water Sale," *Pueblo Daily Chieftain*, 5 May 1984; "Bessemer Ditch Stockholders Plan Fight to Keep Water in River's Basin," *Pueblo Daily Chieftain*, 31 May 1984, 10A; "Fort Lyon Shareholders May Sell," *Arkansas Valley Journal*, 11 September 1986; "Ft. Lyon Canal Separate from Sale Issue," *Arkansas Valley Journal*, 18 December 1986, 1; and "Fort Lyon Canal President Sees Merger as Beneficial," *Bent County Democrat* 31 July 1986, 1.

8. "CF&I Steel to Sell Rights," *Denver Post*, 29 December 1983, 1C; and "Crane to Sell Water Rights," *Denver Post*, 15 March 1984, 1C.

9. Jack A. McCullough, "Water Resources and Historical Water Use for Colorado Springs, Colorado," PUOCS, April 1974, 3–9 and 43–48; "Homestake Water Plan Gets Qualified Approval," *Denver Post*, 11 August 1984, 1A; "Consolidated Space Operations Center Brings Road, Water Needs," *Denver Post*, 25 November 1984, 6I; "Aurora & Colorado Springs Near Agreement on Homestake Water Project," *Denver Post*, 24 May 1985, 8A; Abbott, *Descriptions of Water-Systems Operations in the Arkansas River Basin, Colorado*, 11–24; "Holy Cross Wilderness Wetlands Threatened," *Peak and Prairie*, April 1987, 3; Don Miles, "Recharge: Its Role in Total Water Management, Arkansas Valley of Colorado," 1–9; "Remnant of a River: Man's Designs on the Arkansas," *Wichita Eagle-Beacon*, 28 June 1989, 1A and 6A; and "Talk of Unity Doesn't Impress Colo. Water Factions," *Daily Camera*, 7 August 1985, 16A.

10. See "A Marshland Goes Dry: Cheyenne Bottoms Wildlife Facing Uncertain Future," *Wichita Eagle-Beacon*, 22 September 1984, 1A and 6A; "Kansans Gauge the Losses as Arkansas Dwindles Away," *Wichita Eagle-Beacon*, 29 June 1989, 1A and 6A; and *Kansas v. Colorado*, Motion for Leave to File Complaint, Complaint, and Brief in Support of Motion for Leave to File Complaint, 16 December 1985.

11. "Revegetation Project Gains Steam," *Arkansas Valley Journal*, 12 October 1986, 1; and "Ark. Valley No Future Dustbowl," *Arkansas Valley Journal*, 12 February 1987, 1.

12. Andre Gorz, *Ecology as Politics*, trans. Patsy Vigderman and Jonathan Cloud (Boston: South End Press, 1980), 84.

GLOSSARY

Alkaline. Water or soils containing principally sodium, potassium, magnesium, and calcium in such quantity to raise the pH-value above 7.0. These soils and waters are harmful to most crop production.

Assessment. The dollar amount annually levied against each share of issued stock in a mutual stockholding company. For paid assessments a company will deliver an irrigator's water and with the proceeds from the assessments pay for canal upkeep.

Cubic feet of water per second. The measure of cubic feet of water flow passing a given point in one second. One second foot of water, expressed 1 cfs, flowing for twenty-four hours amounts to approximately 650,700 gallons.

Ditch call. The point when an irrigation company informs the state engineer's office that it wants to make use of its water rights and begin diverting water.

Diversion dam. A structure placed across a stream, creating a rise in the streambed, which channels water into an irrigation ditch or water canal.

Diversion point. The place on a stream bank where water is diverted into an irrigation ditch or water canal.

Exchange. A diversion of water at one point in a stream replaced by the same quantity of water from a reservoir, or through a transmountain system, at another point in the same stream.

Feeder ditch. A ditch that usually transports water to a reservoir.

Flume. A structure built to transport ditch or canal water over a depression or a stream.

Gross duty. The total amount of irrigation water divided by the amount of acreage irrigated.

Headgate. The gate at the entrance to an irrigation ditch or water canal.

High flow. Greater than normal stream flow, but not considered at flood stage.

June rise. The increase in stream flows on the High Plains from the melting of the mountain snowpack in the springtime.

Laterals. A side ditch or conduit. A *lateral box* is a structure built into the main ditch that channels water into the laterals leading to farmers' fields.

Mutual stockholding company. A nonprofit canal company that provides a division of canal runs, assesses for upkeep, and allows a vote in policy formation in proportion to a shareholder's ownership in the enterprise.

Overdecreed. A condition when the amount of flow awarded to water rights on a certain stream greatly exceeds the stream's normal flow.

Phreatophyte. A plant that obtains its water from the zone of saturation, either directly or through the capillary fringe. The most common of these in the Arkansas Valley are the salt cedar (*Tamarix ramosissima*), the cottonwood (*Populus sargentii*), and the narrow leaf willow (*Salix amygdaloides*).

Prior appropriation doctrine. In Colorado, as embodied in the state constitution, the doctrine recognizes the right of people to use the publicly owned water of the state. The state permits the use of its water when three tests are met. First, there is a hierarchy of beneficial water use—domestic (or urban) consumption first, followed in order by agricultural, industrial, and, recently, environmental applications of water. Second, each right to use water possesses a court-adjudicated priority date. The state engineer regulates diversions from all streams in the state according to the respective dates of the water rights. If two canals operate on a river and one has a water right dated 1870 and the other a right dated 1874, then the 1870 right will be filled before the person owning the 1874 right receives any water from the river. The third element is beneficial use. The owner of a right has to show a legitimate use of the water to which he or she makes claim. If the owner fails in this, then the state can take away the portion of the water right not "beneficially" used. Usually the canal capacity determines beneficial use; once water is delivered through a headgate, the courts will consider it beneficially used, regardless of the application of the water as it flows through the canal.

Recharge. The amount of water that returns to an aquifer through percolation.

Return flow. Applied irrigation water that reenters a surface stream.

Riparian doctrine. The word *riparian* is derived from the Latin root meaning riverbank. This system assures to the owner of land on the bank of a stream the right to the use of that water. Originating in common law, the doctrine guaranteed a riparian owner the right to his or her water undiminished in quantity and unaffected in quality regardless of the uses of this same water by other riparian owners.

Salinity. The concentration of salts, expressed in terms of the number of parts per million of chloride, in a given water.

Sedimentation. The process of deposition of suspended matter carried by stream flows caused by gravity.

Seepage. Water percolating from canals and irrigated lands to underlying strata.

Semiarid. An area where the annual precipitation is from 8 to 16 inches.

Settling reservoir. A reservoir in which stored water is kept still so that the sediment in it will settle to the bottom of the reservoir, leaving clear water for the conveyance system leading out of the reservoir.

Siphon. A large pipe that transports water down and up depressions or under streams. A wooden-stave siphon was generally made of narrow redwood strips that formed the sides, bound together from the outside by iron or steel bands.

Transit loss. The amount of water lost during transmissions in a streambed from the time when a release is made from an upstream reservoir to when the water arrives at a downstream diversion point. If the state engineer calculated a 10 percent transit loss and a ditch company wanted to transmit 40,000 acre-feet of reservoir water to its downstream irrigation ditch, then the company would have to release a total of 44,000 acre-feet, 4,000 of which would be considered transit loss.

Waste gate. A gate built into a ditch or canal to release excessive water flow into a natural watercourse.

Water consumption. The amount of water, usually expressed in acre-feet, that enters into a ditch or canal.

Weir. A structure placed in the main ditch or in laterals to measure the water flow to a farmer's land.

SELECTED SOURCES

INTERVIEWS

Adkins, Ralph D., former superintendent of the Colorado Fuel and Iron Corporation's Water Division. Interview with author. Pueblo, Colorado, 9 July 1986.

Christy, Harold, former superintendent of the Colorado Fuel and Iron Corporation's Water Division. Interview by H. Lee Scamehorn. Pueblo, Colorado, 29 and 30 June 1982.

Converse, Paul, former superintendent of the Fort Lyon Canal Company. Interview with author. Las Animas, Colorado, 5 April 1983.

Ireland, Gail, former attorney general of Colorado and commissioner during the negotiation of the Arkansas River Compact. Interview with author. Denver, Colorado, 14 February 1986.

Kidder, Edward, irrigation farmer under the Rocky Ford Ditch Company. Interview with author. Rocky Ford, Colorado, July 1985.

McHendrie, Douglas, son of A. Watson McHendrie. Interview with author. Denver, Colorado, 7 February 1986.

Reyher, George, irrigation farmer under the Fort Lyon Canal Company. Interview with author. Bent County, Colorado, 5 April 1983.

NEWSPAPERS

Arkansas (La Junta, Colo.) *Valley Journal*, 1983–84.
Bent County Democrat (Las Animas, Colo.), 1986.
Colorado Chieftain (Pueblo, Colo.), 1868–91.
Colorado Springs Daily Gazette, 1899–1920.
Colorado Springs Weekly Gazette, 1875–1900.
Daily Camera (Boulder, Colo.), 1982–87.
Daily Democrat (Rocky Ford, Colo.), 1924.
Denver Post, 1885–1950.
La Junta (Colo.) *Tribune*, 1887–1900.
Peak and Prairie (Denver, Colo.), 1982–87.
Republican (Denver, Colo.), 1902
Rocky Ford (Colo.) *Enterprise*, 1900, 1941–50.
Pueblo (Colo.) *Daily Chieftain*, 1874–1986
Rocky Mountain News (Denver, Colo.), 1882–1950.
Wichita Eagle-Beacon, 1980–89.

PRIMARY SOURCES

Arkansas Valley Ditch Association. Manuscript Collection No. 16. Colorado Historical Society. Denver, Colorado.

Assessors rolls, abstracts. Finney and Kearny counties, 1896–50. Kansas State Historical Society. Topeka, Kansas.

Bessemer Ditch Diversions, 1927–50. The Bessemer Irrigating Ditch Company Office. Thatcher Building. Pueblo, Colorado.

Bessemer Irrigating Ditch Company. By-Laws, as Amended to September 1934. Thatcher Building. Pueblo, Colorado.

Bessemer Irrigating Ditch Company. Minutes of monthly board meetings and annual stockholder meetings, 1920–50. Thatcher Building. Pueblo, Colorado.

Board of Pueblo Water Works. James W. Preston Files. Pueblo, Colorado.

Breitenstein, Jean. Correspondence, 1941–53. Colorado State Archives. Denver, Colorado.

Carpenter, Louis G. Scrapbooks. Western Collections. Denver Public Library. Denver, Colorado.

Colorado Attorney General. Correspondence. Colorado State Archives. Denver, Colorado.

————. *The United States Irrigating Company v. The Graham Ditch Company, et al.* Testimony. Colorado State Archives. Denver, Colorado.

————. *Kansas v. Colorado.* Case Files. Colorado State Archives. Denver, Colorado.

————. *Kansas v. Colorado.* Testimony. Colorado State Archives. Denver, Colorado.

Colorado Fuel and Iron Company Collection. Manuscript Collection No. 1057. Colorado Historical Society. Denver, Colorado.

Colorado Secretary of State. Corporation Files. Colorado State Archives. Denver, Colorado.

Colorado State Supreme Court. *The La Junta and Lamar Canal Co., et al. v. Hess et al.,* #3768. Briefs and Testimony. Colorado State Archives. Denver, Colorado.

Colorado Water Conservation Board. Administrative Files. Colorado State Archives. Denver, Colorado.

————. *Colorado v. Kansas.* Motions and Pleadings. Vols. 802–6. Colorado State Archives. Denver, Colorado.

District Court of the Third Judicial District. In the Matter of the Priorities to the Use of Water in District No. 17. #4954. Colorado State Archives. Denver, Colorado.

Division of Water Resources. *Colorado v. Kansas.* Testimony. Kansas State Board of Agriculture. Topeka, Kansas.

————. File Amazon Canal near Lakin, Kansas. Kansas State Board of Agriculture. Topeka, Kansas.

————. File Farmers' Ditch near Garden City, Kansas. Kansas State Board of Agriculture. Topeka, Kansas.

————. File Garden City Ditch near Garden City, Kansas. Kansas State Board of Agriculture. Topeka, Kansas.

————. File Great Eastern near Lakin, Kansas. Kansas State Board of Agriculture. Topeka, Kansas.

————. File South Side Ditch near Hartland, Kansas. Kansas State Board of Agriculture. Topeka, Kansas.

Fort Lyon Canal Company. *Articles of Incorporation and Amendments; Bylaws, Amended 11 April 1984; Rules and Regulations, Adopted December 1983.* Fort Lyon Canal Office Building. Las Animas, Colorado.

_____. *Annual Report of the Officers of the Fort Lyon Canal Company*. 1910–50. Fort Lyon Canal Office Building. Las Animas, Colorado.

Hinderlider, Michael Creed. Manuscript Collection No. 312. Colorado Historical Society. Denver, Colorado.

Kansas Attorney General. *Kansas v. Colorado*. Kansas State Historical Society. Topeka, Kansas.

Kramer, Brigadier General Hans. Kramer Collection. Hill and Robbins Law Firm. Denver, Colorado. (Photocopy of set at National Archives, Records of the Geological Survey, Record Group 57.)

McCullough, Jack A. "Water Resources and Historical Water Use for Colorado Springs, Colorado." April 1974. Public Utilities Office, Colorado Springs, Colorado.

McHendrie, A. Watson. Manuscript Collection No. 1250. Colorado Historical Society, Denver, Colorado.

Minutes of the Colorado-Kansas Arkansas River Compact Commission. Abstracts. Meetings 1–17. Hill and Robbins Law Firm. Denver, Colorado.

Minutes of the Colorado-Kansas Arkansas River Compact Commission. Verbatim transcript. Meetings 1–17. Hill and Robbins Law Firm. Denver, Colorado.

Oringderff, Barbara. "A Short History of the United States Sugar and Land Company, Now Called the Garden City Company," N.d., typewritten, in company files, Garden City Company, Garden City, Kansas.

Public Utilities Office. Scrapbooks. Colorado Springs, Colorado.

Schoeppel, Governor Andrew. Correspondence. Kansas State Historical Society. Topeka, Kansas.

Schuyler, James D. "Report on the Property of The Fort Lyon Canal Company, Colorado, Its Water Supply, Its Present Physical Condition, and the Betterments Needed to Complete the Irrigation System, 1910." Typewritten, in record vault, Fort Lyon Canal Office Building, Las Animas, Colorado.

Stoeckly, Eugene. "A Company and Factory." N.d., typewritten, in company files, Garden City Company, Garden City, Kansas.

The United States Irrigating Company v. The Graham Ditch Company, et al. Record Group 21. Box 1028. Federal Record Center. Denver, Colorado.

U.S. Department of Interior. Bureau of Indian Affairs. *Letters Received by the Office of Indian Affairs, 1824–81*. Microfilm 234, rolls 878–79.

_____. Reclamation Service. Correspondence re *Kansas v. Colorado*. Record Group 115. National Archives. Washington, D.C.

U.S. Supreme Court. *Kansas v. Colorado*, 206 U.S. Sup. Ct. 46 (1906). Records and Briefs. Microfiche Cards, Nos. 1–57. University of Colorado Law Library. Boulder, Colorado.

_____. *The State of Kansas, Complainant, v. The State of Colorado et al., and the United States Intervenor. In Equity. Transcript of Record.* October Term, 1905. No. 7, Original. Published by Judd & Detweiler, Washington, D.C., 1905.

Water Commissioner's Field Book[s], District 12, State of Colorado, 1908–50. State Engineer's Office. Denver, Colorado.

Water Commissioner's Field Book[s], District 14, State of Colorado, 1895–50. State Engineer's Office, Denver, Colorado.

Water Commissioner's Field Book[s], District 17, State of Colorado, 1895–50. State Engineer's Office, Denver, Colorado.

Water Department Reports, 1936–50. Public Utilities Office, Colorado Springs, Colorado.

Water Division. Historical File. Colorado Springs, Colorado.

Water Report Years 1941 to 1980. Board of Water Works. Pueblo, Colorado.
Water Resources Division. General Correspondence. Kansas State Historical Society. Topeka, Kansas.

SECONDARY SOURCES

Abbott, P. O. *Descriptions of Water-Systems Operations in the Arkansas River Basin, Colorado*. Water Resources Investigations Report 85-4092. Lakewood, Colo.: U.S. Geological Survey, 1985.
Adkins, Ralph W. "Water Supply for an Integrated Steel Plant at High Altitude." Paper presented at San Francisco Regional Technical Meeting of American Iron and Steel Institute, 9 November 1962.
Alexander, Lucien Hugh. "James Wilson, Patriot, and the Wilson Doctrine." *North American Law Review* 183 (16 November 1906): 971–89.
Athearn, Robert. *The Denver and Rio Grande Western Railroad*. Lincoln: University of Nebraska Press, 1962.
————. *The Mythic West in Twentieth-Century America*. Lawrence: University Press of Kansas, 1986.
Biennial Report of the State Irrigation Commissioner to the Kansas State Board of Agriculture July 1919–25 to June 1920–6. Topeka, Kans.: State Printer, 1920–26.
"Birth of Irrigation in Kansas." *Irrigation Age* 6 (March 1894): 95.
Blaney, Harry F., and Wayne D. Criddle. *Consumptive Use and Irrigation Water Requirements of Crops in Colorado*. Washington, D.C.: Department of Agriculture, Soil Conservation Service, 1949.
Block, Mrs. Henry. "Sugar Beets: Story of Their First Three Years of Experimental Production in Kansas for Commercial Sugar-Making." In *Fourteenth Biennial Report of the State Board of Agriculture, 1903–5*. Topeka, Kans.: State Printer, 1906.
Bowman, Charles W. "History of Bent County." In *History of the Arkansas Valley, Colorado*. Chicago: O. L. Baskin & Co., 1881.
Boyle, R. V., and J. S. McCorkle. "Guard First the Bottom Land." In *Grass: Yearbook of Agriculture*. Washington, D.C.: Government Printing Office, 1948.
Brown, F. Lee, and Helen M. Ingram. *Water and Poverty in the Southwest*. Tucson: University of Arizona Press, 1987.
Bryant, Keith L. *History of the Atchison, Topeka & Santa Fe Railway*. Lincoln: University of Nebraska Press, 1974.
Buchanan, G. C. "The Water Supply for Western Kansas." *Irrigation Age* 8 (March 1895): 118.
Burris, DuVoid, interviewer. "Fourteen Statements: History of Fryingpan-Arkansas Project and Southeastern Colorado Water Conservancy District." Sponsored by the Southeastern Colorado Water Conservancy District, [1976?].
Cain, Doug. *Quality of the Arkansas River and Irrigation Return Flows in the Lower Arkansas River Valley, Colorado*. Water Resources Investigations Report 84-4273. Lakewood, Colo.: U.S. Geological Survey, 1985.
Carpenter, Delph E. "Brief on Law of Interstate Compacts." In *Report of the State Irrigation Commissioner to the Kansas State Board of Agriculture, 1 July 1924 to 30 June 1926*. Topeka, Kans.: State Printer, 1926.
Chronic, J., and H. Chronic. *Prairie Peak and Plateau: A Guide to the Geology of Colorado*. Colorado Geological Survey Bulletin 32. Denver: State Printers Office, 1972.

Clark, Ira G. "The Elephant Butte Controversy: A Chapter in the Emergence of Federal Water Law." *Journal of American History* 61 (March 1975): 1006–33.

———. *Water in New Mexico*. Albuquerque: University of New Mexico Press, 1988.

Colorado. State Engineer. *Tabulation of Ditch and Reservoir Decrees Main Stem Arkansas River, Colorado: Water District 11, 12, 14, 17, and 67 (Tributary Decrees Not Included)*. N.p., n.d.

Colorado. Water Conservation Board. *A Hundred Years of Irrigation in Colorado: 100 Years of Organized and Continuous Irrigation, 1852–1952*. Denver: Colorado Water Conservation Board; and Fort Collins: Colorado Agricultural and Mechanical College, 1952.

———. *Interstate Compacts*. Vol. 4. Denver: Water Conservation Board, 1946.

Cronon, William. *Changes in the Land: Indians, Colonists, and Ecology of New England*. New York: Hill and Wang, 1983.

Darton, N. H. *Geology and Underground Waters of the Arkansas in Eastern Colorado*. U.S. Geological Survey Professional Paper 52. Washington, D.C.: Government Printing Office, 1906.

Davis, E. C. "Report of Water Commissioner." In *City of Colorado Springs: Town Incorporation, City Organization, and Reorganization, also Classification as City of the First Class*. Colorado Springs, Colo.: City Council, 1902.

Diamond, Stephen. "Legal Realism and Historical Method: J. Willard Hurst and American Legal History." *Michigan Law Review* 77 (January–March 1979): 784–94.

Donaldson, Orren. "Irrigation and State Boundaries: A Problem of the Arid West and Its Solution." *Irrigation Age* 8 (February 1895): 47–53.

Doyle, Don Harrison. "Social Theory and New Communities in Nineteenth-Century America." *Western Historical Quarterly* 8 (April 1977): 151–65.

Downing, Theodore, and Gibson McGuire, eds. *Irrigation's Impact on Society*. Tucson: University Press of Arizona, 1974.

Draper, N. R., and H. Smith. *Applied Regression Analysis*. New York: John Wiley & Sons, 1961.

Dunbar, Robert G. *Forging New Rights in Western Waters*. Lincoln: University of Nebraska Press, 1983.

———. "The Origins of the Colorado System of Water-Right Control." *Colorado Magazine* 27 (October 1950): 241–62.

Engelbert, Ernest A., and Ann Foley Scheuring, eds. *Water Scarcity: Impacts on Western Agriculture*. Berkeley and Los Angeles: University of California Press, 1984.

Estes, James R., Ronald J. Tyrl, and Jere N. Brunken, eds. *Grasses and Grasslands: Systematics and Ecology*. Norman: University of Oklahoma Press, 1982.

Faxon, R. H. "Garden City, Kansas, and Vicinity." *Irrigation Age* 24 (January 1909): 85–86.

———. "Garden City, Kansas, and Vicinity." *Irrigation Age* 24 (February 1909): 116.

———. "Garden City, Kansas, and Vicinity." *Irrigation Age* 24 (April 1909): 175–76.

———. "Garden City, Kansas, and Vicinity." *Irrigation Age* 24 (July 1909): 347.

Fireman, Milton, and H. E. Haywood. "Irrigation Water and Saline and Alkali Soils." In *Water: The Yearbook of Agriculture*. Washington, D.C.: Government Printing Office, 1955.

Fite, Gilbert C. *The Farmers' Frontier, 1865–1900*. Albuquerque: University of New Mexico Press, 1974.

Flaherty, David H. "An Approach to American History: Willard Hurst as Legal Historian." *American Journal of Legal History* 14 (1970): 222–34.

Floud, Roderick. *An Introduction to Quantitative Methods for Historians*. 2d ed. London: Chaucer Press, 1979.

Follansbee, Robert, and Edward E. Jones. *The Arkansas River Flood of June 3–5, 1921*. Water Supply Paper 487. Washington, D.C.: Government Printing Office, 1922.

Foreman, W. James, and Robert S. Eckley. *Agriculture*. Economic Development in Southwestern Kansas, part 5. Lawrence: University of Kansas Press, 1955.

Friedman, Lawrence M., and Harry N. Scheiber, eds. *American Law and the Constitutional Order: Historical Perspectives*. Cambridge: Harvard University Press, 1978.

Frost, John E. "Story of Irrigation: The Beet Sugar Industry in the Arkansas River Valley of Eastern Colorado." *Irrigation Age* 17 (January 1902): 5–11.

"Garden City and Surroundings." *Irrigation Age* 1 (November 1891): 279–82.

Gilbert, G. K. "The Underground Water of the Arkansas Valley in Eastern Colorado." In *Seventeenth Annual Report of the United States Geological Survey, 1895–96*, part 2. Washington, D.C.: Government Printing Office, 1896.

Goldsmith, Edward, and Nicholas Hildyard. *The Social and Environmental Effects of Large Dams*. San Francisco: Sierra Club Books, 1984.

Gorz, Andre. *Ecology as Politics*. Translated by Patsy Vigderman and Jonathan Cloud. Boston: South End Press, 1980.

Gregory, J. W. "Irrigation in Southwest Kansas: Experience Teaches Practicability of Pump Irrigation." *Irrigation Age* 8 (January 1895): 13–17.

Gressley, Gene M., ed. *The American West: A Reorientation*. Laramie: University of Wyoming, 1966.

Griffin, H. N. *Cantaloupes*. Colorado Agricultural Experiment Station Bulletin 62. Fort Collins, April 1901.

Hall, Frank. *History of the State of Colorado*. Vol. 3. Chicago: Blakely Printing Co., 1895.

Hall, Kermit L. "The 'Magic Mirror' and the Promise of Western Legal History at the Bicentennial of the Constitution." *Western Historical Quarterly* 18 (October 1987): 429–35.

Ham, George E., and Robin Higham, eds. *The Rise of the Wheat State: A History of Kansas Agriculture, 1861–1986*. Manhattan, Kans.: Sunflower University Press, 1987.

Harrison, George B. "The Beet-Sugar Industry in Kansas." In *Fifteenth Biennial Report of the State Board of Agriculture, 1905–6*. Topeka, Kans.: State Printer, 1907.

Harvey, Mr. and Mrs. James R. "Rocky Ford Melons." *Colorado Magazine* 26 (January 1949): 26–36.

Hassell, Wendell, and John Knapp. "Establishing Permanent Vegetation of Previously Irrigated Lands of Southeastern Colorado." Paper presented to the National Society of Agronomy meeting, Anaheim, California, fall 1982.

Hays, Samuel. "The Politics of Reform in Municipal Government in the Progressive Era." *Pacific Northwest Quarterly* 55 (October 1964): 157–69.

Hendrickson, Gordon Olaf. "Water Rights on the North Platte River: A Case Study of the Resolution of an Interstate Water Conflict." Ph.D. Dissertation, University of Wyoming, 1975.

Hinderlider, M. C. "Interstate Negotiations for River Compacts: Republican River." In *Thirty-First Biennial Report of the State Engineer, Colorado, 1941–42*. Denver: State Printers, 1942.

————. "Investigations" and "Additional Water Supplies for the Arkansas Valley." In *Twenty-Fourth Biennial Report of the State Engineer, Colorado, 1927–28*. Denver: State Printers, 1928.

————. "Trans-Mountain Diversions." *Twenty-Third Biennial Report of the State Engineer, Colorado, 1925–26*. Denver: State Printers, 1926.

Horkheimer, Max. *The Eclipse of Reason*. New York: Oxford University Press, 1947.

Hosea, R. M. "Minnequa Steel Works Water Supply." *Camp and Plant* 2 (29 November 1902): 513–19.

Hundley, Norris. *Water and the West: The Colorado River Compact and the Politics of Water in the American West*. Berkeley and Los Angeles: University of California Press, 1966.

Hurst, James Willard. *Law and Economic Growth: The Legal History of the Lumber Industry in Wisconsin, 1836–1915*. Cambridge: Harvard University Press, 1964.

————. *Law and Social Order in the United States*. Ithaca, N.Y.: Cornell University Press, 1977.

————. *Law and the Conditions of Freedom in the Nineteenth-Century United States*. Madison: University of Wisconsin Press, 1966.

————. "Legal Elements in United States History." In *Perspectives in American History*, Vol. 5 of *Law in American History* (Cambridge: Harvard University Press, 1971): 3–92.

Hutchins, Wells A., R. V. Smrha, and Robert L. Smith. *The Kansas Law of Water Rights*. Topeka, Kans.: State Board of Agriculture, 1957.

Kahrl, William L. *Water and Power: The Conflict over Los Angeles' Water Supply in the Owens Valley*. Berkeley and Los Angeles: University of California, 1982.

"Kansas." *Irrigation Age* 2 (June 1893): 26.

Kansas. State Board of Agriculture. *Irrigation Pumping Plants: Construction and Costs*. Topeka: State Board of Agriculture, 1942.

Kansas. Water Resources Board. *State Water Plan Studies*. Part A: *Preliminary Appraisal of Kansas Water Problems: Section II. Upper Arkansas Unit*. Topeka: State Printing Office, 1962.

————. *Water in Kansas, 1955: A Report to the Kansas State Legislature*. Topeka: State Printing Office, 1954.

Kellogg, Charles E. *The Soils That Support Us*. New York: Macmillan, 1943.

Kelso, Maurice M., E. Martin William, and Lawrence E. Mack. *Water Supplies and Economic Growth in an Arid Environment: An Arizona Case Study*. Tucson: University of Arizona Press, 1973.

Knapp, George. "The Kansas-Colorado Water Controversy." In *Report of the State Irrigation Commissioner to the Kansas State Board of Agriculture, 16 June 1919 to 30 June 1920*. Topeka, Kans.: State Printer, 1920.

————. "The Proposed Arkansas River Compact." In *Report of the State Irrigation Commissioner to the Kansas State Board of Agriculture, 1 July 1924 to 30 June 1926*. Topeka, Kans.: State Printer, 1926.

Knapp, George S., and Warden L. Noe. *Laws Governing the Appropriation of Water for Beneficial Use*. Topeka, Kans.: State Board of Agriculture, 1948.

Larsen, Roy J., Donald R. Martin, and M. Bruce McCullough. *Soil Survey of Otero County, Colorado*. Washington, D.C.: Government Printing Office, 1972.

Lecompte, Janet. *Pueblo, Hardscrabble, Greenhorn: The Upper Arkansas, 1832–1856.* Norman: University of Oklahoma Press, 1978.

Lee, Lawrence B. *Reclaiming the American West: An Historiography and Guide.* Santa Barbara, Calif.: ABC-Clio, 1980.

———. "William Ellsworth Smythe and the Irrigation Movement: A Reconsideration." *Pacific Historical Review* 41 (August 1972): 289–311.

Leiss, William. *The Domination of Nature.* New York: George Braziller, 1972.

Limerick, Patricia. *The Legacy of Conquest: The Unbroken Past of the American West.* New York: W. W. Norton & Co., 1987.

Lindauer, Ivo E. "A Comparison of the Plant Communities of the South Platte and Arkansas River Drainages in Eastern Colorado." *Southwestern Naturalist* 28 (August 1983): 249–58.

———. *A Survey of the Woody Phreatophytes in the Lower Arkansas River Valley of Colorado.* Fort Collins: Department of Botany and Plant Pathology, Colorado State University, 1968.

———. "The Vegetation of the Flood Plain of the Arkansas River in Southeastern Colorado." Ph.D. Dissertation, Colorado State University, 1970.

Littlefield, Douglas. "Water Rights during the California Gold Rush: Conflicts over Economic Points of View." *Western Historical Quarterly* 14 (October 1983): 415–34.

Lowitt, Richard. *The New Deal and the West.* Bloomington: Indiana University Press, 1984.

Maass, Arthur, and Raymond Anderson. *. . . and the Desert Shall Rejoice.* Cambridge: MIT Press, 1978.

McEvoy, Arthur F. *The Fisherman's Problem: Ecology and Law in the California Fisheries, 1850–1980.* New York: Cambridge University Press, 1986.

MacKendrick, Donald. "Before the Newlands Act: State Sponsored Reclamation Projects in Colorado, 1888–1903." *Colorado Magazine* 52 (Winter 1975): 1–21.

Malin, James C. *The Grassland of North America: Prolegomena to Its History with Addenda and Postscript.* Gloucester, Mass.: Peter Smith, 1967.

Markoff, Dena S. "A Bittersweet Saga: The Arkansas Valley Beet Sugar Industry, 1900–1979." *Colorado Magazine* 56 (1979): 161–78.

———. "The Beet Sugar Industry in Microcosm: The National Sugar Manufacturing Company, 1899 to 1967." Ph.D. Dissertation, University of Colorado, 1980.

Marvin, Anne M. "The Fertile Domain: Irrigation as Adaptation in the Garden City, Kansas Area, 1880–1910." Ph.D. Dissertation, University of Kansas, 1985.

Mead, Elwood. "An Unsolved Western Problem: The Division of the Waters of Inter-State Streams." *Irrigation Age* 7 (July 1894): 12–15.

Miles, Don. "Recharge: Its Role in Total Water Management, Arkansas Valley of Colorado." Paper presented to the Great Plains Council Groundwater Management Seminar, Denver, Colorado, April 1974.

———. *Salinity in the Arkansas Valley of Colorado.* Denver: Environmental Protection Agency, 1977.

Miner, H. Craig. *West of Wichita: Settling the High Plains of Kansas, 1865–1890.* Lawrence: University Press of Kansas, 1986.

———. *Wichita: The Early Years, 1865–80.* Lincoln: University of Nebraska Press, 1982.

Montgomery, Douglas C., and Elizabeth A. Peck. *Introduction to Linear Regression Analysis.* New York: John Wiley & Sons, 1982.

Morgan, Arthur E. *Dams and Other Disasters: A Century of the Army Corps of Engineers in Civil Works*. Boston: Porter Sargent, 1971.

Mutel, Cornellia Fleischer, and John C. Emerick. *From Grassland to Glacier: The Natural History of Colorado*. Boulder, Colo.: Johnson Books, 1984.

Nash, Gerald D. *The American West in the Twentieth Century: A Short History of an Urban Oasis*. Albuquerque: University of New Mexico Press, 1973.

————. *The American West Transformed: The Impact of the Second World War*. Bloomington: University of Indiana Press, 1985.

Nichols, F. B. "Pumping Irrigation in Kansas." *Irrigation Age* 31 (January 1916): 42.

"The Original Jurisdiction of the United States Supreme Court." *Stanford Law Review* 2 (July 1959): 665–719.

Pannell, James, Roy J. Larsen, M. Bruce McCullough, Ronald E. Moreland, and Stanley Woodyard. *Soil Survey of Powers County, Colorado*. Washington, D.C.: Government Printing Office, 1966.

Pfister, Richard. *Water Resources and Irrigation*. Economic Development in Southwestern Kansas, part 4. Lawrence: University of Kansas Press, 1955.

Pisani, Donald J. "Deep and Troubled Waters: A New Field of Western History?" *New Mexico Historical Review* 63 (October 1988): 311–31.

————. "Enterprise and Equity: A Critique of Western Water Law in the Nineteenth Century." *Western Historical Quarterly* 18 (January 1987): 15–37.

————. *From Family Farm to Agribusiness: The Irrigation Crusade in California and the West, 1850–1931*. Berkeley and Los Angeles: University of California Press, 1984.

————. "State vs. Nation: Federal Reclamation and Water Rights in the Progressive Era." *Pacific Historical Review* 51 (August 1982): 276–82.

Preator, Rodney E., Ronald E. Moreland, Stanley O. Woodyard, and M. Bruce McCullough. *Soil Survey of Bent County, Colorado*. Washington, D.C.: Government Printing Office, 1971.

Radosevich, George E., ed. *Colorado Water Laws: A Compilation of Statutes, Regulations, Compacts, and Selected Cases*. 5th ed., 3 vols. Fort Collins: Colorado State University, 1983.

Radosevich, G. E., K. C. Nobe, D. Allardice, and C. Kirkwood. *Evolution and Administration of Colorado Water Law: 1876–1976*. Littleton, Colo.: Water Resources Publications, 1976.

Reid, H. I. "The Water-Works of Colorado Springs and the Strickler Tunnel." *Engineering News* 36 (27 August 1896): 131–34.

Reisner, Marc. *Cadillac Desert: The American West and Its Disappearing Water*. New York: Viking Penguin, 1986.

Report of the State Engineer, Colorado. 1891–1944. Denver: State Printers, 1893–1945.

Robinson, Michael C. "The Relationship between the U.S. Army Corps of Engineers and the Environmental Community." *Environmental Review* 13 (Spring 1989): 1–41.

Robinson, T. W. *Introduction, Spread, and Areal Extent of Saltcedar* (Tamarix) *in the Western States*. U.S. Geological Survey Professional Paper 491-A. Washington, D.C.: Government Printing Office, 1965.

Sallee, Kenneth H., Vernon L. Hamilton, Charles W. McBee, and Edward L. Fleming. *Soil Survey of Kearney County, Kansas*. Washington, D.C.: Government Printing Office, 1963.

Scamehorn, H. Lee. *Pioneer Steelmaker in the West: The Colorado Fuel and Iron Company, 1872–1903.* Boulder, Colo.: Pruett Publishing Company, 1976.

Scheiber, Harry N. "American Constitutional History and the New Legal History: Complementary Themes in Two Modes." *Journal of American History* 68 (September 1981): 337–50.

————. "At the Borderland of Law and Economic History: The Contributions of Willard Hurst." *American Historical Review* 75 (February 1970): 744–56.

Schowe, Walter H. "The Geography of Kansas: Hydrogeography." *Transactions of the Kansas Academy of Science* 54 (September 1951): 263–308, and 56 (June 1953): 131–90.

Schulze, Suzanne, comp. *A Century of the Colorado Census.* Greeley: University of Northern Colorado, 1976.

Schumacher, E. F. *Small Is Beautiful: Economics As If People Mattered.* New York: Harper & Row, 1973.

Scott, Robert D. "Kansas v. Colorado Revisited." *American Journal of International Law* 52 (July 1958): 432–54.

Sherow, James E. "The Chimerical Vision: Michael Creed Hinderlider and Progressive Engineering in Colorado." *Essays and Monographs in Colorado History* No. 9 (1989): 37–59.

————. "The Contest for the 'Nile of America': *Kansas v. Colorado* (1907)." *Great Plains Quarterly* 10 (Winter 1990): 48–61.

————. "Discord in the 'Valley of Content': Strife over Natural Resources in a Changing Environment on the Arkansas River Valley of the High Plains." Ph.D. Dissertation, University of Colorado, 1987.

————. "Utopia, Reality, and Irrigation: The Plight of the Fort Lyon Canal Company in the Arkansas River Valley." *Western Historical Quarterly* 20 (May 1989): 162–84.

Sibert, Captain William L. "Improvement of Arkansas River and of Certain Rivers in Arkansas and Missouri." In *Report of the Chief of the Engineers,* part 2. U.S. Department of War, Army Corps of Engineers. Washington, D.C.: Government Printing Office, 1898.

————. "Improvement of Arkansas River and of Certain Rivers in Arkansas and Missouri." In *Report of the Chief of the Engineers,* part 3. U.S. Department of War, Army Corps of Engineers. Washington, D.C.: Government Printing Office, 1897.

Sixteenth Annual Denver City Directory. Denver: Corbett and Balenger, 1888.

Slichter, Charles S. "Operations in Kansas." In *Fourth Annual Report of the Reclamation Service.* U.S. Department of Interior, Geological Survey. Washington, D.C.: Government Printing Office, 1905.

————. *The Underflow in Arkansas Valley in Western Kansas.* U.S. Geological Survey Water Supply and Irrigation Paper 153. Washington, D.C.: Government Printing Office, 1906.

Smrha, R. V. "George Knapp and the Kansas Water Rights Act." *Kansas Water News* 9 (April 1966): 3–4.

Smrha, R. V., W. H. Sunderland, and Warden L. Noe, comps. *Water . . . Its Appropriation for Beneficial Use.* Vol. 64, Report 320. Topeka, Kans.: State Board of Agriculture, 1955.

Smythe, William Ellsworth. *The Conquest of Arid America.* With an introduction by Lawrence B. Lee. Seattle: University of Washington Press, 1969. Reprint. Seattle: Americana Library, 1970.

by Lawrence B. Lee. Seattle: University of Washington Press, 1969. Reprint. Seattle: Americana Library, 1970.

Sorensen, Conner. "Federal Reclamation on the High Plains: The Garden City Project." *Great Plains Journal* 15 (Spring 1976): 114–33.

Sprague, Marshall. *Newport in the Rockies*. Denver: Sage Books, 1961.

Stegner, Wallace. *Beyond the Hundredth Meridian: John Wesley Powell and the Second Opening of the West*. Lincoln: University of Nebraska Press, 1953.

――――. *The American West as Living Space*. Ann Arbor: University of Michigan Press, 1987.

Steinel, Alvin. *History of Agriculture in Colorado*. Fort Collins, Colo.: State Agricultural College, 1926.

Stevens, Joseph E. *Hoover Dam: An American Adventure*. Norman: University of Oklahoma Press, 1988.

Stone, Wilbur E., ed. *History of Colorado*. 4 vols. Chicago: S. J. Clarke Publishing Co., 1918.

Summary of Council Proceedings and Department Reports, December 1917–35. City Commission, Colorado Springs, Colorado. Norlin Library. University of Colorado, Boulder.

Thomas, James H., and Carl N. Tyson. "Navigation on the Arkansas River, 1719–1886." *Kansas History* 2 (Summer 1979): 135–41.

U.S. Congress. House. *Arkansas River and Tributaries. Letter from the Secretary of War Transmitting a Letter from the Chief of Engineers, U.S. Army, Dated July 26, 1935, Submitting a Report, together with Accompanying Papers and Illustrations, Containing a General Plan for the Improvement of Arkansas River and Tributaries, for the Purposes of Navigation and Efficient Development of its Water Power, the Control of Floods, and the Needs of Irrigation*. 3 vols. H. Doc. 308, 74th Cong., 1st sess., 1936.

――――. *Report of Exploration for a Route for the Pacific Railroad, by Capt. J. W. Gunnison, Topographical Engineers, near the 38th and 39th Parallels of North Latitude, from the Mouth of the Kansas River, Mo., to the Sevier Lake, in the Great Basin, by Lt. E. G. Beckwith*. H. Doc. 91, 33d Cong., 2d sess., 1855.

U.S. Congress. Senate. *Report of an Expedition Led by Lieutenant Abert, on the Upper Arkansas through the Country of the Camanche Indians*, by J. W. Abert. S. Doc. 483, 29th Cong., 1st sess., 1846.

――――. *Report of the Special Committee on the Irrigation and Reclamation of Arid Lands*. S. Rept. 928, 51st Cong., 1st sess., 1891.

――――. *The Effect upon Certain Rivers in Colorado of the Diversion of Water for Irrigation*, by J. W. Powell. Sen. Ex. Doc. 120, vol. 3, 50th Cong., 2d sess., 1889.

――――. Committee on Interior and Insular Affairs. *Arkansas River Compact, Hearing before the Committee on Interior and Insular Affairs on S. 1448*. 81st Cong., 1st sess., 1949.

U.S. Department of Agriculture. Forest Service. *Strategies for Protection and Management of Floodplain Wetlands and Other Riparian Ecosystems*. Washington, D.C.: Government Printing Office, 1978.

U.S. Department of Agriculture. Weather Bureau. *Climatic Summary of the United States*. Washington, D.C.: Government Printing Office, 1932.

U.S. Department of Commerce. Bureau of Census. *Seventeenth Census of the United States, 1950: Irrigation of Agricultural Lands*. Vol. 7. Washington, D.C.: Government Printing Office, 1950.

――――. Weather Bureau. *Climatography of the United States No. 11–12, Climatic*

Summary of the United States—Supplement for 1931 through 1952, Kansas. Washington, D.C.: Government Printing Office, n.d.

U.S. Department of Interior. Geological Survey. *Compilation of Records of Surface Water of the United States through September 1950. Part 7, Lower Mississippi River Basin.* Washington, D.C.: Government Printing Office, 1955.

———. Office of Indian Affairs. *Report of the Secretary of the Interior, for the Fiscal Year Ended 30 June 1865.* Washington, D.C.: U.S. Government Printing Office, 1866.

Van Hook, Joseph O. "Development of Irrigation in the Arkansas Valley." *Colorado Magazine* 10 (January 1933): 3–11.

Vencill, Betsy. "The Federal Power Act and Western Water Law—Can States Maintain Their Own Water Use Priorities?" *Natural Resources Journal* 27 (Winter 1987): 213–34.

Wagner, Mark J. "The Parting of the Waters—The Dispute between Colorado and Kansas over the Arkansas River." *Washburn Law Journal* 24 (1984): 99–120.

Warner, Sam Bass, Jr. *The Private City: Philadelphia in Three Periods of Its Growth.* Philadelphia: University of Pennsylvania Press, 1968.

Welsh, Michael. *U.S. Army Corps of Engineers: Albuquerque District, 1935–1985.* Albuquerque: University of New Mexico Press, 1987.

White, Richard. "American Environmental History: The Development of a New Historical Field." *Pacific Historical Review* 54 (August 1985): 297–335.

———. *Land Use, Environment, and Social Change: The Shaping of Island County, Washington.* Seattle: University of Washington Press, 1980.

William, Martin, and Lawrence E. Mack. *Water Supplies and Economic Growth in an Arid Environment: An Arizona Case Study.* Tucson: University of Arizona Press, 1973.

Wittfogel, Karl. *Oriental Despotism: A Comparative Study of Total Power.* New Haven, Conn.: Yale University Press, 1957.

Worster, Donald. *Dust Bowl: The Southern Plains in the 1930s.* New York: Oxford University Press, 1979.

———. "History as Natural History: An Essay on Theory and Method." *Pacific Historical Review* (February 1984): 1–19.

———. "Hydraulic Society in California: An Ecological Interpretation." *Agricultural History* 56 (July 1982): 503–15.

———. "Irrigation and Democracy in California: The Early Promise." *Pacific Historian* 27 (Spring 1983): 30–35.

———. *Nature's Economy.* San Francisco: Sierra Club Books, 1977. Reprint. New York: Cambridge University Press, 1985.

———. "New West, True West: Interpreting the Region's History." *Western Historical Quarterly* 18 (April 1987): 141–56.

———. *Rivers of Empire: Water, Aridity, and the Growth of the American West.* New York: Pantheon Books, 1985.

———, ed. *The Ends of the Earth: Perspectives on Modern Environmental History.* Cambridge: Cambridge University Press, 1988.